T0301451

THE RETURN OF WORK IN CRITICAL THEORY

NEW DIRECTIONS IN CRITICAL THEORY

For a complete list of titles, see page 233

The Return of Work in Critical Theory

SELF, SOCIETY, POLITICS

Christophe Dejours, Jean-Philippe Deranty,
Emmanuel Renault, and Nicholas H. Smith

Columbia University Press
New York

Columbia University Press
Publishers Since 1893
New York   Chichester, West Sussex
cup.columbia.edu
Copyright © 2018 Columbia University Press
All rights reserved

Library of Congress Cataloging-in-Publication Data
Names: Dejours, Christophe, author.
Title: The return of work in critical theory: self, society, politics /
Christophe Dejours, Jean-Philippe Deranty, Emmanuel Renault, and Nicholas H. Smith.
Description: New York: Columbia University Press, 2018. | Series: New directions in critical
theory | Includes bibliographical references and index.
Identifiers: LCCN 2018000894 | ISBN 9780231187282 (cloth:) |
ISBN 9780231547185 (e-book)
Subjects: LCSH: Work—Psychological aspects. | Critical theory.
Classification: LCC BF481 .R455 2018 | DDC 158.7—dc23
LC record available at https://lccn.loc.gov/2018000894

CONTENTS

Whether we love work or loathe it, whether we want more work or less, whether we feel proud and uplifted by the work we do or humiliated and downtrodden, there is no escaping the impact work has on us, both as individuals and members of society as a whole.

How far does this impact reach? A common view runs like this. Inasmuch as work is the means of an income, the impact of work is huge. Everybody needs an income to live, and without a decent level of income to rely on, people are doomed to impoverished, miserable lives. But subtract the income-providing purpose of work, its impact just depends on an individual's preferences or the things that happen to matter to a particular individual. Some people find meaning and a sense of identity from work and prefer to spend more time on it than other things. Others don't, and have stronger preferences for the joys of family life, leisure activities, and so on. Some people are prepared to put up with boring but well-paid hours at work because they prefer having money in their pockets. Others are prepared to put up with meager spending power because they prefer the intrinsic rewards of personally satisfying work that is not well-paid. Perhaps no one should have to work under dangerous or excessively exploitative conditions. But ultimately it is up to the individual to decide whether work is "for them" or not, or at least it would be if a living wage wasn't at stake.

Beyond the impact that access to a decent income has, the impact of work is just a matter of one's preferences or dependent on the conception of "the good life" that is "right for me."

This innocent-enough-looking view can have far-reaching philosophical consequences. If the only universally accepted value in relation to work is thought to be its income-earning purpose, if, beyond that, evaluations of work are thought to be just a matter of subjective preferences, it can seem as if the *moral* significance of work is tied up exclusively with distribution of income, on the one hand, and freedom of choice in pursuit of preferences or conceptions of the good, on the other. This can lead to the further thought that in a morally ideal world, or in a perfectly just one, individuals would be completely free to pursue their preferences in relation to work; indeed that justice *consists* in that freedom of choice being available to everyone. Furthermore, this ideal world may not be so far away. For developments in technology, in particular the automation of work tasks through the use of robots, are making many types of work unnecessary, and in taking the necessity out of work they are opening it up to freedom. The impact of work on individuals and communities, as these developments unfold, can be expected to progressively weaken, and, in anticipation of this, theorists and other people in the know should be turning their minds to the "postwork" world or, as it has also been called, "the end of work."

Many are. But if the book we have written shows one thing, it is that the world of work is full of unfinished business for the philosopher, theorist, and social critic. It is a world with a highly complex moral landscape that we have only started to explore. The predominant features of this landscape, as they emerge from our explorations, are multifaceted expectations of *justice* and *autonomy*; that is to say, rich substantive norms that shape the experience of work and the experience of being without work. The freedom to choose to enter the labor market or not, and the point at which to enter it, are just two aspects of the landscape, or the landscape seen "sideways on," so to speak. There are many other ways in which autonomy and justice are at stake in work, but in order to understand them one has to enter the experience of the people who, in suffering injustice, lack of autonomy, and domination at work, have a unique if not necessarily well-formulated grasp of what those norms mean.

How do you gain access to this experience? One can get a first impression from what people say in surveys. So long as the surveys are carefully constructed, and contemporary social science has developed sophisticated techniques for constructing them, they can reveal the attitudes people have toward specific work practices, the expectations they have in regard to work, and the extent to which those expectations are fulfilled or frustrated. Social surveys of this kind are a good way of discerning patterns of experience at a population level—they are certainly better than just speculating about them—and we will draw on them to get a big picture of prevailing forms and levels of discontent about work in part 1 of the book. Useful though such empirical research is for this purpose, it is not well suited for disclosing the fine grain of experience. For this to become manifest, the right conditions need to be in place for self-disclosure on the part of the subject, and a theoretical framework is needed for the interpretation of the material disclosed. The psychodynamics of work developed by Christophe Dejours serves precisely this purpose, and we draw on the results of research using this method, especially when it comes to the illustration we give in the last part of the book of how the theory of work we propose can yield emancipatory transformations.

Access to experience is also a matter of having the right concept *of* experience, which in turn requires having an appropriate concept of the *subject* of experience. We are dealing here, of course, with the *lived* experience of work, not experience as viewed from some detached objective standpoint. Felicitous description of lived experience is a notoriously difficult thing to achieve, but fortunately there is a tradition of philosophy that is alert to these difficulties, to the dangers that beset attempts at such description, and that offers ways of overcoming such difficulties. This is the tradition of existential phenomenology. Since what we are looking for is a theoretical framework for understanding the normative content of the lived experience of work, we must first have in place a model of what lived experience consists in and from this develop an account of how, from the specific challenges that work presents to a subject, subjectivity emerges fortified or worn down. This is what we attempt in part 2. We argue that the lived experience of work engages subjectivity in both a technical and a social dimension, the latter in way structured by various relations of recognition.

By this point, we have moved a long way from the common view that there is nothing much interesting to say, nothing much of philosophical, moral, or political import to articulate about work as activity as distinct from work as a means of income. This distinction, which will be fundamental to our discussion, plays little role in the traditions of political and social philosophy that dominate academic discourse today, namely the liberal and republican traditions. But it has an important role to play in the dialectical and pragmatist traditions as well as the phenomenological tradition just mentioned. And it is within these traditions that the contribution offered in this book belongs. Above all, we take inspiration from the idea of a critical theory of society formulated in various ways by Max Horkheimer and Theodor Adorno, Jürgen Habermas and Axel Honneth. But we also find ourselves departing from some of critical theory's well-trodden paths and, in seeking to redeem what Honneth once called a "critical conception of work," we suggest a way of renewing the project of critical theory itself.

We should say a few words about the composition of the book. The four authors have been discussing the ideas covered in the book for around a decade, and in that sense the book has been a long time in the making. The book is very much centered around the psychodynamic approach to work pioneered by Christophe Dejours in the past three decades, and one way of reading it is as an attempt to draw out the broader philosophical implications of Dejours's strikingly original and insufficiently known work. If the three philosophers involved in the writing of the book were not quite the underlaborers, they were building on foundations laid by him. Nicholas Smith wrote the introduction and the chapters that make up part 1 of the book and edited the whole manuscript to maintain consistency of argument and style; Jean-Philippe Deranty wrote the chapters that make up part 2; Emmanuel Renault took responsibility for part 3 and also wrote the conclusion; and Christophe Dejours provided the material that makes up part 4. While the act of writing is ultimately the act of one person, the four authors have, so far as possible, sought to act together. The views expressed in the book are not necessarily shared to the same degree by each of us, but they do accurately reflect our considered shared opinion.

Finally, some words of thanks are due. We are grateful to the Australian Research Council for a Discovery Project award that funded the research activities that got the book project going. Nicholas Smith would like to thank the Faculty of Arts at Macquarie University for an Outside Studies Program grant that enabled him to do the extensive research required to draft part 1 of the book. We are grateful to Dale Tweedie, Andrea Veltman, and Titus Stahl for very helpful feedback on the completed manuscript. And many thanks to Wendy Lochner and Amy Allen for their support for the project.

THE RETURN OF WORK IN CRITICAL THEORY

This book is about work and why it matters. Our focus will be on work understood as something that we *do*, as a form of activity that, for most people, takes up most of their active life. The thesis we will put forward in the book is that work matters a great deal, not just for obvious reasons that everyone immediately understands but for complex and hidden ones that only become apparent through scientific analysis and philosophical reflection. By way of such reflection, we will argue that work matters because in the doing of it we relate to the world, to others, and to ourselves in ways that fundamentally affect the quality of life available to us. Work matters because some of our deepest fears and hopes are bound up with it. The aim of this book is to cast some light on this melange of fear and hope, both to contribute to an understanding of the sources of anxiety we have around work and to clarify the anticipations of freedom, justice, and fulfillment, however muted or suppressed they may be, that stubbornly accompany our experience of work.

One might think—given the palpable and widespread concerns that gravitate around work and the difficulties we have in comprehending them—that philosophers, social theorists, and other theorists in the humanities would have had much to say on the subject. One might think that there would be a large philosophical literature for us to review and draw upon in formulating our own views on why work matters. But that is not the case.

On the contrary, there is a dearth of philosophical reflection on the question that we raise: how the experience of work—the relation to the world, to others, and to ourselves it involves—affects the quality of life available to us. Very few of the many theorists that populate humanities and social science departments have attended to the morally redolent fears and anticipations that accompany the experience of working. But this neglect is not due to some chance intellectual oversight or mere lack of interest. Rather it is due to the hold of powerful currents of thought that can make the kind of inquiry we will be undertaking in this book seem otiose, irrelevant, or plain wrongheaded. In the remainder of our introduction we will look at some of these currents of thought with a view to clearing away a few obstacles that might seem to block our path of inquiry.

AUTOMATION AND THE MYTH OF THE END OF WORK

First, there is a set of quasi-empirical beliefs about the impact of automation. Machines have been doing work once done by humans on a massive scale since the beginning of the industrial revolution. Mechanization both transformed the experience of manufacturing work and eliminated the need for certain kinds of manufacturer. It is common knowledge that over the past few decades, since the onset of so-called post-industrial society, not just the manufacture of commodities but also the production and delivery of services—such as financial, legal, medical, and educational services—has been transformed by technology. Furthermore, the automation of tasks in the service sector has eliminated the need for certain kinds of service worker, just as the introduction of automation into the manufacturing sector made many kinds of industrial worker redundant. Advances in computing technology have rapidly accelerated these transformations, with the automation of whole swathes of tasks associated with a wide range of professions in manufacturing and service provision now within reach. Many of the tasks done for centuries by highly qualified professionals— lawyers, accountants, surgeons, translators—are already being done by intelligent machines, and the evidence suggests this trend will continue.

But why should this accelerating trend toward automation represent an obstacle to our project of gaining deeper insight into the experience of work and the ways in which this experience affects the quality of life? It does so if one takes the end of the need for human agency in the performance of specific working tasks to entail the end of the need for work *as such*. And this inference—from the substitutability of human beings in particular circumstances of work to the substitutability of human beings in the whole system of work—yields the radical conclusion that the "end of work" is nigh, that we stand at the dawn of a "jobless future." But if this is the case, if automation spells not only the demise of particular types of work but the imminent demise of work as such, it would be futile to dwell on the experience of work and the contribution it makes to the quality of individual and collective life. We would do better to reflect on what will *replace* work, to consider the kind of society that will come into being once "work society" has had its day. Much philosophical and social-theoretical reflection about work, not to mention a plethora of less high-brow social commentary and forecasting, is geared around this "end of work" scenario. On the assumption that intelligent machines or robots will soon eliminate the need for human work, a raft of issues suddenly becomes pressing: should automation be embraced or resisted? Whose interests does automation fundamentally serve—those of the powerful corporation, the savvy entrepreneur, the powerless worker, or someone else? Would the end of work spell social and economic disaster, with mass unemployment, poverty, and social disintegration? Or would it perhaps bring mass liberation, opening up undreamed-of opportunities for human fulfillment through leisure funded by a universal basic income? Reflection on such matters might seem the right way of responding to the present state of work and certainly has popular appeal.[1]

While there is no harm speculating about the future, our first responsibility is to the present. And as a depiction of present and foreseeable reality, the end of work scenario is way off target. It is a myth based partly in the faulty inference mentioned earlier—a version of the metonymic fallacy, which falsely ascribes to the whole the character of some of its parts. It does not follow from the automation of particular work tasks, or even the characteristic tasks of particular professions, that all or even most work tasks, or all or most professions, are capable of being automated. But there is more than just a logical mistake in the argument: the argument simply does not fit the facts. It is of course true that many working tasks have become automated and many others are on the cusp of automation, leaving those who previously did those tasks without employment *in that activity*. One can also point to upwardly trending levels of unemployment in those professions or sectors of employment where automation has been introduced. In the case of employment in the manufacturing sector in the developed economies, to use what many take to be the decisive example, the decline has indeed been sharp and protracted.[2] But, on their own, such figures are deceptive: while the global number of unemployed has been rising, albeit unevenly over the past decade, the number of people *in* paid work has been growing too, only more steadily and at a greater rate. This means that there has been a continually growing number of tasks done by humans worth paying for—the exact opposite of the end of work scenario. Even employment in sectors already massively automated has been rising at a global level: industrial employment, for example, constituted a higher proportion of global total employment in 2013 than it did in 2000. Insofar as the need for work, and the reality of work, is indicated by levels of employment, there is little evidence that we are witnessing the end of work. Far from becoming an extinct species, employed people are, as a matter of fact, more numerous than ever before.[3]

These remarks are meant merely to serve as a reminder of something that should be obvious: work is by no means a peripheral or shrinking aspect of life in modern societies, as the myth of the end of work maintains, but a core feature around which much else turns. There is statistical evidence that the experience of work is changing—and we will turn to that evidence later on—but there is no empirical basis to the belief that work is no longer a major locus of experience. The most that can be said is that certain kinds of work experience have disappeared or are dying out, being replaced, in large part, by others.

However, the hold of the myth of the end of work was never really about the statistics that could be stacked up in its favor. The enduring appeal of the myth of the end of work lies—as it does with all myths—in the hopes and fears it condenses. In particular, its appeal is due to the attraction of a utopian vision of life without work. In other words, it is the end of work as *possibility*, rather than as fact, that holds us in thrall. And, in thrall of it, the task of attending to the content of work experience—especially when proposed, as we are doing here, as a form of social critique—will seem, at best, an irrelevance. We could say that this reason for circumventing a critical analysis of work experience is an "ontological" one: it is based on a conception of what human beings can and ought *to become*. The idea is that we are, and ought to be, *moving on* from work as a *self-defining* feature.

Before we consider this potential obstacle to our inquiry, we should make some clarifications about what we mean by work.

A PROVISIONAL DEFINITION OF WORK

It is notoriously difficult to define work in a clear cut, all-inclusive way, but Alfred Marshall's definition of labor as "an exertion of mind or body undergone partly or wholly with a view to some good other than the pleasure derived directly from work" is about as clear and inclusive as a working definition gets.[4] Although our analysis of work in chapters 3 and 4 will introduce some modifications to this simple definition, when we use the term *work* we are referring to activity that has the general features included in Marshall's definition.

Thus we think of work as typically involving effort, as an "exertion" of some kind, though that does not rule out occasions when work is easy. In ordinary language, when we speak of there being "work to do," of "getting down to work," or when we use similar locutions, we imply that there is some effort to put in. This implication is such an entrenched feature of ordinary language that it would be remiss not to include it in a general definition of work activity. Exertion implies some resistance to the will of the agent, and such resistance is a characteristic feature of what we mean when we say that working, or work on something, is going on. The exertion may be physical; it may be a straightforward matter of bodily toil, such as lifting; or it may be intellectual, the taxing process of getting the figures or words right; or it may be emotional, the effort of containing or shaping feelings. The exertion required of work may be intellectual, physical, and emotional at once—indeed we shall be arguing later that, since human beings do not come in discrete physical, intellectual, and emotional parts, this synthesis of exertion is the typical case. The effort involved in dealing effectively with an aggressive patient in a casualty ward, for example, or with a misbehaving child in a classroom, illustrates that exertions of mind, body, and spirit are hard to separate in real life. That fatigue typically accompanies work is another indication that effort is a characteristic element of work. And while we can distinguish between mental, physical, and emotional fatigue, fatigue always affects the whole person, and it is always the whole person who does the work that fatigues her.

The fatigue that accompanies work arises from the doing of something "partly or wholly with a view to some good other than the pleasure derived directly from work." It is an important nuance of Marshall's definition that it leaves room for the possibility that pleasure may be taken from work—even though, as we have just seen, work involves exertion. Effort and pleasure are not mutually exclusive, contrary to what a simplistic utilitarian psychology might suggest. But more significantly, Marshall's definition steers clear of the classical economist's fiction that work is always a sacrifice, a pain to be counterbalanced by an external pleasure, a negative value in a utility calculus.[5] As the definition enables us to see, work may be done partly with a view to pleasure derived directly from the activity of working, that is, because the work is enjoyable. But if activity is undertaken solely for the pleasure it directly brings, then we do not think of it as work—we think of its as leisure or play. In making explicit the condition that work is undertaken *at least partly* for a purpose other than enjoyment arising from the activity itself, the distinction between work and leisure or play is respected, without ruling out the possibility that work might resemble play, in being an enjoyable activity that could be done for its own sake. Of course work that holds no pleasure at all, that is not in the least enjoyable and is wholly unsuited as leisure activity or play, is also accommodated within the definition.

If work is activity done partly or wholly for some other reason than the pleasure directly derived from the activity, what is that reason? The answer supplied by Marshall's definition is as broad as could be: "some good." There are several advantages to this open-ended formulation. The "good" served by work might be the direct satisfaction of my own want or need: I could be working on the house not because I enjoy it but because the house I live in needs repairing. Or the good served by work might be the direct satisfaction of someone else's want or need: housework, of course, is often like this, as it meets not just my own needs but those of the whole household. Care work, to the extent that it involves exertion done for the sake of meeting other people's needs, serving some good in that way, also counts as work on this definition. Housework and care work, as well as voluntary and service work, are all obviously cases of work, and the definition shows us why: they are effortful activities of body or mind undertaken for the sake of some good other than the pleasure directly derived from the activity. It would be egregious to exclude housework, care work, and voluntary work from the domain of work, and Marshall's definition has the virtue of protecting us from that grievous error.

The temptation to commit that error derives from the tendency to identify work with *employment*. Employment can be understood as activity done partly or wholly for the sake of *one particular good* other than that derived directly from the activity: a wage. The wage is an indirect way of satisfying wants and needs, be they my own or those of others, and it is by mediation of the wage that the effortful activity undertaken in employment realizes some good. As a matter of course, the good served by the wage of the employee would not be forthcoming if it were not for other goods that the work activity served for the employer. In the not-for-profit sector of the labor market, the return obtained by the employer for the wage of the employee takes various forms: the real provision of a service, or, increasingly, "results," as measured by some external method of audit. In the corporate sector the primary benefit to the employer is some profit, as mediated by the satisfaction of some want or need of a purchaser. The good served by work activity that takes the form of employment is thus principally fourfold: a wage for the worker, a profit for the employer, the production or delivery of a commodity or a service, and the consumption or appropriation of a commodity or service by a customer. For the reasons just outlined, a definition of work ought not to restrict itself to activity aimed at that specific constellation of goods, and Marshall's definition does not entail such a restriction. However, an adequate account of work must nonetheless include activity that is oriented to those goods, since we are talking here not merely of one particular orienting set of goods among others but the *dominant* orientation of working activity in modern market societies.

So while it is important not to identify work with employment—both because people today do much work that isn't paid for, or that they are not employed to do, and because in the past many people worked without relating to the institution of employment at all (slaves, serfs, etc.)—it is also important to retain awareness of the predominance in modern times of work that is mediated by an employment relation. It is for the most part by working that people have access to the goods provided by employment, and, in particular, the purchasing power that the wage provides. When we speak of work in this book, we will often be referring to activity through which the goods (and indeed the "bads") of employment are obtained. But even when we do this, it will be important for us to distinguish between work as activity and work as employment. This is because working activity has a structure independent of the structure of employment, a structure and significance that is by no means exhausted by the relation between employer and employee.

There is another feature of work in a contemporary setting that an adequate conceptualization of work must take into account. This is the fact that most work today is performed in *organizations*. This feature of work is not touched upon in Marshall's definition at all, and we will need to move beyond that definition if we are to grasp the meaning that effortful activity done partly or wholly for the sake of some good other than the pleasure derived directly from the activity assumes in a contemporary context. It will be crucial to the analysis of work that we offer in this book that working activity is typically activity that yields a *prescribed* outcome, typically by way of a procedure that also takes the form of prescriptions. Another way of putting this is to say that work in organizations is fundamentally a matter of *rule-following*: the good that the exertion of mind or body serves, as well as the manner of that exertion, is defined in advance by rules determined partly or entirely by the work organization. One works in an organization by following rules for action that are *given* to one in the organization and sanctioned by the organization. As we shall see later, work activity always actually involves more than is contained in the formal specification of a rule, such that the "following" of a rule is always, in a certain sense, an "interpretation" of it.[6] Rules, *even technical ones*, do not apply themselves, but require a *subject* to apply them in particular cases. This point is of great significance for understanding the nature of work in organizations and the conflicts and tensions that can arise within work organizations. It is a chief aim of this book to cast some light on the conflicts and tensions that derive from the organizational and institutional contexts of work, and our use of the term *work* reflects that underlying purpose.

WORK, IDENTITY, AND POLITICS— A PHILOSOPHICAL CUL-DE-SAC?

The details of our conception of work will emerge as the argument of the book unfolds. But we should now at least have said enough about what we mean by work to be able to resume our discussion of the obstacles to be cleared before our analysis of work can properly begin. Recall that our inquiry might seem to be threatened by what we called an ontological objection. The ontological objection, we saw, questions the *self-defining* role of work; that is, the role work has to play in making us who we are and who we might become. For work to have this role is for it to constitute us in our *identity*. Unless it is reasonable to suppose that work can have this self-defining, self-constituting function, then—so it might seem—our whole course of inquiry is a dead-end.

It is precisely the reasonableness of the supposition of the identity-conferring significance of work that some of the most powerful currents of contemporary thought deny. Some of them deny the appropriateness of any kind of ontological reflection, or reflection on constitutive features of the self, never mind the possibility of work being such a feature. This current of thought, typified by procedural liberalism and shared by much economic theory, conceives the self minimally as the locus of a capacity for choice—a conception that fits a rights-based understanding of morality and politics. On this view, work has significance on account of it being a reasonable object of choice, as shaping an identity one might *opt for*, but not as something internal to or constitutive of the chooser. According to another current of thought, the self must be conceived as something more substantial or "thicker" than the thin minimal self of liberalism, but not in a way that draws work into the picture. On this view, typified by communitarianism, the self is a *social* self, but the social allegiances and identifications that make up that self do not extend to working. Communitarianism emphasizes the internal relation between individual and community but is generally indifferent to the role that working might play in establishing that relation. A third current of thought acknowledges that work may have a self-defining (and in that sense ontological) role but should not be accorded any *privileged* status. In particular, it should not be granted the privilege that it has enjoyed in male-dominated, imperialist, production-oriented societies, a privilege secured historically through the oppression of women, indigenous peoples, and cultures oriented by values other than productive work, which has now brought us to the brink in our relation with the natural environment. This questioning and critique of the privileged status of work—its status as a basis for self-identity—informs various strands of feminist, postcolonial, and environmentalist thought and might also seem to represent something like an a priori objection to our inquiry.

Let us briefly consider each objection in turn.

First, if we stick to our provisional definition of work as effortful activity done for the sake of some good, then all that matters about work from a moral or political point of view, it might seem, is the social distribution of the goods served by work and the opportunities that exist to enjoy them. The procedural liberal, like his close relation the neoclassical economist, is skeptical about the validity that any substantive conception of the good might have, which we can take to mean any conception that ties some good or activity to the self. The self is better conceived, according to this way of thinking, as a chooser of goods, and it is qua chooser of goods, and *only* qua chooser, that the self is relevant for morality and politics. The chooser of goods may be subject to constraints of *rationality*—this is precisely what rational choice theory, the key theoretical tool of procedural liberalism, aims to specify—and principles of political and social justice may be constructed on the basis of those constraints. Such is the provenance of proceduralist liberal theories of justice.[7] But beyond that, beyond the construction of principles that rational choosers (however specified) would elect as fit for organizing their collective life, the philosopher has no business. There is thus nothing to be gained philosophically by proposing an internal relation between particular goods or activities and the self, and, a fortiori, between the good or activity of working and the self.

We will consider this objection in more detail in chapter 6. But for now we can quickly spell out why we do not think it represents an insurmountable challenge to our approach. First, as many critics have noted—indeed as even its advocates concede—rational choice theory is both impoverished and implausible as a *psychological* theory. But a rich and plausible psychology is indispensible for understanding the things that matter to people, the sources of suffering they are subjected to and fear as well as the satisfying and fulfilling things they enjoy, wish for, or aspire toward. The claim—sometimes made in response to this point—that procedural liberalism is psychologically "neutral," is disingenuous since no recognizable social or political doctrine can have that feature. The social and political theorist cannot *opt out* of psychology: the choice facing the theorist is not between having recourse to a psychology and not having recourse to one; it is always a question of going for the best psychological account available. And a chief problem with rational choice theory, and the procedural liberalism it helps to frame, is that the psychology it goes for, often by its own admission, is thin and weak. What it likes to describe as virtuous abstention from

ontological matters, or at most as the endorsement of a minimalist conception of the self, is unavoidably an ontological commitment of its own,
one that it struggles to articulate and is slightly embarrassed by: *the self as
chooser*. In rejecting that conception, and in seeking a more realistic, richer
conception of a self shaped by its activities and allegiances, we are merely
following a path that many others, similarly unconvinced by this aspect of
procedural liberalism, have pursued.

Our second response to the procedural liberal objection is to question
the very model of rationality it relies on. It is a crucial premise of procedural liberalism that rational constraints or standards, in their purest form,
have universal scope. While, according to this view, the proper *application*
of rational norms will vary between contexts, the *justification* of them does
not: indeed it is owing to the context-independence of the procedure by
which they are justified that norms can be said to be rational at all. The first
duty of the political theorist—the task that must be acquitted before anything else worthwhile can be achieved—is then seen as the construction of
a procedure of justification that can be used to test the validity of norms or
standards that serve to regulate collective life generally, whatever the context. If this model of the relation between justification and application is
correct, and with it this concept of rationality, then our approach would
indeed be a road to nowhere as far as political theory is concerned. But we
reject this model of rationality, as do many others. In our view, matters of
justification and application cannot be separated in this way, for the basic
reason that the very meaning of a norm or a regulating standard (which
the norm or standard must be presumed to have if it is to pass or fail a justification test) depends on some social context. It is thus no compelling
objection to our investigation of the norms that apply to (and partly constitute) contexts of work that we do not at the outset put in place a procedure
for establishing the possible validity of those norms. The local, context-
specific meaning of the norms of work—like those that apply, for example,
in the intimate sphere—does not itself fatally compromise their claim to
validity, or at least it would be sheer epistemological vanity to rule out such
a claim a priori.

The challenge that procedural liberalism presents to our mode of inquiry
thus hinges on two very questionable assumptions: a rationalistic conception
of the self, on the one hand, and a rationalistic conception of normativity on
the other. Of course we are not the first to point to these drawbacks and to

propose alternative, more expansive vistas for political theory. The communitarian critique of liberalism shared a similar ambition. The communitarian critique famously challenged the atomistic ontology presupposed by procedural liberalism as well as the gulf it imposed between justification and application. It exposed the "punctual self" that lurks beneath much modern philosophical discourse (not just liberalism);[8] it highlighted the many "spheres of justice" with their specific goods and normative principles;[9] and it emphasized the concrete, historically specific "practices" in which the irreducible plurality of human goods are realized.[10] The central contribution communitarianism made to political theory, however, has widely been taken to be what Charles Taylor once called the "social thesis": the entanglement of the self in a network of social practices and allegiances.[11] The distinctiveness of communitarianism seemed to reside in its insistence on the importance—both normative and functional—of community belonging and participation. On this view, some identification of individuals with the larger community is at once a functional requirement of healthy, cohesive communities and a good to be fostered in its own right. But communitarianism, so understood, makes it hard to see how work can shape or constitute such a self. What we do when we work is not the kind of thing that can realistically generate a *communal allegiance*, or a sense of *communal belonging*, but it is just such forms of allegiance and belonging that communitarians think go missing in liberalism and that they seek to bring back into the picture with the notion of the social self.

Now it is true that the activity of working is an unlikely source of the kind of allegiance and belonging that communitarians invoke as a corrective to liberalism. It would appear to be a long shot to suppose that merely by working one is conscious of participating in something larger than oneself that generates a feeling of allegiance and belonging akin to patriotism.[12] However, it is not just by identifying with large-scale imagined communities—be they national, ethnic, or religious—that individuals acquire a social self. The identification may be more local and mundane: a local sporting club, perhaps, but surely more commonly a place of work. Or the identification may be with the larger body of practitioners of the activity one does when working, especially if that activity resembles a "practice" in MacIntyre's sense, as some professions do. Furthermore, it is not just by way of conscious identification with a group that one acquires a social self. One acquires it through actual interaction with others, and it is plausible to say that it is partly, if not largely, through working that individuals daily interact with others outside their immediate family. It is not unreasonable to suppose that work is not just a context of justice—though, as Walzer has argued, and we will maintain later, it surely is that[13]—but also a context in which the social self is at stake and of political significance in that respect too. The idea that the social self is also a working self was certainly not lost on John Dewey, though it does seem to have been forgotten by contemporary communitarians, including many who embrace Dewey's pragmatist legacy.[14]

In proposing that *the social self is also a working self*, we are thus drawing out a potential that resides in communitarian thought, albeit largely mutely. Rather than being an objection to our inquiry, the "social thesis" at the heart of communitarianism stands to be refined and developed by an investigation of the ways in which the self is shaped by working activity. However, it is important to distinguish this train of thought from another with which it is easily confused. According to this other trajectory, what is crucially at stake in the relation between work and the self is the object of the working self's authentic identification—namely, *the class of workers*. It can look, in other words, as if what we must be after in pursuing the thought that the social self is a working self—or, as we put it earlier, the idea that work has an ontological, identity-conferring significance, a significance it is incumbent on political theory to grapple with—is some kind of workerist redux, a rehabilitation of the now long obsolescent "production paradigm."[15] If that is what we are doing, there are indeed formidable challenges ahead.

The criticisms of the production paradigm associated with Marxism are familiar, but it is worth briefly rehearsing them here to clear away possible misunderstandings of the direction we are taking. At the crux of them is the thought that productive activity does not have the special self-constituting (or human-constituting) status the paradigm ascribes to it and, worse, that in granting productive work this privileged status it devalues other kinds of activity and other sources of identity. At an abstract theoretical level, the emphasis on production can be seen to screen out the kind of action that has a more communicative, moral, or political orientation, or it can be seen to exclude the need for a public realm in which human beings can disclose themselves in their plurality through speech and political contestation.[16] More concretely, the emphasis on productive work can serve to marginalize all the "unproductive" work that nevertheless underpins it: above all, child-rearing, care work, and domestic work. By privileging productive work, the production paradigm failed to articulate the struggles and wishes of those who were left to do all that other stuff. This is the core of the feminist objection to Marxism, but the objection can also stretch to the values implicit in the production paradigm, such as its celebration of a "masculine" stance of mastery and control over an environment (attitudes that seem essential to effective productive activity) and a trivialization of the "feminine" virtues of nurturing and care. This challenge to the ethos underlying the production paradigm merged with criticisms from the green movement and ecologically minded theorists who sought an alternative not only to a civilization of unconstrained production and economic growth but also to the whole spiritual outlook that condoned the unfettered domination of nature.[17] The unabashed anthropocentrism of the production paradigm always drew criticism inspired by romanticism, but it has come to seem increasingly objectionable in light of human-induced climate change, species extinction, and the industrialization of human relations with animals. The spiritual outlook accompanying the production paradigm has also been associated with an arrogance toward non-Western cultures and traditions, as if their lack of prowess in matters of production were a mark of their overall inferiority. In failing to challenge androcentrism, anthropocentrism, and ethnocentrism—indeed by tacitly if not expressly reinforcing these attitudes—the production paradigm has come to seem hopelessly out of tune with the times and completely inadequate as a framework for criticizing them.

We accept that if these familiar objections to the production paradigm applied to our proposal we would have serious trouble even beginning to justify our claim to offer a framework for social criticism attuned to the needs of the times. But the critical impulses animating nonworkerist social movements, and at least some of the shifts in critical theory that track them, are by no means inconsistent with the focus on work we propose.[18] This follows from our approach to the definition of work. As we have already said, care work is no less work than manufacturing work, the hotel cleaner no less a worker than the aircraft pilot. So long as we don't forget that a service such as a dressed wound is as much a "product" of work as a physical object such as a wooden cabinet, we should have little difficulty keeping our bearings on this issue. The important point is to be alert to the way the gender of the worker can affect how the product of the work, and the activity required to produce it, is *recognized* and *valued*. The same point holds for race. An understanding of the modes in which recognition may be granted or denied in the activity of working is thus by no means alien to feminist (and antiracist) concerns, and it will be a recurrent theme in the analysis of work that follows in this book. We also agree that the contemporary culture of work is dominated by masculinist values that not only get in the way of the equal recognition of men's and women's work but also corrupt the activity of work in other ways (for example by tolerating harassment or encouraging ruthless competition). But in our view it is not work as such, but particular *virile cultures of work*—cultures that could be replaced by more nurturing and caring ones if we chose—that have these features. A similar point can be made in response to the ecological critique. It is a particular way of organizing production that has led to the devastation of natural environments and the needless suffering of animals, not productive activity per se. Human beings prior to industrialization also worked, and they will continue to work once the current organization of work has passed. The challenge we face is not how to live without work, but how to live and work in ways that are better attuned to the natural environment and to the needs of other animals. Again, far from representing an objection to a focus on work, "green" concerns force the issue of work upon us.

As for the shift to a more communication-oriented paradigm of critical theory, we accept that action aimed at reaching understanding, and not just at control over an environment, is crucial for understanding social life and indeed for a diagnosis of the times. But again, rather than take this as a reason for turning attention away from work, we see it as a reason for looking at work more closely and enriching our conceptualization of work. When we do this, we quickly come to see that there is more to work than pure instrumental action and that the structure of working activity is by no means opposed to that of communicative action in its ordinary sense. In particular, some of the normative standards we expect to be fulfilled when communicating with each other (for example, the expectation that we will be listened to, that our word counts for something) are also standards we expect to be fulfilled when we work. And it is not unreasonable to suppose that the failure of the actual organization of work to deliver on these expectations is one of the defining characteristics of the times we live in.

So in turning our attention to work we need not be turning our back on advances made on the production paradigm in the tradition of critical theory. Nonetheless, in attending to the problems of work we will need to take critical theory in a new a direction, a direction different to the one developed by Habermas and other critics of the production paradigm. First, we will be focusing on the *specific* problems and pathologies of work, without claiming to offer anything like a general or comprehensive diagnosis of the pathologies of modern society. Second, we will seek to establish this focus by examining the empirical evidence for the existence of such pathologies, on the one hand, and the structure of subjectivity that makes them possible on the other. This gives our approach an *empirical* and *phenomenological* dimension that is generally lacking in post-Habermasian critical theory. Third, we will develop a normative analysis also specifically targeted on work rather than a general model of rationally grounded social criticism. Our goal here is to elucidate a *critical conception of work* or a conception that can articulate the critical impulses that arise specifically from the contemporary experience of work. In these three respects, the exercise in critical theory that follows takes inspiration from Max Horkheimer's original formulation of the tasks of a critical theory of society without (we believe) succumbing to the illusions of the old production paradigm.[19]

OUTLINE OF THE BOOK

The program of critical social theory pioneered by Horkheimer and his colleagues at the Institute for Social Research in Frankfurt was nothing if not an attempt to understand the sources of social suffering from which critical impulses sprung. Horkheimer saw clearly that the success of the program depended, among other things, on the availability of reliable methods for describing these sources, that is, methods for finding out what patterns of social suffering actually existed. Taking our cue from this methodological consideration, in the two chapters that make up part 1 of the book we examine the patterns of negative experience regarding work as they are revealed by contemporary methods of empirical social research. What, as a population, worries us about work? What are the main negative experiences people actually suffer either in the course of their working activity or in their exclusion from work? How extensive are these experiences and how deeply do they affect those who are vulnerable to them? Social scientists have developed a variety of techniques for answering these questions, and while, as we shall see, the picture that emerges from the application of them is sometimes ambiguous and confused, they do provide some objective basis for a diagnosis of contemporary ills around work. The aim of chapters 1 and 2 is thus to diagnose the current malaise around work not merely on the basis of hearsay or speculation but *insofar as the evidence commands one.*

In part 2 we offer a phenomenological description of work activity to supplement the empirical level of description considered in part 1. The aim here is to analyze the ways in which work activity, especially activity that is characteristic of work performed in organizations, affects subjective life. We distinguish two levels, or dimensions, in which this happens and devote a chapter to each. First, as analyzed in chapter 3, there is the technical dimension. Our claim, which challenges the philosophical orthodoxy, is that the *technical* demands a worker faces cannot but *engage the subjectivity* of the worker at some level. In contrast to the conventional view that technical constraints always only impinge externally on the subject, we maintain that the subject is drawn in and psychically shaped by the demands of technique, properly understood. Alongside the technical dimension is the social dimension within which the subject of work relates to other subjects. Relations of *recognition* are crucial to our analysis here, but again we need to distinguish different planes in which this occurs. In addition to what we call the "horizontal" axis of recognition, recognition as provided by peers, recognition also occurs on a "vertical" axis involving the work hierarchy as well as the client relationship. In chapter 4 we analyze the dynamics and tensions that can arise along each of these axes of recognition and we argue for the importance of a vibrant *work collective* in dealing with problems of recognition that are bound to arise within work organizations.

In part 3 our focus turns to the normative content of the experience of work analyzed in parts 1 and 2. That is to say, we will be concerned with expectations of how work *ought to be* as they are revealed in the negativity of the work experience. In chapter 5 we propose that these experiences have the content they do on account of expectations of *justice* and *autonomy* that are frustrated or denied. This means that there are standards of justice and autonomy that subjects generally expect to be met in regard to work—and *specifically* in regard to it—across a range of issues including access to the labor market, remuneration for employment, conditions of employment, the recognition of working activity, the organization of tasks, the distribu-tion of tasks, the work hierarchy, and others that we attempt to elucidate here. Having spelled out the main elements of the normative expectations that attend the contemporary experience of work, we then turn, in chapter 6, to the philosophical significance of this exercise and the role it has to play in the construction of a critical conception of work. We do this by way of a contrast between two models of critique. The first we label *objectivist* on account of the primacy it gives to impartiality, universality, and univocity in its construction of the normative standards that form the basis of valid social criticism in general. While many critical theorists and political phi-losophers are attracted to this model, we argue that it yields an unduly nar-row and restrictive conception of the norms apt for *critique of work*. We call the second model "experientialist" on account of the primacy it gives to experience and its orientation to practical transformation of the social conditions of experience. We argue that this model is better equipped than the objectivist one to deliver effective critique of the organization of work (both within the workplace and in society at large) that is so sorely needed today.

In the two chapters that make up the fourth and last part of the book, we turn our attention to a practice that has been systematically adopted by all sorts of work organizations in the past two to three decades: individual performance evaluation. Despite the qualms that are commonly expressed privately or behind closed doors about the legitimacy of these evaluation methods, they are seldom subjected to close public scrutiny or effective social criticism and resistance. Our aim here is to show how that thresh-old might be crossed and performance evaluation taken up as a serious political issue. We begin by contextualizing the introduction of individ-ual performance evaluation techniques within what has been called the "neoliberal" transformation of the organization of work, a transforma-tion marked in part by the emergence of a new style of management and indeed a whole new ideology of managerialism. We draw attention to the follies of this ideology, as others have done, but we do not leave it at that. Guided by our critical conception of work, we also look for practical solu-tions to the problems this managerialism has created. We do this by propos-ing an alternative approach to management, an approach that takes its main purpose to be the *reconstruction* and *maintenance* of *cooperation*. We then outline the functions the manager would have to have for such "cooperative management," as we call it, to take effect. In chapter 8 we describe an actual intervention in a company that illustrates how the transition from managerialism to something resembling cooperative management might happen. The problems afflicting the company, while generated by circumstances unique to it, will be all too familiar to many readers—at least those whose working lives are blighted by their employment in a neoliberal firm or an organization trying to mimic one. And the solutions found to these problems may give hope that things do not have to be that way with work, even the most productive, economically efficient work. But we also acknowledge that emancipation from social suffering at work, and the realization of deep-rooted normative expectations in regard to work, requires more than a transformed approach to management. At the very least, it requires a bottom-up transformation, the kind of transformation that brings about genuinely *democratic* change.

In the conclusion we reflect briefly on the broader implications for democracy of our critical conception of work.

PART I
Worries About Work

Chapter One

UNEMPLOYMENT AND PRECARIOUS WORK

Our task in this chapter and the next one is to examine the significance of work as it is revealed in common worries that currently surround work. The pervasiveness of these worries, as reflected, for example, in the frequency with which they surface in the media, "state of the nation" discussions, and political campaigns around the world, is itself indicative of the underlying social significance of work. If work didn't really matter, people wouldn't worry so much about it (though of course they may worry about it without speaking publicly, without even articulating the worry at all—a point we shall return to later). But the worries about work that permeate modern societies also indicate something else: that all is not right with work. The worries that afflict modern societies around work are suggestive of a *malaise* around work. Modern societies are unsettled by how things stand with work in a way that reveals both the significance of work for those societies and the conflicts, tensions, and instabilities that abide in them.

Before we proceed with our sketch of the main worries that cluster around work, we should acknowledge the dangers that accompany such an exercise and make explicit the limits of what we aim to achieve. The main point to acknowledge is the variability of the experience of work and the standpoint-dependence of the worries that relate to it. Clearly, the features of work that most concern people change over time. What worried people about work a few decades ago may not be what worries them about it now, and what worries people about work now may not be what worries them in the decades to come. The world of work appears to the observer today still in the shadow of the global financial crisis of 2008, but who knows how it will look in a few years' time? It is also clear that different countries have their own working cultures, traditions, and institutions that give national specificity to their experience of work and characteristic ways of dealing with its problems. One would expect the experience of work in a country with a minimum wage, extensive social welfare systems, and strong trade unions, for example, to differ significantly from that in a country without them. Third, and most tellingly, the experience of work, and the work-related anxieties to which one is vulnerable, depends on how one is socially situated and, in particular, on the socially constituted group to which one belongs. The worries about work of a poorly qualified school-leaver will differ from those of an expectant professional working mother; the anxious relation to work of a middle-aged man suddenly made redundant will differ from someone contemplating retirement after an uninterrupted working life. The young, the middle-aged, and the old have their own sets of worries about work, as do women and men, white people and people of color, the able-bodied and disabled. Age, gender, race, and ability/disability structurally affect the individual's relation to work, as of course does "class," however that is defined. It goes without saying that the relation to work of a subcontracted blue-collar worker, a domestic worker on a temporary migration visa, a self-employed shopkeeper, a chief executive of an investment bank, a tenured university professor, or whatever other class representative one might care to mention will vary enormously. And even when these and other structural differences in the relation to work are accounted for, each individual has his or her own unique experience of work and his or her own singular set of anxieties arising from work.

It is very important when reflecting on the meaning of work not to forget that one's relation to work is contingent on many factors, including prevailing economic conditions, the national culture and institutions in which one is embedded, the position one finds oneself in on account of one's age, gender, race, level of ability, and, of course, class as well as one's own particular dispositions and values. The closer one gets to the concrete individual and his or her relation to work and the anxieties that color it, the more visible these contingencies will be. But there might also be something to be gained from moving back a distance and taking a high-altitude perspective on the subject matter before us. If one were to do that, and with a wide-angled lens take a snapshot, as it were, of the worries about work in our midst, what would show up? What *patterns* of anxiety do contemporary societies display in relation to work?

In attempting to sketch these patterns, we by no means want to suggest that they are unaffected by the structures just mentioned. On the contrary, one of our central claims will be that social *structures*—the things that determine, with more or less force, how one is socially positioned—and patterns of individual *experience* can only be properly understood together. The malaises around work are by no means evenly distributed, and some people may be so fortunate as to hardly suffer from them at all. But those will be few in number. And, in any case, to the extent that the malaises around work are features of contemporary societies as a whole, they present problems that societies have to deal with and in that sense are of universal concern.

So what are the major anxieties that contemporary societies face around work?

FEAR OF UNEMPLOYMENT

No doubt the biggest worry surrounding work, from an individual's point of view, is the fear of being out of it. Generally speaking, the magnitude of a fear can be said to depend on two things: the harm that would be suffered if the object of the fear came to pass and the likelihood of it happening. While one can be irrationally terrified of something that is actually quite harmless and very unlikely to happen, as a rule fears are proportionate to the harmfulness of the things feared and the probability of their occurrence. Assuming that the fear of unemployment follows this rule—that for most people, unemployment would affect them badly and is a real possibility—we can ask what the harm of being unemployed consists in and the likelihood of falling victim to it.

First a few brief remarks about the latter aspect. Clearly, the chances of finding oneself out of work are indicated by the levels of unemployment. In 2013 the global unemployment rate was estimated to be 6 per cent, meaning roughly that of all the people who are available for paid work, 1 in 16 are failing to find any at all. By current estimates, about 202 million people find themselves in this predicament. They are spread across the world, but not evenly so. One is more likely to be counted among them if one lives in North Africa, the Middle East, and the so-called developed economies— where unemployment rates currently average at 12.2 percent, 10.9 percent, and 8.6 percent respectively—than in South East Asia or Latin America. But if current economic trends and forecasts are anything to go by, the chances of finding oneself in the ranks of the unemployed are on the rise just about wherever one lives.[1]

Of course one's vulnerability to unemployment depends on more than one's geographic location. It is affected by one's gender, race, class, and, most strikingly, age.[2] In 2013 more than one in ten (12.6 percent) of people aged between fifteen and twenty-four across the globe struggled in vain to enter the labor market. The youth of the European Union faced a particularly tough plight, with more than one in five of them (22.6 percent) failing in their search for a job. In Spain and Greece, where the youth unemployment levels in 2012 were a staggering 52.4 and 54.2 percent respectively, young people were more likely to fail than to succeed in finding paid work; a situation that shows no sign of abating. The employment prospects of young people in many other European countries are bleak, if not quite as grim, with unemployment rates of between 20 and 35 percent common. A sizable proportion of the youth of the Middle East and North Africa, where the predicted youth unemployment rates for 2014–2018 are 30 percent and 24 percent respectively, seem destined to have their fear of unemployment realized. And even in countries where youth and general adult unemployment levels are close to or below the global average, one may find oneself in a group that is particularly vulnerable to unemployment, such as the Aboriginal and Torres Islander peoples in Australia, more than one in five of whom were unemployed in 2012–2013.[3]

Since the statistical category of unemployment does not include people who are out of work but who do not meet the criteria of actively seeking paid employment, the "real" level of unemployment, or the number of people involuntarily without a job, is likely to be much higher than the official unemployment figures suggest, however scrupulously those figures are obtained. Generally speaking, unemployment statistics are geared toward economic macro management, and most economists would agree that they underestimate the threat of joblessness individuals actually face. Furthermore, since the category of unemployment also excludes those who find the merest slither of paid work, the unemployment rate as such tells us nothing about the extent of *under*employment, that is, of *insufficient* paid work. Indeed, official unemployment figures serve to disguise the actual lack of paid work of the underemployed.[4] The fear of unemployment is unlikely to be assuaged by a few hours of casual work per week, even if it is enough to raise one out of the rank of the statistically unemployed. Though it is less amenable than unemployment to measurement, the evidence suggests that underemployment, at least in the sense of paid work that is involuntarily temporary (rather than continuing) and part time (rather than full time), or work that falls short of a desired level of employment, is extensive and increasing.[5]

There can be little doubt that real unemployment is more pervasive than national unemployment rates indicate, worrying enough as those are, especially for the young and members of socially disadvantaged groups. At the same time, it is just as certain that employment remains a key institution of society, one that affects and shapes the lives of the vast majority of people across the globe. We need to remind ourselves of this fact in view of the prevalence of the myth of the end of work mentioned in our introduction. The myth of the end of work tells us that productively working human beings are being replaced at ever increasing speed by intelligent machines, taking away their jobs and leading inexorably to higher and higher levels of unemployment. According to the myth, within the foreseeable future there will be hardly any work worth paying for—and so next to no employment left to do. But as we have already seen, the reasoning behind this scenario is fallacious (it makes faulty inferences about the fate of the whole of the division of labor based on the fate of some of its parts), and it neglects the de facto centrality of the institution of employment to the lives of multitudes of people across the globe.

Of course, the fact that the vast majority of the world's population is either engaged in or dependent on paid work is no consolation to those who are involuntarily without it. We have just seen that unemployment is at alarmingly high levels, that its likelihood is such as to make it a real concern. But how seriously should one be concerned about becoming a victim? What, exactly, is bad about being unemployed?

We do not need to introspect or to speculate to answer this question: the impact of unemployment on the unemployed themselves, including their families, has been subject to extensive empirical investigation, using a wide range of methods, over a long period of time, in many different places. The research shows that in addition to the material deprivations that follow from the lack of paid work, there are psychological costs that the unemployed must bear. If you find yourself unemployed, you are likely not only to be financially badly off but to be in poor physical and psychological shape too. You are less likely to have interests that engage you, to have a lively sense of purpose, to have hope for the future. You are more likely to be depressed, to feel anxious and distressed, to believe that your life is not worth living. The association between unemployment and poor mental health, between being out of paid work and having the pathologically low self-esteem and interest in life that characterizes depression, has been known since the first studies of the psychological impact of unemployment.[6] But what is now also known, or at least commands the assent of the large body of unemployment researchers, is that the unemployed as a group do not just *happen* to be in poor mental health relative to the employed: they are in that condition *because* of their unemployment.[7] An abundance of research over the past decades provides compelling evidence that unemployment is the *cause* of the poor psychological and physical state that the unemployed generally find themselves in. Sophisticated meta-analyses of the results of the many studies of the psychological impact of unemployment provide "a clear and unequivocal warning that unemployment is a severe risk for public mental health that must be fought with all possible means."[8]

While the serious negative impact of unemployment on body and soul is not in dispute, there is some disagreement about how the effects of unemployment on the individual are to be explained. Put otherwise, while there is agreement that unemployment causes rather than merely correlates with poor health, there is some dispute about where this causal power lies. There are two main lines of thinking about this issue. One, championed by David Fryer, is that the distress endured by the unemployed is rooted fundamentally in their material deprivation, that is, in poverty.[9] It is because the unemployed are generally so poor, and do not have adequate material resources at their disposal, that they suffer in the ways that they do. Poverty does not just make it difficult to maintain good physical health by eating well, keeping warm, and so on; it also has an array of damaging psychological consequences. Poverty puts all sorts of constraints on action, it prevents one from doing the things one desires to do and it forces one into doing things one would otherwise not choose for oneself or one's family. It is such material incapacity for self-directed action, according to this approach, that lies at the root of the psychological distress known to be caused by unemployment. On top of this, the unemployed must generally, on account of their poverty, deal with the psychological burden of stigmatization. If they are in receipt of social welfare, or even suspected of it, they regularly find themselves subject to psychologically damaging hostile social attitudes and may face humiliation by their enforced state of financial dependence and inability to maintain a household.

There is plenty of evidence to show that poverty leads to psychological distress as well as physical hardship and that the unemployed, lacking an income, are particularly prone to it. And there can be little doubt that fear of such material deprivation moves the expressions of despair so frequently uttered in face of losing one's job. At the front of the minds of most people about to lose their jobs are questions like "how will I feed the kids?," "how will I pay the rent?," that is, anxieties about imminent poverty. Unfortunately for many of those who find themselves in this predicament, the dire material deprivations they fearfully anticipate will have unforeseen psychological costs too.

It would be egregious to downplay the role of poverty in the misery of the unemployed. But one can be mindful of the severe material deprivations occasioned by unemployment without identifying what is bad about unemployment with them. This is the second approach to the question of how unemployment causes poor mental health. According to this line of thought, developed most powerfully by Marie Jahoda, there are psychological costs to being out of work that are explained by specific psychological needs that those in work are generally able to satisfy but that are generally unmet among the unemployed.[10] There is thus a kind of psychic deprivation to being out of work *in addition* to both the material deprivation that arises from earning no income *and* the psychic deprivation that the material deprivation of poverty brings in train. Jahoda uses the pregnant term *categories of experience* to designate those aspects of psychic life that are generally given some expression among the employed, thus fulfilling a vital human need, but which generally fail to find expression among the unemployed, thus causing psychological distress. According to this approach, it is the absence of these categories of experience in the psychic life of the unemployed that is responsible for the poor mental health known to exist among that group—in addition to the material deprivations they suffer.

Jahoda identifies five categories of this sort. The first has to do with the experience of time. In contrast to the employed, whose waking hours are preshaped by culturally imposed time structures, the unemployed generally find themselves in a kind of formless time, an empty stretch that is a struggle to fill. They are particularly prone to chronic boredom, wasting time, and oversleeping—themselves hardly signs of sound mental health. The second category includes regular shared experiences and contacts with people other than one's family. Such experiences and contacts are important not only as a release from the centripetal emotional pressures of domestic life but also as a way of connecting with the wider social world. Employment provides a regular and reliable source of such shared experiences and social contacts, while the unemployed must seek such sources for themselves, leaving them vulnerable to social isolation. This also amounts to separation from collective goals and purposes, for example, those that orient the professions, as well as society as a whole. Connection with goals and purposes that transcend one's own, such as is enjoyed through participation in the division of labor, provides the third category of experience the unemployed lack. The fourth is the status and sense of personal identity that participation in collective purposes brings. One's employment generally provides a ready, publicly acceptable answer to the question of one's worth to society, one's social standing, and the question of "who one is." For many people, not having such a ready, publicly acceptable answer to such questions carries a considerable psychological burden. The fifth category of experience Jahoda identifies is "activity" (sometimes qualified as "reality-oriented activity").[11] Whereas employment generally enforces regular activity, the unemployed easily find themselves without it. Over time this also has damaging psychological as well as physical consequences.

It should be clear that access to the categories of experience listed by Jahoda is not *just* a matter of employment: wealth and other factors, such as education, play a role too. A reasonably well-off, materially well-resourced, and well-educated unemployed person may have less difficulty ordering their days and filling them with purposeful activity than a poorly educated person in poverty. It should be equally clear that forms of employment differ enormously in the *quality* of experience they deliver in these categories. Having a job is no guarantee against boredom, for instance, and the shared experiences with colleagues and bosses at work may be so corrosive that none at all would seem preferable. But neither the potential fulfillment to be obtained from activity outside employment nor the fact that some jobs can feel worse than having no job at all fundamentally undermines Jahoda's claim that the damaging psychological effects of unemployment have their basis in deprivation from categories of experience. This is because, as Jahoda points out, employment is by far the dominant *institutional* context in which these categories of experience are available for individuals in modern societies. It may not be the intended or "manifest" function of employment to meet these psychological needs—its manifest function is to create value through the wage system—and it is deprivation from the manifest benefit of employment, a wage, that is first on the mind of those who suddenly find themselves unemployed. But it is a "latent" consequence of being in employment to have those needs satisfied, however voluntarily or consciously one goes about meeting them, however well-equipped an individual might be to meet them by other means (outside employment), and however pleasant it feels to have them met. There is a *social fact* at issue here, namely the poor mental health of a particular social group (the unemployed), a fact that requires explanation whatever differences obtain at the level of the individual experience of employment and unemployment.

Several considerations count in favor of the framework Jahoda proposes for the explanation of the psychological costs of unemployment. First, it is more precisely targeted at the specific effects of unemployment, which may overlap but do not coincide with those of poverty. While, as recorded in the classical study of the unemployed of Marienthal,[12] the unemployed may experience their plight as overwhelmingly one of poverty, the working poor do not suffer in the same way as the unemployed, and it is the specificity of the latter that calls for explanation. Second, the approach has impressive predictive power for a theory of its kind: it yields predictions about how unemployment affects mental health that have generally been confirmed. Some of these tests have been direct, that is, have confirmed the operation of the specific latent functions described in Jahoda's model.[13] Others have been indirect, for example by determining the relative weight of the various costs of unemployment. One recent American study provides good evidence to suggest that the nonpecuniary effects of job loss are the decisive ones in determining the precipitous decline in subjective well-being (the degree of "life satisfaction" one feels) that follows unemployment.[14] In line with European studies, it supports the view that "income loss explains only a small portion of unemployment-induced distress."[15] And like these other studies, it turns to the latent mechanisms identified by Jahoda to fill this explanatory gap. A third advantage of the approach is that it provides a *psychologically* plausible explanation for a psychologically complex phenomenon. It takes seriously the psychological significance of being in and out of work, the contribution that working makes to the life of the psyche as a whole. At the same time, the psychological consequences of unemployment, the transformations of the psyche employment and unemployment bring, are bound up with *social* forces that transcend the individual. This is another merit of Jahoda's explanatory framework: it accounts for the *social facts* concerning the individual experience of unemployment by linking them to the social *institutions* from which they emerge.

For these reasons, Jahoda's theory is particularly useful for helping us to understand what is so bad about unemployment. But as Jahoda insists, the theory rests on a fundamental distinction: the distinction between *work* and *employment*.[16] Employment, the lack of which we have been considering so far, can be defined as "work under contractual arrangements involving material rewards." The more general category of work is more difficult to define, but Jahoda rests content with the definition which also served as our point of departure in our introduction: namely Marshall's definition of labor as "an exertion of mind or body undergone partly or wholly with a view to some good other than the pleasure derived directly from work." The distinction between work and employment is implicit throughout Jahoda's account of the harms of unemployment: it is the deprivation that comes from not being involved in a practice of social activity, namely working, rather than the material rewards secured by contractual arrangements involving such activity that lies at the root of the psychological phenomena. Whereas the manifest consequences of unemployment refer to the material deprivations that exclusion from employment brings, it is the latent consequences of exclusion from socially organized working activity that carry the explanatory weight for the psychological distress of unemployment. Furthermore, following Freud, Jahoda suggests that the underlying contribution to sound mental health of the latent functions of employment taken together consists in the "tie to reality" they provide.[17] But this tie to reality can be secured by work independently of its institutionalization as employment, just as each of the latent psychological functions of employment could, in principle, be socially secured in an institution other than that of contractually mediated material rewards.

There is one more reason to be fearful of unemployment, one more element of its badness, which we should mention. The debate we have been considering so far concerns the origins of the psychological harms of unemployment, harms that are known to exist in addition to material deprivations. But there is a type of harm that the unemployed, particularly young men, are vulnerable to which is neither a material deprivation nor a psychological one: namely, violence. Unemployment heightens the risk of exposure to violence, and—for many people at least—fear of unemployment is dreadful anticipation of a violence-ridden life. There are two sources of this violence that should be distinguished. On the one hand, there is involvement in criminal or black-market activity, which the unemployed may have recourse to in order to obtain money or acquire material resources. Clearly, those involved in such activity are not protected from the violence of others in the way that participants in the regular labor market are, and they are not constrained by the same sanctions on perpetrating violence themselves. This kind of violence thus arises from activities that are either on the edge of or on the other side of legal employment; it is a feature of the *ersatz* employment of the unemployed. On the other hand, however, there is violence that serves not so much as a substitute for employment as a compensatory negation of it. Adolescents and male youths in families with chronic unemployment are particularly prone to this form of violence. Disappointed in their hopes and expectations of finding a place in the institution of employment and the identity and status it confers, they turn against it and regain a sense of identity and status in small groups that define themselves collectively as enemies of that institution. Violence directed at the infrastructure of the world of employment, such as vandalism on public transport, or at agents of its reproduction, such as public officers and teachers, is symbolically destructive of a hostile force—*the world of working*—and for this reason can provide a psychologically effective mechanism of defense among groups suffering from chronic unemployment. In this case violence is not just a way of coping with poverty, as it is in the first from of violence we noted, but also a way of dealing with the psychic deprivations of exclusion from a central institution of society at large. In order to see this, we have to be able to see what is lacking in the lives of the long-term unemployed as more than an employment contract: a normatively structured world of activity and social relations has gone missing too. With the issue of violence, the psychological and social costs of unemployment appear in all their seriousness.

To conclude this section, we agree with Jahoda that the distinction between work and employment is fundamental for grasping the psychological, social, and indeed political significance of work. We also agree with the insight, derived from Freud, that the psychological and social significance of work is bound up with the tie to reality bestowed by work as activity as distinct from employment. We will elaborate our reasons for this in chapters 3 and 4. But suffice it to note for now that the badness of unemployment cannot be understood without taking account of the latent consequences of the lack of a form of socially mediated activity—*working*—in addition to the manifest consequences of the lack of the material rewards— wages—obtained from employment.

PRECARIOUSNESS

We noticed before that one can be in serious want of employment without finding oneself in the rank of the unemployed. This is the predicament of all those people whose employment is insufficient—those who have some but not enough paid work. We also noted that there is evidence to suggest that the number of underemployed is large and rising. Indeed, there are those who claim that this group, or a mutation of it, is so large, and rising at such a rate, as to constitute an emerging class of its own: the "precariat." And fear of finding oneself stuck in the precariat class, doomed forever to precarious work, is one of the defining anxieties of our times surrounding work.

While there is some disagreement among sociologists and economists about how exactly to define precarious work, and the precariousness of the situation of the people who do it, they all pick up on some aspect of the insecurity of work or the worker.[18] Precarious work is, in one way or another, insecure, and precariousness is an anxiously inhabited situation of uncertainty, instability, and fragility that arises from this lack of security. Those who are underemployed—that is, those who lack sufficient employment—are deprived of the benefits of employment here and now; for those who are precariously employed, this lack projects indefinitely into the future. The most tangible manifestation of this insecurity is the employment contract itself. A temporary employment contract or a casual (hourly contracted) job by definition delivers the benefits of employment to the employee for a fixed time only.[19] As such, it fails to deliver a key benefit of a continuous employment contract: namely, provision of those benefits that projects freely into the future. The shortcoming of precarious work, in this respect, is that it is a weak buffer against future unemployment; it provides flimsy security against it, in contrast to employment under a continuous contract. The failure of temporary or casual employment to deliver this benefit—that is to say, security—makes it not just *insufficient* as employment but *inadequate* as employment too. It affects the quality of the employment, not just the quantity. That temporary or casual employment falls short qualitatively as employment is revealed in the way we speak of a "proper job": a worker may go through more or less lengthy periods of temporarily contracted or casual work, but only finds a "proper job," according to our manner of speech, once he or she lands a continuous employment contract.

It is evident that those who have to make do with short-term employment contracts have good reason for feeling insecure in relation to their work and for being anxious about the future. But a dispute has emerged about the extent of this problem and the basis it provides for generalizations about the precariousness of work in the contemporary age. On the one hand, there are those like Arne Kallerberg, Serge Paugam, and Klaus Dörre who find the concept of precarious work useful for social diagnosis and can provide evidence of a decline in the average length of time workers are attached to their employers, a growth in the amount of "outsourced" or "contingent" work and work undertaken on short-term contracts, and a rise in perceived job insecurity indicated by the reported fear of job loss.[20] But the significance of such evidence has been challenged by others, such as Kevin Doogan, Ralph Fevre, and Francis Green, who have also been able to invoke evidence indicative of contrary trends.[21] So, for example, recourse to the short-term employment contracts characteristic of "contingent" work is more common in some industries (such as mining and agriculture) than others, and levels of "subjective job insecurity" (fear of job loss as reported in attitude surveys) have been found to vary significantly according to region, but generally track the rate of unemployment. Findings such as these suggest that precarious work is better conceived as being located within pockets of the labor market, rather than as a general characteristic of the condition of labor as such, and that work-related insecurity is a function of the cycles that the labor market would be expected to undergo, rather than an unprecedented structural transformation of employment relations as a whole. Among the evidence that has been found to indicate contrary trends (namely a decline in job insecurity), perhaps the most striking are Doogan's analyses of labor force data in the developed economies from the mid-1980s to mid-2000s, which show that long-term employment in most industries has risen rather than declined during this period, and Green's analyses of attitude survey data from around the world, which reveal no general increase in the levels of subjective job insecurity.[22] A look at the OECD's current database shows that the average share of temporary employment in the OECD countries in 2013 was 11.8 percent, a little more than the level in 2000 (11.3 percent) but a little less than the level in 2006 (12.2 percent).[23] As the proportion refers to the total level of employment, the share of "permanent employment" in the OECD since 2000 has remained steady at about 88 percent. Those figures are hardly suggestive of a structural change in employment relations from the permanent to the temporary, from the secure to the precarious.

If careful statistical analysis shows that long-term employment continues to be predominant in the labor market—that short-term temporary jobs are islands, as it were, in the sea of permanently contracted labor—then one might wonder what to make of the widespread anxiety around precarious or insecure work. Doogan and Fevre are critical of social theorists (typically sociologists) who claim that the past three or four decades have witnessed a veritable social transformation, a change in the very nature of society consequent on the decline of secure work and emergence of a class of precarious workers, despite the absence of any statistical evidence for this in the available employment data. However, they do acknowledge that fears and anxieties around insecure work exist and that a discourse of precariousness abounds. Their explanation for this curious state of affairs (the discrepancy between what is actually the case by way of employment security and widespread attitudes toward it) is that such fears and anxieties have an *ideological* function, one that the discourse on precariousness serves to reinforce and reproduce. That is, it suits the interest of powerful employers to have their current and prospective employees imagine themselves as weak and insecure, in competition with other weak and insecure workers for whatever scraps of short-term employment the labor market has to offer. It suits those interests, in other words, for workers to feel insecure about their jobs and to be grateful for whatever employment conditions are offered to them. Theorists and critics of the "precarious society" are unwitting accomplices of those interests and would do better, according to this line of thought, to stick to the facts about the actual terms of employment, which testify to the underlying strength and ongoing capacity for achievement of the standpoint of organized labor.

There is, however, another explanation that can be offered for the discrepancy between the pervasiveness of anxieties around insecure work, theoretically articulated or not, and the continuing predominance of long-term, relatively secure employment contracts. This is to distinguish between the insecurity that is attached to *work* from the insecurity that is attached to *employment*. The mismatch between pervasive anxieties around precariousness and the general availability of long-term employment in the labor market would then be explained, at least in part, by elements of insecurity at work that do not concern the length of the employment contract. Such forms of work-related insecurity would not reveal themselves in the employment statistics, but they would contribute to anxieties around precarious work, which all parties to the debate acknowledge exist, whether real or dreamed up.

Guy Standing, one of the most eloquent purveyors of the precarious society thesis, draws the distinction between work and employment in this context himself. [24] He provides a list of seven forms of security that came to inform the normative model of work (the standard for guiding how work should be organized) in the era of what he calls "industrial citizenship," but which are lacking among the precariat of today. Of these, what Standing calls "labour market security," "employment security," and "income security" all relate to work *qua employment*. Labor market security is the security of having guaranteed access to income-earning opportunities (the norm of full employment); "employment security" provides protection against the arbitrary termination, modification, or infringement of an employment contract; and "income security" provides assurance of a stable income within a job, through a minimum wage, wage indexation, and so forth. Of the four remaining forms of security in Standing's list, three collectively have a different character. What he calls "work security" refers to protection against accidents and illness incurred at work, as prescribed through health and safety regulations, restrictions on the length of the working day and unsociable hours, and so on. "Skill reproduction security" is provided through opportunities to learn and exercise skills through apprenticeships and training. "Job security" refers to protections in relation to the tasks performed, ensuring that the tasks remain stable and afford opportunities for career advancement. Although Standing does not characterize these three forms of security in this way, they all relate to work *qua activity*. That is, they refer to the regulation of working activity—its duration, quality, form, and recognition (in a sense we will endeavor to make clear later). The seventh and final kind of security on Standing's list, "representation security" combines aspects of work as employment and work as activity. For it refers to guarantees to enable workers to negotiate both the terms of their employment and the terms of their working activity in a collective voice and collectively to withdraw their working activity (through strike action or work to rule) in the context of such negotiations.

It should be clear from these brief considerations that employment on a long-term contract leaves plenty of room for deep-rooted feelings of insecurity in relation to work. There are aspects of *employment* that may be insecure in addition to the length of the employment contract, but, just as significantly, there are aspects of the *working activity* one is employed to do that can fill one with a sense of precariousness. Furthermore, while Standing's list nicely illustrates how insecurity in relation to working activity can arise, it by no means exhausts the possibilities. There are a host of ways in which one can find oneself feeling insecure in one's work, not just in one's employment, and good reasons can be provided for supposing that this is not an accidental feature of contemporary work organizations, but a systemic or cultural one. Take, for example, routine subjection to formalized techniques of performance evaluation. If one is regularly having to stand back from one's work and question its worth from an "objective," "neutral," or "impartial" point of view, if what one has achieved in the past is in principle never enough to secure ongoing recognition of one's competence and willingness to work, it would not be unreasonable to start finding insecurities in relation to one's working activity even if one was not initially aware of having them. The problem is exacerbated by the discrepancy often perceived by workers between the "performance indicators" their work is measured by and the activity that actually goes into doing good work. The former are presented in a language suited for the purposes of external auditing; the value of the latter is typically communicated in the vernacular of the workers themselves, if indeed it is reflectively articulated at all. Regular subjection to the scrutiny of auditors, and the distorted self-presentation required to appear satisfactory from their standpoint, add to the precariousness of work activity even if the employment contract is stable and one stays in the job. The wages one can expect, one's position in the work hierarchy, and the type of working activities one is expected to perform are all affected by bad evaluations. A related phenomenon is relations of mistrust within work organizations. If one is continuously on the lookout for ways in which the standard of one's performance can be made to appear inferior to what is expected, as the "weak link" in the chain of production or provision of service, again one is likely to find oneself perpetually "on guard," insecure, and "on the defensive" in relation to management and other workers. It bears repeating to say that workers can find themselves in such an anxious condition while occupying a "permanent" official position within a work organization.

We will have a lot more to say about performance evaluation later. For the moment, it is important to see how the enforced adoption of a defensive stance in regard to working activity underlies the sense of insecurity that the term *precariousness* attempts to capture. From the lived point of view of the worker, precariousness demands a state of readiness for change, a flexibility of personality adapted to the fungible requirements of the work situation. But the problem here is not just that this is all well and good for some kinds of personalities, the "risk-takers," for example, while leaving other more "risk-averse" types out in the cold. The problem affects all workers to some degree. This is because precarious conditions of work compromise the psychological investment in work that all working activity to some degree brings in its train. The psychological investment in work enables the worker to overcome the difficulties and endure the pains involved in the work activity. At its best, it can transform those difficulties and pains into sources of pleasure and satisfaction. But the precarious worker, being always on the back foot and on the defensive, is unable to make such an investment. And this block on the psychological investment in working for those who do precarious work is an important feature of the particular form of insecurity at stake here, whatever the personality type of the individual worker and whatever their conditions of employment. Furthermore, insofar as the defensive stance is a socially imposed position of weakness, those who occupy it are liable to various forms of social domination. In other words, precariousness also means lack of protection from the possibility of arbitrariness that is involved in their being dependent—with regard to employment, income, and type of activity—on the will of their employers. In some parts of the world at least, self-awareness of the precariat as a dominated group has given it a political reality that should be reckoned with even if the "objective" basis of precarious work remains obscure.

Richard Sennett sometimes speaks of *ontological security* in regard to work—not an expression you are likely to find in the catalogues of the bureau of statistics, but perhaps one capable of yielding insight nonetheless.[25] Sennett uses this term to convey the thought that when work goes well, it lends background support to one's whole sense of identity, but when it goes badly it can thoroughly undermine this sense. Sennett is particularly concerned by the way in which the cultural norms of work *institutions* can either foster this sense of security or wear it down. This is because the ontological weight of institutions, so to speak, bears heavily and inescapably on the individual. The larger reality of the institution, when it is organised by the right social and cultural norms, can be a source of self-reassurance for the individual; but when organized by the wrong ones it can crush the individual or be callously indifferent to the individual's fate. The latter can be expected to have social as well as psychological consequences. For individuals lacking the ontological security that participation in well-ordered institutions of work would provide can seek it elsewhere. The affiliations of the "disaffiliated" with work seem to be various, but if reaffiliation with well-ordered institutions of work is not an option, there is a question of how these various affiliations will all fit together and how conducive they will be to social cooperation.[26] We have already noted how long-term unemployment can trigger violent counterreactions in which identity and status are regained independently of, and in destructive opposition to, participation in the world of work. Something similar can be said of the members of the precariat or those who find themselves indefinitely excluded from the world of well-ordered institutions of work. They too can turn against the world of work *as such*, which even in its well-ordered manifestation presents itself to them as a friend turned enemy, and seek compensation for this betrayal in the destruction of that world.

If the insecurities in relation to working activity of the kind we have been describing are not inconsistent with labor market statistics showing a high prevalence of continuing employment contracts, nor are they confounded by relatively high and steady aggregate levels of "subjective" job or employment security. This is because subjective job security is measured by the expectation of remaining in one's job or, in the case of employment security, remaining employed in either one's present job or another one. In both cases the security relates to an employment status rather than to working activity. Another consideration to bear in mind is that unlike fear of job loss or a change in employment status, the kind of insecurity that attaches to precarious work activity is not amenable to measurement by way of statistical analysis of attitude survey data (or, for that matter, any other quantitative method). It would be a gross epistemological conceit to suppose that if such things cannot be measured they do not really exist. And finally, if, as we are proposing, precariousness should be understood in the context of relations of domination, we would not be surprised if those subject to those relations do not immediately or intuitively describe them that way. As we will see, working also means coping with the unpleasant side of work, and it could lead to denial (notably denial of domination) or to justification of the evils of the working situation (notably consent to domination). This too has significant methodological implications. For relations of domination may need to be "uncovered," and that task may involve *questioning* what seem to be obvious shared meanings, rather than *establishing* such meanings as part of the data-generating procedures of quantitative research. That means taking a different kind of approach to the subject matter—the entwinement of domination and insecurity—than the one suited for identifying patterns and trends in self-reported job security (or "subjective job security") at the level of a population. It means adopting an approach in which the phenomena may gradually reveal themselves in a space that is itself maximally free from domination, a space of inquiry in which the participants can reflect freely on their experience over an extended period of time and communcate openly with each other about it. We will present an example of this kind of study, one that gradually unveiled sources of insecurity and anxiety in a workplace and relations of domination underlying them, in the final chapter of this book.

Chapter Two

WORK-LIFE IMBALANCE, DISRESPECT AT WORK, AND MEANINGLESS WORK

Fears about unemployment and precarious work relate to the prospect of exclusion from something that brings vital benefits. The unemployed are *deprived* of things that those in employment benefit from, both the wages they receive in exchange for their labor and the various social and psychological rewards of inclusion in the institution of employment. Those in precarious work miss out on the security those in nonprecarious work enjoy. Another way of putting this is to say that employment and secure work are "goods"—valuable things the lack of which is harmful or damaging in some way. The worry about unemployment and precariousness could then be expressed in the thought that there are not enough of these goods—employment and secure work—to go around. Furthermore, it is not just the amount, but the *distribution* of these goods that causes alarm. Is it fair that access to the goods associated with a "proper job" should be much easier among some groups than others? What does the highly unequal distribution of opportunities for gainful employment and secure work tell us about society as a whole? Is such inequality sustainable in the long run? Such worries can prick the consciences of those lucky enough to have "proper jobs" and can stir deeper passions of injustice among those who must cope, perhaps indefinitely, without them. We will consider the basis of those passions in part 3.

But there are widespread worries about work that take a different form. Rather than being directed at the scarcity of the availability of the goods associated with work, and perhaps also the fairness of their distribution, these are directed at the presumed positive value of work itself. Otherwise put, they arise from the perception of work not as a locus of goods, or a means to them, but as something negative: an activity that contributes not to the enhancement of life but to the spoiling or degradation of it. In one common form, the worry that work has this feature relates simply to the time it takes up: in absorbing so many hours, work deprives people of the opportunity to enjoy other, nonwork-related goods, such as those of relaxation, leisure, spending time with friends, and, above all, family life. The ubiquity of the expression *work-life imbalance* seems to reflect a widespread anxiety that modern societies place too much value on work, that they overestimate the goods that work provides, and that this overvaluation has damaging consequences for individuals, families, communities, and society at large. We will look at the empirical basis for such concerns—the amount of time people are actually spending "in work" and the imbalance between "work" and "life" they report—shortly. The evidence, which is by no means unambiguous, suggests that it is not only the amount of time spent at work that contributes to the sense of life put "out of joint" by work but also the *quality* of that time. Here the empirical evidence is incontrovertible: the working lives of many people have become more *demanding* in recent decades. Although, as we shall discuss in the second section of the chapter, there is some dispute about the specific pathology known as "burnout," there is no doubt that the intensification of work has contributed to much personal suffering and that, in this sense, the experience of work has taken a negative turn. This source of negativity in the experience of work, to which popular talk of burnout and "stress" gives expression, is another indicator that work is far from the good it is usually presumed to be.

We want to say that the experience of overly demanding work, work that is high in stress and strain, falls short of its measure *as* an experience of work. It abrogates a normative standard of what the experience of work ought to be like.[1] But this is not the only way in which the experience of work can have this feature, the feature of possessing what might be called a "normative deficit." For there are *moral* standards that we expect to be met at work, standards whose abrogation generates feelings of *disrespect*.

We turn our attention to a malaise concerning unacceptably high levels of disrespect at work in the next section of the chapter. We try to capture here the range of disrespectful behavior that mainfests itself at work, which includes but is by no means restricted to bullying and harassment, and we consider the evidence, such as it is, for a deterioration in that behavior. In the final section of the chapter we look at one more way in which the contemporary experience of work seems to fall short of its measure and the discontent over work this normative deficit generates. This is the long-standing, seemingly intractable problem of *meaningless* work. Our task here, as it is throughout this chapter, is to make more precise a diffuse sense of anxiety that attaches to the quality of work generally available in contemporary society and to assess the justification for such worries insofar as the empirical evidence allows of one.

WORK-LIFE IMBALANCE

It is certainly a widely held perception that people are spending more time at work and that life outside work, which generally means family life, is suffering as a consequence. Columns on how to improve your work-life balance are a regular feature of magazines and newspapers, the question of work-life balance has become a key issue in bargaining between employers and unions, and it has become common for governments to commission research on the nature and extent of the problem of work-life imbalance and how to address it. The statistics give a mixed picture. In the 2010 European Working Conditions Survey (EWCS), for example, 18 percent of workers attested to having a poor work-life balance, 29 percent of employees said they would like to reduce their working hours, and 43 percent of the self-employed recorded that wish.[2] Shortage of time and fatigue arising from long working hours have been found to be the most commonly reported reasons for work-life imbalance,[3] but there has been a long-term decline in the average number of hours workers spend in their employment, not just in the EU but the OECD generally. According to the OECD statistics, on average workers in the OECD countries spent one and a half hours *less* per week in their paid work in 2012 than they did in 2000.[4] The share of employees working very long hours (more than fifty hours per week) across the OECD was at the last count 9 percent, though it is a bit more than that in the US (11 percent) and Australia (14 percent) and a lot more in Mexico and Turkey (29 and 43 percent respectively).[5] Conversely, a very small proportion of Russian employees (0.2 percent) work such hours, and the figure is also low in the Scandinavian countries (between 1 and 3 percent) and Canada (4 percent).[6]

For most OECD countries, then, there seems to be a discrepancy between popular consciousness of widespread work-life imbalance, which to some extent is reflected in the levels of dissatisfaction with work-life balance and desire for reductions in working hours reported in surveys, and the number of hours people are actually employed to work. Is it not puzzling that average employment hours (at least in the OECD) are going down while discontent about work-life imbalance is on the rise? Various factors might be invoked to solve the puzzle. One possible explanation is that even though there might be more time available for life outside work, especially family life, there is now more that needs to be done in that time, especially domestic and care work, if both householders are in employment. A second possible explanation is that even though people are spending on average fewer hours in their employment, their working time has become more demanding, making them less equipped psychologically for the demands of family life but more in need of the satisfactions family life can offer. A third possible explanation is that the demands of employment are increasingly seeping through into the time that officially lies outside it, such that work arising from employment but not counted toward it is responsible for the imbalance.[7]

Though other explanations could be offered,[8] it is notable that each of these explanations, which all have plausibility, calls for some reframing of what the expression work-life imbalance actually means. For, in each case, it is clear that working activity needs to be conceptualized in a way that extends beyond the sphere of employment, that "life" might exist outside employment but not so obviously outside work, and that the subject of work is one and the same in both life and employment. Talk of work-life balance can encourage a conception of ourselves as divided into a self that "works," in the sense of having employment, and a self that "lives," in the sense of having a family or private life. But the conception needs only to be expressed this way for its absurdity to become apparent. The challenge, which we shall take up in part 2, is to arrive at a self-conception in which the sufferings and pleasures of life and working activity are united.

Of the three possible explanations we considered for the discrepancy between the pervasiveness of anxieties around work-life imbalance and the amount of time people are actually spending in employment, a key presumption of the second has received considerable empirical confirmation: jobs nowadays are more *demanding* than they have been in the recent past.[9] They are more demanding in the sense that they require more effort, a higher pace and tighter deadlines. Evidence for the trend of work intensification comes from various sources, including the five European Working Conditions Surveys conducted between 1995 and 2010. These show, for example, that the proportion of workers in Europe working at a very high speed more than half the time rose steadily from just over 43 percent in 1995 to over 48 percent in 2005, while the proportion working to tight deadlines rose from nearly 46 percent in 1995 to 50 percent in 2005.[10] In the 2010 survey, 62 percent reported working to tight deadlines at least a quarter of the time while 59 percent were working at a high speed at least a quarter of the time.[11] While rising intensification is a general trend affecting all occupations to various degrees, it is increasingly affecting jobs in the public sector, and full-time jobs done by women. Not only is more being demanded of these and other workers by way of speed and effort but also less autonomy is being granted to them in the prosecution of their tasks. The number of jobs that can be classified as high "stress"—as requiring a lot by way of effort and speed but little by way of autonomy or discretion— has risen dramatically. Drawing on data from British surveys, Francis Green estimates that the proportion of high-stress jobs in the British economy roughly doubled between 1992 and 2006 (rising from about one in eleven jobs to about one in six for men and one in five for women).[12]

Work overload, arising from working activity that is high in stress and strain, is thus an increasingly common feature of contemporary work. But how serious are its consequences for the people who do it? The evidence suggests that there are three main health risks, none of which should be taken lightly. The first is cardiovascular disease. An association between heart disease and work stress has been established by at least twenty-three studies, with one meta-analysis of fourteen papers on the subject showing a 50 percent higher risk of heart disease among those who report stress at work relative to those who do not.[13] The second is musculoskeletal injuries and disorders. Disorders of the hand/wrist, elbow/forearm, neck/shoulder, and lower back are increasingly common and have consistently been shown to be associated with high work stress and strain.[14] A recent meta-analysis of longitudinal studies presents strong evidence that the association is causal, namely that high work stress and strain are responsible for musculo-skeletal disorders and can be used as predictors for their onset.[15] The implication is that the growth of musculoskeletal disorders is due at least in part to the increasing stress and strain of work. The size of the problem is evident from a report on changes in the state of health in the US between 1990 and 2010. One of the findings of the report was that low back pain and other musculoskeletal disorders had risen significantly during the decade, the latter by more than 3 percent.[16] By 2010 they were the illnesses with the largest number of "years lived with disability" in the country, alongside major depressive disorder and anxiety disorders. The latter (depressive and anxiety disorders) make up the third major health risk associated with high work stress and strain. A meta-analytic study of research from 1994 to 2005 discovered strong evidence of a causal link between high job strain and poor mental health.[17] A strong association between stress and strain at work and major depression has also been shown.[18] The EWCS of 2010 shows that depression is a major problem for workers in the EU as well as the US: 20 percent of workers there (18 percent of men and 22 percent of women) showed themselves "at risk" in regard to their mental health, though the proportion is higher than that for those aged over fifty.

Whether the condition known as burnout is a distinct species of depression, a zone in the spectrum of depressed states, or something else entirely, it owes its known existence to depressive symptoms belonging to workers and manifested in their work.[19] The burned-out worker certainly bears family resemblances to the depressed person: he or she feels chronically fatigued, continually "drained" and "worn out," and assumes a debilitating passive comportment. Burnout and depression are also characterized by low self-esteem, lack of interest, lack of motivation, and lack of a sense of accomplishment. The burnout syndrome is characterized by a sense of physical, emotional, and cognitive exhaustion that is not always so closely associated with depressive anxieties, and there is a diachronic aspect to it that also seems distinctive. Before the process of burnout can begin, there must be something that is "burning"—there must be a "fire" that can be extinguished. In the person with burnout, radical disengagement and "depersonalisation" have *replaced* full personal involvement, engagement, and enthusiastic commitment. And the context in which the transition from full involvement and engagement to radical detachment and disengagement happens is work—that, as a matter of fact, is the case, whether or not the burnout syndrome can be conceived as occurring in other contexts. Burnout could be described as the emptying of the worker's activity of its involved, engaged character; a process that has a devastating effect on the entire agency of the worker.[20]

The image of the burned-out worker has come to assume a prominent place in the contemporary consciousness about the hazards of work. But while the term *burnout* clearly resonates with widespread anxieties regarding the inner costs of work-life imbalance and work overload, the "scientific" value of the term is contestable. There is Scandinavian research to suggest that burnout is a distinct and fairly widespread phenomenon—according to one study, up to a fifth of Swedish workers may have experienced it—but there is not enough evidence to speak confidently of its prevalence.[21] Most studies of burnout have been focused on workers in the caring and "service" professions—social workers, nurses, and doctors mainly, but hospitality and call center workers too—and we know from those studies that the problems that go under the name of burnout are acute in those occupations. For example, in a 2012 study in which around seven thousand US physicians took part, almost half of them reported at least one symptom of burnout, with the highest rates amongst doctors "at the front line" of health-care provision, such as family medicine, general medicine, and emergency medicine.[22] Whether or not such findings justify us in speaking of a pandemic of burnout in those populations, what does at least seem clear is the high degree of work-related suffering in them.

It has been suggested that the high levels of burnout symptoms among care and service workers arises from a particular feature of the kind of work that they do, namely "emotional work." *Emotional work* is another term that enjoys much currency, though, like *burnout,* its meaning is contested.[23] Usually the term designates the work that workers have to put into managing their emotions in interaction with patients and clients. Burnout has always been associated with stress arising from interpersonal conflict at work. But the concept of emotional work picks out a specific source of stress in dealing with other people, one that is bound up with the need for continuous vigilance in the expression, and often suppression, of feeling.[24] Matters are complicated by the fact that it is in the nature of care and service work to show concern and empathy or, in other words, to show visibly that the patient or client is being cared for. To complicate matters further, the display of feeling that is demanded by the job is constrained not just by the professional judgment of the service worker but also by organizational norms; in this case, standards regarding the display of emotion required by an organization that might clash with the worker's own or simply be very difficult to produce.[25]

Emotional work, like any work, is susceptible to intensification, and the indicators are that such intensification has taken place here as well as in other forms of work. It is worth remarking that some of the damaging effects of work intensification we identified before, namely heightened risk of cardiovascular disease and musculoskeletal disorders, have also been found to be associated with emotional work intensification.[26] But its link to the kind of suffering associated with the "burnout" syndrome is particularly strong, and this link introduces a new set of worries about the contemporary world of work. We have just seen that the challenge of emotional work consists in part in hiding one's feelings and in part in managing the display of feeling to make it conform with organizational norms. If one's feelings are strong, if one is convinced that one ought to display them, and display them in a manner that conflicts with the organizational norm, the burden of emotional labor will be considerable. We know that a broad class of "moral" feelings—the emotional responses we have to what we take to be morally inappropriate treatment or behavior—are especially powerful. Emotions such as humiliation, indignation, and anger arising from a sense of injustice are particularly difficult to manage and, as the literature shows, particularly conducive to the kind of suffering known as burnout. But three important consequences follow. First, the processing or "management" of emotion must then be conceived as a feature of *all* work insofar as it involves experiences of moral disappointment, and since those experiences can arise in any context of work, they must be conceived as a feature of all work activity and not just the kind of work that is done in particular "sectors" (for example the health care, education, or hospitality sectors). Second, since it is clear that not all this psychic processing is conscious, we must avail ourselves of the resources available for understanding the *unconscious* mind if we are to grasp the psychic stakes of working. And third, the circumstances that elicit moral emotions are sources of concern irrespective of their contribution to the burnout syndrome. It is not just the management of such emotions that is the problem: it is also the morally deficient work situation itself that elicits those emotions. We will consider some of the unconscious mechanisms involved in working activity and the processing of moral emotions in the next chapter. But now we turn to concerns about the moral deficits of work insofar as they contribute to the general contemporary malaise around work.

BULLYING AND DISRESPECT AT WORK

Work provides the occasion for the onset not just of physical harms and injuries, such as musculoskeletal disorders and exhaustion, but moral harms and injuries too. For present purposes, a moral injury, as distinct from a physical one, is a harm that arises either from conduct that is socially unacceptable, or inappropriate in some way, or from the institutionalization of unacceptable or inappropriate attitudes. In speaking of the moral deficits of work, we mean the ways in which work organizations either allow, facilitate, or even demand morally deficient behavior or institutionalize morally deficient attitudes. Work organizations can be said to be morally deficient to the extent that they either allow, facilitate, or demand patterns of behavior from their members that fall short of the proper moral standards or institutionalize morally inappropriate attitudes toward their members and clients.

Now there is a widespread perception that moral standards in the workplace are in decline or, at any rate, that low standards of behavior at the workplace have been tolerated for too long and that the time has come to do something about it. Perhaps the most visible expression of this concern in recent years has been the public debate around bullying and harassment. It is clear from the popularity of books on psychopaths at work and the media attention given to workplace harassers and their victims that the issue strikes a public nerve. This public debate has not been without practical consequence: work organizations are now widely expected to have explicit codes of ethics, to have procedures in place for identifying and dealing with unethical behavior, for punishing the perpetrators and supporting the victims, and so forth. Several countries have introduced legislation to enforce work organizations to adopt such procedures, such as the "harcèlement moral" (bullying) legislation in France and the "Equality Act 2010" in UK, which in turn have triggered further debate about the nature and extent of the problems they are meant to address and the effectiveness of such legislative measures in addressing them.

The high level of public attention to bullying and harassment in the workplace has also been accompanied by a proliferation of academic research on the subject in the past two decades or so.[27] But this research by no means gives a clear and consistent picture of the size, or for that matter the nature, of the problem. A 2007 study of the prevalence of bullying in the US concluded that about 30 percent of US employees had experienced frequent workplace bullying.[28] Most of the studies on workplace bullying in US and Europe dating from the 1990s and early 2000s, however, suggest that the proportion is more likely to be between 10 and 20 percent.[29] On the evidence of some of the larger surveys of working conditions, the number would seem to be toward the bottom end of that range, if not lower. According to the overview report of the 2010 EWCS, for example, just 4 percent of workers reported to having been a victim of bullying or harassment in the year preceding the survey; a slightly lower figure than the level reported in the survey of 2005 (5 percent).[30] As for the distribution of this kind of behavior, or rather exposure to it, the picture is clearer: it is the caring professions, or those that work in places where care services are provided, that bear the brunt.[31] Largely due to studies of the effects of bullying and harassment on the careers and health of care workers, the seriousness of their consequences have become known. The experience of being bullied is not only unpleasant: it can wear the person down, eroding his or her ability to cope both at the workplace and in life outside it. In the worst cases, the individual withdraws not just from working activity (for example, through sick leave—a common coping tactic among the bullied) but also from life itself. Depression and suicide, "the ultimate escape," are known to result from bullying at work as well as from intolerably demanding work activity.[32]

It is partly in acknowledgment of the seriousness of the suffering that subjection to aggressive and intimidating behavior at work can bring that the problem of bullying and harassment has risen on the public agenda. Such behavior deserves public attention because it is no light matter and no one should have to put up with it. On this everyone now seems to agree. But it is one thing to acknowledge the suffering of those who are subjected to unchecked aggression, intimidation, and abuse at work, it is another to interpret the phenomenon in terms of a relation between a powerful individual perpetrator (the bully) and a victim. It might be that while the suffering of those who are commonly called the victims of bullying and harassment is real enough, their situation is misunderstood by conceiving it in those terms. There are several reasons for thinking that this is indeed the case.

First, there is the problem of definition of *bullying* itself. The term lacks a clear meaning and it can signify different things to different people. What one person calls a bully, another might call manipulative, assertive, or simply loud. This can lead to protracted and futile arguments over whether a particular form of conduct constitutes bullying or not. Does subjection to a one-off aggressive act amount to being bullied? Must bullying involve an intent to inflict harm on the part of the perpetrator, or is it sufficient that the victim feels picked on? Can the bullying intent be a collective one, that of a group of individuals or an organization, or must there be an individual person who means to do harm and who can be identified as the bully? There are no obvious answers to these questions. The contested nature of the concept in ordinary usage also carries over into its usage in empirical research. There is no consensus about how to "operationalize" the concept—that is, finesse it for the purposes of quantitative research—and this helps to explain the wide variation that exists in estimates of the prevalence of bullying, as we have observed. If we are still largely in the dark regarding the global prevalence and trend of workplace bullying and harassment, it is partly because those searching for it have been looking for (and finding) different things, which suggests that the concepts for investigating the matter are inadequate in some way.

A second reason why the language of bullying and harassment might get in the way of an understanding of the situation in which the moral suffering of workers occurs is that it gives a restricted view of the field of experience at stake. Bullying and harassment are by no means the only moral harms and injuries that are suffered in work, and it is important that we are able to talk about these other aspects of moral experience in the right language. For example, workers expect their contribution to the work organization to be duly recognized; they expect to receive a fair reward for their work; to be able to get on with their work without excessive monitoring or outside interference; to be trusted to get on with the job and to be able to trust others they work with and work for; to be able to do their work well according to the standards of their trade or profession; to have some say in how to go about doing their work; to have impartial procedures in place for settling disputes, and so forth. The disappointment of such ordinary expectations is itself typically experienced as a moral injury. That is to say, such things as the lack of recognition for the work one does; subjection to constant monitoring and surveillance; dealing with suspicion cast on one's commitment to work or ability to get things done on one's own, as if one would avoid work or shirk it given the chance; defensiveness in relation to mistrust among colleagues and more broadly in the work organization; the inability to do a job well because of time constraints or other pressures; having one's voice ignored and having no trustworthy place to turn when conflicts arise are themselves all forms of moral suffering. They are harms that result either from conduct that falls short of the right moral standard in the context of work or from subjection to a morally inappropriate institutionalized attitude within the work organization: in particular, *disrespectful* conduct and an institutionalised attitude of *disrespect*.

While bullying and harassment certainly counts as disrespectful conduct, it is not typically viewed as a matter of *institutionalized* attitudes of disrespect. But just for this reason the language of bullying and harassment can make other forms of disrespect harder to see. This is because bullying and harassment are usually conceived as the actions of a certain kind of personality, one that compensates for its own inner vulnerabilities by exploiting the vulnerabilities of others, as the "perverse narcissistic" personality is said to do. The suffering that results from bullying is thus conceived to originate in the actions of individuals, actions that are explained by the personality type, in this case the perverse narcissistic personality. The person who suffers, the victim, is also conceived as a certain type of personality, one that draws the interest of the narcissist and gets trapped in an abusive, pathological personal relationship with him or her.[33] Though there may be debate about the exact characteristics that define the perverse narcissistic personality of the bully, or about whether some other personality type disposes people to bullying, or about whether the disposition to bully is a feature of just some personality types or is latent in all, the underlying assumption is that bullying and harassment is about the behavior of individuals and is to be explained by the kind of personality that individuals—the bullies and their victims—have.

The problem is that there are forms of disrespect that do not have the structure that is presupposed in talk of bullying, and because of this, that may escape the attention of those who use such talk. Rather than being down to individuals with a particular type of personality, such disrespect is due to structural features of institutions: the attitudes and values they embody, their hierarchies, the social forces at play in them, and so forth. Individuals typically *find* themselves in such structures—the structures are "given"—and have to adapt to them. An individual's personality type might affect the way they adapt to the social structure they find themselves in, but the situation itself, the socially structured situation, is not their doing. So, for example, if there is a hierarchy within one's workplace that prevents one from having a voice that is listened to, one is subject to an institutionalized, socially constituted form of disrespect. If one finds that one's professional judgment about what is needed in order to do one's work well is increasingly ignored, such that one increasingly has to act against it in order to do one's work at all, the problem is again one of institutionalized, socially constituted disrespect at work. To give one more example, a worker whose contribution to the work organization is not duly recognized, say because there is no mechanism for acknowledging the unpaid work put into meeting deadlines, also suffers from disrespect that has its origins in a socially defined situation—how the workplace is organized—rather than an individual's personality type.

If experiences of disrespect at work typically have this social structure, the conflicts that underlie those experiences will be social too. While workplace bullying is easy to characterize as a personal conflict, or a conflict between individuals who are *set apart* from the social relations that ordinarily prevail at work, these other forms of disrespect point to conflicts in the social relations themselves that go toward making up work organizations.[34] This provides us with a third, very important reason for dissatisfaction with the discourse of bullying. For by focusing on the personal or psychological sources of conflict between the bully and victim, the discourse of bullying screens out the social sources of conflict that exist in work organizations and the social resources that could help the individual to cope with conflictual situations. It hides from view the social hierarchies and the normative orientations (the values and principles) that govern a work organization and that give rise to experiences of disrespect as well as the capacity of social solidarity between colleagues to make social and individual disrespect (and bullying) bearable. We need to have those hierarchies and governing norms in view if we are to understand and explain the sources of the disrespect. We also need to account for the type of work collectives that exist in a given workplace: are they structured by solidarity relations or by mutual distrust and individual competition? But these hierarchies, norms, and social relations will not come into view if our perspective is framed by the language of bullies and their victims. Indeed, the social processes of bullying will themselves be invisible, with the consequence that bullying itself will be inadequately understood and explained. Rather than serve to expose and rectify the kind of disrespect that is manifest in workplace bullying and harassment, the concepts of bullying and harassment can serve ideologically to hide the social sources of that disrespect and its damaging effects.

If this argument is on the right lines, one would expect that policies and legislation aimed at removing disrespect at work by codifying bullying behavior and imposing sanctions against individuals who break those codes would be largely ineffective. And this is generally how things have worked out. The various antibullying and harassment policies that have been implemented in many organizations, and the legislation introduced in several countries to serve a similar purpose, seem to have had little impact. For example, workers generally have little idea of what is in their organization's codes of ethics, and if they do know them they may doubt if they make much practical difference. At the level of legislation, antiharassment laws have proved difficult to police and are rarely enforced.[35]

The reasons we have just given for questioning the aptness of the language of bullying for the purpose of identifying and understanding moral harms at work also count in favor of a different discursive framework, one based around the concept of disrespect. If we were to adopt such a framework, is there a way of gauging the prevalence of the phenomena at stake? Are we able to say something more concrete about the basis of anxieties concerning the moral decline of workplaces now that the experience of disrespect serves as our guide?

The British Workplace Behaviour Survey conducted in 2007–2008, an analysis of which is presented in the book *Trouble at Work* (2012), provides some indications, though of course the situation may be different in other countries. The survey set out to discover the extent of "ill-treatment" in British workplaces, which is a broader phenomenon than "bullying and harassment" and, in the opinion of the authors, more amenable to measurement. Three distinct forms of ill-treatment were identified: "unreasonable management," "incivility or disrespect," and "actual physical violence or injury resulting from aggression." Forty-seven percent of the workers surveyed reported to having experienced some form of unreasonable management (such as "Being given an unmanageable workload or impossible deadlines" or "Having your views and opinions ignored"); 40 percent said they had experienced some form of incivility or disrespect (such as "Being ridiculed" or "Being treated in a disrespectful or rude way"); and 6 percent said they had suffered actual physical violence or injury resulting from aggression at work. Nearly 40 percent agreed with the statement "Where I work, the needs of the organisation always come before the needs of people"; 30 percent agreed that "Where I work, you have to compromise your principles"; and 20 percent agreed that "Where I work, people are not treated as individuals." Overall, just over half of this large representative sample of British workers said they had experienced some form of work-related illtreatment in the two-year period.[36]

Leaving aside the issue of whether "disrespect" should be considered narrowly as subjection to rude or uncivil behavior (as the authors of *Trouble at Work* propose) or as a broader category of social suffering in the manner we have been outlining, the report sheds light on the prevalence of moral harms experienced at work that are largely invisible in the discourse on bullying. It shows that disappointed expectations among the workforce of fair and reasonable treatment, and of recognition of the value of their work and the principles that guide it, are the chief indicators of "troubled workplaces," at least in one country. It is startling to observe that close to a third of workers in Britain believe that they must compromise their principles at work. To have to earn one's living by acting in ways that fall short of the standards that one expects to apply in the situations in which one works is a heavy burden to carry, but it is evident that many people have to bear it. In their analysis of the results, the authors of the survey report are led to a conclusion that other observers of modern work organizations have already reached: in troubled workplaces the moral sense of workers itself becomes corrupted. If the conditions are not right, people can lose their moral knowledge: for example, that one ought not humiliate or ridicule or systematically ignore the voice of others. Another way in which troubled workplaces can damage the cognitive capacities of the people who work in them, which has also been observed before, but which Ralph Fevre and the coauthors of the report confirm, relates to the persistence of assumptions regarding fair and equal treatment even when there is no longer any evidence for it. Workers generally expect their work organization to "treat them as individuals," to "take account of their needs" and "listen to their opinions"—or, as we would say, to show them respect—and need to be persuaded out of the presumption that this is *not* how things actually stand in their place of work. Their presumption of fairness and respect persists even when the evidence contradicts it. It is worth remarking, however, that Fevre and his colleagues, like others who have reached this insight, do so by way of individual case studies of troubled work organizations and not on the basis of large-scale survey data.

The authors of *Trouble at Work* conclude that widespread public worries about the prevalence of workplace bullying are best interpreted as a misplaced response to underlying *normative conflicts* that have come to pervade work organizations. Rather than seeing ill-treatment at work as arising from strong-arm bullies imposing their individual will on weak and vulnerable victims, it should be viewed instead as a matter of the norms that shape work organizations, and in particular the imposition by management of norms that conflict with normative expectations of fair, reasonable, and respectful treatment between workers. In order to see the matter this way, one must replace the focus on the individual perpetrator and victim, typical of the literature on bullying, with a focus on the social forces at play. And, as we have just seen, these forces can have a distorting impact on the moral understanding of workers themselves. In our attempt to map out the malaises around work, we thus encounter again the problem of ideology and the need for a method capable of unveiling the ideological aspects of work and the ideological self-misunderstanding of work organizations. We were not fully convinced that the precariousness paradigm produces an ideological effect, namely, in weakening the bargaining power of collective labor, and we have seen that it would be more likely that the harassment or bullying paradigm could produce such effects, namely, in dissimulating the social processes that underpin experiences of disrespect suffered at work and their severe consequences. To talk about an ideological effect in this way does not commit us to the belief that these discourses have been deliberately shaped so as to produce these effects. But when the management of a firm claims that what comes first is the recognition of autonomy and responsibility, and the autonomy and responsibility of employees is for the most part confined to means of meeting the expectations of management, one is confronted with an ideological discourse of another type: it serves to rationalize forms of what we term social disrespect at work, to create a consensus based on the denial of the nature of the working situation, namely, a situation where the normative expectations of the workers are far from being met.

At the beginning of this section we mentioned that a moral injury can be thought of as a harm brought about by socially unacceptable or inappropriate behavior, which may also be shaped by institutional frameworks. Across a broad range of cases that include a lack of civility, the harassment and humiliation of a person as well as unfair treatment and violence, the moral content of the injury arises from the disrespect the behavior expresses toward someone. We have seen that worries about the level of disrespect and the harm it causes are integral to the contemporary malaise around work. But if this conception of disrespect corrects the narrow conception of it as mere incivility, it may be that the conception of a moral injury with which we began this section is also too narrow. That is, there might be harms whose "moral content" arises not so much from actions of others that fall short of some socially accepted standard, as from the quality of life that the subject of the harm leads. In such cases the "moral" dimension of the injury would arise not so much from disrespect, or disappointed expectations of the recognition of one's worth as a person, as from the frustration of the desire to *realize oneself*, to live according to one's unique standard. The relevant concept for grasping what is at stake here is not so much respect as individual fulfillment or authenticity. And, as we shall see in the next section, a separate set of anxieties in relation to work is attached to it.

MEANINGLESS WORK

Unlike worries about unemployment, precarious work, work-life imbalance, burnout, and disrespect at work, the last set of concerns we shall consider does not get much public attention, at least not nowadays. They have, however, occupied the reflections of many philosophers and social theorists stretching back at least to the industrial revolution, as well as industrial psychologists in more recent times. It is also something that many people unhappy with their job or career would have privately reflected upon and is responsible for many a sleepless night among high school pupils and college students. For there are people who are unhappy

with their job or career not so much because it is inadequately paid, insecure, or precarious, or because they spend too much time at work, are overloaded by it, or experience disrespect there, as because they do not feel
fulfilled in their work. Young people, having finished their education and
standing at the gates of the labor market, may feel dread at the prospect of
entering, as if doomed to waste a good part of their lives in boring, hateful
jobs. The worry for these people is that they will not be able to find *meaningful* work. Anxiety and discontent about enforced participation in meaningless, unfulfilling work may not grab the headlines, but it is an enduring
feature of our malaise around work.

Is there a way of telling how prevalent such worries about work are?
While it is unusual for working conditions surveys to feature questions
about the "meaningfulness" of work, most of them do include questions
about "job satisfaction." And the degree of job satisfaction reported in these
surveys, in the OECD countries at least, has been consistently high. The
EWCS reports high degrees of satisfaction with "working conditions"
across all occupations in the past two decades: in the 2010 survey, 84 percent of workers across the European Union answered that they were either
"very satisfied" or "satisfied" with their working conditions, and very few
(less than 5 percent) said they were not satisfied at all. But being an overall
indication of how satisfied one is with the conditions under which one
works, degree of "job satisfaction" does not reveal very much about the *fulfillment* one finds from work. It is possible to feel deeply unfulfilled in
one's work, and to feel one is wasting one's life in it, without feeling particularly dissatisfied with the working conditions of the main job that one
does (the pay, hours, and so forth) or, otherwise put, with the terms of one's
employment.

However, working conditions surveys also provide information on the
so-called intrinsic features of the job, including features that have to do
with the activity of working, such as the tasks that have to be performed,
and degrees of satisfaction about these might provide better insight into the
extent of personal fulfillment gained from work. In particular, the skill
level required of the job, the various capacities that have to be exercised in
it, the potential for the development of those capacities and the acquisition of new skills through working, the possibility of self-development,
self-expression, and the exercise one's powers of judgment, all contribute
to the quality of work in a way that would appear to make it more or less

meaningful or fulfilling for the worker. There is evidence to suggest that the introduction of new technologies (especially computers) has generally raised the level of skill required for most jobs, and surveys over the past two decades indicate that most workers are able to exercise some skill in their work.[37] To draw once more from the 2010 EWCS, 82 percent of the European workers surveyed indicated that they were able "to solve unforeseen problems" at work; 75 percent were able "to apply their own ideas"; 68 percent "learnt new things" at work; 58 percent said they had "complex tasks" to do; 55 percent said they did not have monotonous tasks; and 60 percent said they did not have repetitive tasks. Diversification of work activity through task rotation is a well-established method of reducing monotony and repetition, and it was reported to be available to about half of workers in organizations with more than ten employees. Another noteworthy finding of the survey was that just over half the workers (55 percent) said that their "present skills correspond well with their duties," implying that there was a match between their actual skill levels and the levels required for the acquittal of their tasks.

Such findings seem to mollify a long-standing concern that philosophers and social theorists have expressed about the human consequences of the division of labor in modern industrial societies. Toward the end of the eighteenth century Adam Smith famously observed that commercial production was made much more efficient by dividing the production process into discrete tasks that could be assigned to distinct groups of workers. But Smith also observed that while the division of labor responsible for these gains in productivity would dramatically enhance wealth, they would also have a crippling effect on the minds and souls of those at the base of the production process whose working lives were consumed with monotonous, repetitive, mindless, spiritually deadening menial labor. Deprived of the opportunity to exercise their natural cognitive and moral capacities in their long working days, these workers—"the great body of people"—were in danger of becoming "as stupid and as ignorant as it is possible for any creature to become . . . unless government takes some pains to prevent it."[38] The dehumanizing effects of the division of labor under capitalism seemed obvious to many social theorists and social commentators in the nineteenth century, as did the potential for increased productivity through the identification and manipulation of the discrete tasks of the production process, culminating in Frederick Taylor's formulation of the principles of scientific management at the turn of the twentieth century.[39] This tension between the goals of efficient, profitable production, on the one hand, and the overall well-being (if not the wage packet) of the great body of those engaged in productive activity, on the other, set the stakes for one of the defining sociological debates of the postwar period. According to Harry Braverman, the fundamental characteristic of the production process under capitalism, responsible for both its efficiency dividends and its human costs, was the separation it instituted between "conception" and "execution," the former migrating largely to a privileged management class, leaving the latter to be performed in isolation from them by the working class.[40] This separation was manifest, Braverman argued, in a long-term decline in the skill levels required for productive activity: in the course of the twentieth century, most work had come to involve the mere "execution" of tasks whose "conception" happened elsewhere, namely amidst the dominant capital-owning and management class. Braverman thought that the degradation of work and the worker under capitalism could only be corrected by an overhaul of the productive process, and many agreed with him.

Does the information that we now have about the skill levels required of workers put such worries about the "degradation" of work to bed? Does it expose the folly of ignoring the facts for the sake of preserving some preciously held Marxist or post-Marxist dogma, as has been suggested?[41]

The matter is not so simple. First, while the picture that emerges from the working-conditions surveys and other sources is not so bleak as the more dystopian depictions of work in contemporary capitalism, and is at odds with the general "de-skilling hypothesis" put forward by Braverman, it is by no means a rosy one and should still occasion concern. The 2010 EWCS data indicates that a quarter of European workers are not able to apply their own ideas at work, about a third learn nothing new at work, nearly half have no complex tasks to do, and the same proportion have skill levels that don't match up with their duties. That means there is a very substantial minority of workers who see themselves as either having no skilful work to do or as being without work that reflects their abilities. Everyone agrees that engagement in complex, skillful activity is an important element of well-being and that deprivation from such activity in the long term is harmful.[42] Given that it is such an important human good, it should concern us that a large proportion of the population are without it. It should concern us not only because of its social consequences but because there is a moral issue at stake: if there is not enough skillful work to go around, if there are some kinds of work that even the most sophisticated computers can't make interesting, why should a certain group of people be stuck with them, perhaps for life? And why should the composition of that group be shaped by class, gender, race, and ability/disability, as it is known to be? Are deep-seated inequalities in relation to access to work that allows for some degree of skillful self-expression and judgment morally acceptable, given how important such activity is for individual flourishing? The persistence of low-skill monotonous jobs, their not insubstantial prevalence, and the manner in which they are socially distributed leave little room for complacency about the general state of the "intrinsic quality" of work.

Matters are also complicated by problems relating to the interpretation of the information presented in the working conditions surveys. Consider the first of the results we cited earlier, that 82 percent of European workers said they were able "to solve unforeseen problems" in their work. The figure suggests that a very high proportion of workers are engaged in some kind of "problem-solving activity" and thus are able to exercise some degree of autonomy and judgment in their work. For what is it to solve unforeseen problems if not to draw on one's practical rational capacities, capacities for discerning what a particular situation requires, and thus to exercise discretion or autonomy, though typically, of course, without reflection or an explicit articulation of what is going on? This means that if a worker is able to solve unforeseen problems, he or she is exercising conceptual capacities at some level and so is not blindly or brutishly "executing" someone else's conception, as the traditional image of the industrial laborer suggested. If a worker was merely mechanically executing a task that someone else conceived, he or she would not be able to solve unforeseen problems. But consider: what would working be like if one really were *not* able to solve unforeseen problems? In practice, work situations *always* throw up problems that have not been anticipated; work that was not able to solve them would be work that did *not get done*. Not, of course, that this problem-solving activity is something the worker is necessarily conscious of or able to put into words. The capacity of workers to solve unforeseen problems is manifest in the working, not in some set of skills that can be ascribed to them and that they know they have in advance, which is then merely "applied" when unforeseen problems occur.

Rather than taking the information provided by recent working conditions surveys as settling the matter about deskilling or the degradation of labor under capitalism, we should take it as an invitation to probe more deeply into the question of *what working activity actually consists in.* But this itself, we just suggested, may not be self-evident to the worker and, by implication, may not be the kind of thing that reveals itself in working conditions surveys. We need another means of access into the meaning content of working activity, one that uncovers meanings the worker may not be consciously aware of or able to recognize in the kind of formulations that are apt for large-scale population-level surveys.

Furthermore, even if empirical social science succeeds in debunking the deskilling hypothesis by demonstrating the existence of skillful activity throughout the division of labor, it would still not settle anxieties about the availability of meaningful or fulfilling work. This is because although the capacity to exercise some skill might be necessary for work to be meaningful or fulfilling, it is not sufficient for it. This implies a general truth about the relation between meaningful work and "self-realization," which has consequences that are particular to the so-called post-Fordist culture of work that shapes many contemporary work organizations.

The general truth is that meaningful work enables not just the expression and development of any capacities, but capacities that one takes to be of value. One must be able to embrace or appropriate the capacities one expresses in work and, in addition, see those capacities as an expression of oneself. Meaningful work must meet the latter condition as well as the former because, even if I recognize that a certain activity is valuable and worthwhile for *someone* to do, I might not see myself as suited to it and so I might not see it as something that would be fulfilling for me. People can find themselves unfulfilled in their work even if they recognize that someone else could well find fulfillment from it. To speak of meaningful or fulfilling work is to speak of work that enables self-realization, and of course everyone has their own "self," which it is the project of each individual life to "realize." In lives that lack meaning, the project of self-realization is not going well. And for many of the unfortunate people who find themselves leading such lives it is their work that is going badly. We have already looked at several ways in which work can go wrong: besides being inadequately remunerated, it can be made insecure, take up too much time, be too demanding, and be a source of disrespect. But the sense of discontent with work at issue here is that of not feeling "at home" in one's work, of feeling "alienated" from it, or, to use a more contemporary expression, feeling "inauthentic" in one's work.

But inauthenticity takes on a particular significance in the post-Fordist culture of capitalism. This is because in work organizations shaped by this culture the worker is *expected* to feel authentic in her work, which in this case means an expectation to identify wholeheartedly with the work and the organization that magnanimously provides it. This phenomenon, which in the German literature is known as the "subjectivization" of work, transforms authenticity from an individual's desire into a company's demand.[43] Or, more precisely, it manipulates the desire to conform to the demand. The individual worker must now work on herself in order to appear authentic, since inauthenticity or self-nonrealization in work would betray a failing in the productive agency of the worker. Workers in this situation are thereby forced into taking an external instrumental stance on their own inner spontaneous desire for authenticity and self-realization. They have to present themselves to clients and colleagues as engaged in self-realizing activities if they want to meet the managerial demands—a self-presentation that involves a great deal of emotional labor and self-reification (self-entrepreneurship being another contemporary managerial demand for self-reification). Such a self-relation might be useful to the company, but it is destructive in the long run for the worker. Self-realization cannot be compelled, and a self conceived as a useful commodity for a company or organization cannot last. Authenticity cannot be managed; indeed, nothing could be more inauthentic than managed authenticity. If this is the main kind of authenticity work offers, it is bound to generate a malaise of inauthenticity.

Thus while skill is an important, indeed necessary, feature of meaningful work, the problem of meaningless work extends beyond the skill levels that the various jobs that make up the modern division of labor require. Conversely, the degradation of work is not necessarily a matter of deskilling—whether or not that has generally happened across the division of labor—though the ability to express capacities that one values and to which one feels suited is the key to finding meaningful work. The lack of availability of such work to everyone, and the privileged access to it that some enjoy, are rightly concerns that we have about work, as are new forms of work that demand all sorts of contorted and destructive self-relations to be undertaken.

Our aim in this chapter and the previous one has been to map out the main worries that modern societies have in relation to work. We have identified five main zones of anxiety: unemployment, precariousness or insecurity in relation to work, the high demands of work that can culminate in burnout, various forms of disrespect shown at work, and unfulfilling or meaningless work. Our examination of the social research on these matters has shown that these anxieties about work have a basis in reality: unemployment, precariousness, work intensification, disrespect, and meaningless work are all worryingly prevalent social facts that have seriously damaging consequences for those who suffer from them. The prevalence, nature, and impact of unemployment, precariousness, overwork, experiences of disrespect, and meaningless work make them all things that we are and ought to be deeply concerned about.

But our exploration of these zones has also shown that what is most worrying about work is not always what it seems. Malaise around work is most obvious when work is considered as *employment*. From this point of view, the benefits of work appear as the fruits of an employment relation—first and foremost the wages that are paid. Conversely it is the absence of those benefits that define, above all, the source of the suffering of the unemployed and the precariat, and perhaps those most vulnerable to disrespect and meaningless, low-value work too. There is no question that, in the case of the unemployed and the precariat at least, they suffer considerably from their exclusion from the manifest benefits that employment brings. But we have seen that in addition to concerns that attach to work as employment, there are also those that attach to work as *activity*. Unemployment has a destructive impact on the psyche on account of the deprivation of an institutional framework for objectively engaged, socially connected action; precariousness in the activity of working deprives the subject of secure sources of self-identity and self-trust; ever-higher paced, physically and emotionally demanding work has its own rewards, but eventually burns the subject out; disrespect in the course of doing one's work offends the moral sense and can lead to a pathological inner withdrawal from both work and life itself; and meaningless work deprives subjects of the kind of activity that contributes decisively to a meaningful life. We have also seen that the malaises around work do not only concern the consequences of deprivation of stable employment and satisfying activities on individual health and self-flourishing but also on social life itself: social life at work (through participation in supporting work collectives or in a generalized competition where everything is permitted) and social life outside work (for instance, the reduction of family life to a mere shelter from the suffering experienced at work). Last but not least, we have also seen that work is the origin of social questions that are not usually connected with work such as the question of violence.

Our consideration of the contemporary malaises around work therefore suggests that malformations of work as activity are responsible for various types of psychic damage that are characteristic of the modern world and, conversely, that work as activity in well-ordered institutions makes a vital positive contribution to psychic health. In the next two chapters we offer an account of the self that makes this relation between work and the psyche intelligible. Our task will be to bring out the intimate connection between working and subjectivity such that malformations on the one side can make sense of pathologies, both individual and social, on the other. But the execution of this task requires us to make a shift in standpoint from the one we had to adopt for the purposes of the first part of our inquiry. Up until this point we have had to stand back a distance, observing the field from a height, as it were, to survey widely held anxieties and to gather together the social facts. It is now time to zoom in and look into the inner structure of the working self.

PART II

The Subject at Work

Chapter Three

THE TECHNICAL DIMENSION

The aim of the previous two chapters was to establish a valid social diagnosis backed up by good empirical evidence about the malaise surrounding work in our societies. We sought to identify and characterize the main symptoms that combine to form this malaise. In the course of our diagnostic analysis, it gradually emerged how complex the experience of work is for us. On the one hand, the dread of unemployment or even simply the scourge of underemployment showed in the negative what is expected of work, namely that it provide access to a number of goods that appear crucial for a flourishing life; not just material well-being but also the engagement of intellectual and physical capacities, existential security, social belonging through contribution to the community, and the acquisition of a positive social status. On the other hand, the actual experience of work undermines us in a myriad of ways: not just through mental or physical exhaustion but also by preventing us from enjoying goods that are important for us and by forcing us to compromise on our moral standards. The need to see oneself as worthy of respect, for example, or to enjoy supportive, committed, intimate relationships with others, or indeed to find meaning in one's activities and life as a whole, is fundamentally affected by the experience of work. The image of work that gradually emerged from the different pathologies of contemporary work was of an experience in which the bodily, psychic, moral, and even political life of the individual is at stake.

In this chapter and the next, we seek to understand what it is about work that makes it such a defining experience, with a deep-rooted and far-reaching impact on the self. The model of work we propose is premised on the thought that *one and the same subject* is summoned by the various demands of work, suffers the various impacts of work, and enjoys work's various satisfactions and compensations. The demands of work have what we will call a *technical* and a *social* dimension. The former refers to work as pragmatic or instrumental activity, that is, activity defined by a task, the accomplishment of which provides the point of the activity. We can call whatever is accomplished through the performance of a task the "product." Products can be material or immaterial: physical objects such as a baker makes or a service such as transport or a state of being for another person such as a feeling of calm induced by a nurse. It is important to keep in mind that all work—whether agricultural, industrial, service, or care work; whether manual or intellectual—has a technical character in this broad sense, and it is certainly not confined to skilled manufacturing work or the work of the traditional "craftsman." The technical demands of work summon up *effort* on someone's behalf. "Techniques" are those rules and processes that guide the efforts and activities of agents in performing a task, that is, in delivering a product, whatever it may be. In this sense, good care provision is as much a technical matter, as much a matter of technique, as good car manufacture. Similarly, intellectual work has its techniques, namely rules for effectively delivering an intellectual "product" (a lecture, a piece of advice, a piece of writing). In each case the subject at work faces a technical demand and must draw on her own resources—physical, cognitive, emotional, and spiritual—to answer it. In other words, the technical character of work is such that it *cannot but mobilize the subjective life of the worker*, to a greater or lesser degree, for better or worse for the worker herself. This is a fundamental insight for us, which, in our view, helps to explain the far-reaching impact of the experience of work. Much of what follows in this chapter is an attempt at clarifying and vindicating this insight.

But it is not only the technical demands of work that summon and impact upon the subjective life of the worker. The social demands, or, as we have put it, the social dimension of work, also bring it into play. There are many facets to the social dimension of work as it appears to the subject of work, and they have a complexity we will only be able to touch on in the space available to us here. First, for most workers, there is dependency on someone else—the wage provider, the customer—for the means of their life subsistence. If most of us are to survive, we must earn a living by exchanging our labor for a wage or selling our wares. We work because we must, and this necessity lies behind some of the existential concerns that gravitate around work, especially in regard to unemployment. A second facet of the social dimension of work has to do with it being conducted with others, colleagues in a workplace or the other workers on whose work we rely to conduct our own tasks and for whom our work is useful in turn. Individual workers must coordinate their activity with others to perform their prescribed tasks effectively, but they must also cooperate with them, in a sense that brings ethical considerations into play. Third, in many cases, the relation we have with others in work is asymmetrical: we work under the command of others: the boss, when we are employed by others, the client if we are self-employed. Very rare are the workers whose will is not under the command of others. In the next chapter we will examine the structure of these social relations and their entwinement with the technical dimension. But suffice it for the moment to observe that the subjective life of the worker is crucially at stake in each of them.

To reiterate: the task we have before us is to develop a model of work detailed and supple enough to account for the various patterns of work-related anxiety that characterize contemporary societies. How is it that work can come to affect us, to trouble us as subjects, in the deep and complex ways that it does? In order to answer this question, we need a plausible account of *the subject* who works. That is, we need a philosophical account that makes the real effects of work on bodily, psychic, moral, and social life comprehensible. But while the task at hand is a philosophical one, it is not one that centrally occupied the great philosophers of work of the past—Plato, Locke, the Encyclopedists, Adam Smith, the Physiocrats, Hegel, and Marx, to name only the most famous. While these philosophers had much to say about justice in the division of labor, for instance, or the role of work in establishing property rights, in creating wealth, in creating value, in establishing social status or entrenching social domination, none of them can be said to have systematically addressed the question: what *is* work and how does it impact on subjects in all its dimensions? In posing and attempting to answer this question here, we are entering largely uncharted philosophical territory.

TECHNIQUE AND SUBJECTIVITY

Let us begin then with the technical dimension of work. As we have already remarked, the technical dimension needs to be taken as a general feature of work, as applying to work generally, and not as a regional concept, that is, as applying only to one region of work among others. Service work, for example, is matter of technique as much as the traditional crafts are, such as shoemaking or carpentry. It involves the use of particular skills, not just emotional but also bodily, cognitive, and in many cases manual forms of know-how. These skills employ specific techniques that can be mastered well (defining the expert in the field) or not so well (by the apprentice) or not at all (by the outsider and the lay person). Furthermore, even work that has been subjected to the most thorough "deskilling" process retains vestiges of technical demands. When the technical division of labor is pushed to its furthest limits, as, for example, it is in Frederick Taylor's time and motion studies, working activities can be stripped down to the performance of such simple, routine, "mindless" tasks that they can appear to have left the technical dimension altogether.[1] As we saw in the last chapter, this vision of modern work, according to which such "mindless" activity becomes the predominant form of productive action, is shared by many social theorists and philosophers of work.[2] But even in relation to the basic tasks that survive the most radical technical division of labor, some capacity on the part of the worker for dealing with technical problems remains. Old styles of Taylorist production line work, for instance, whatever their other deleterious effects, were harder for the novice than the experienced factory worker, not just because older workers were habituated to them but also because they actually required some form of technical learning.[3] And many service sector jobs, such as hairdressing or waitressing, require not insubstantial technical capacities even if this is not reflected in the status of these occupations.[4]

Assuming then that work generally involves some level of skill and know-how, or, as we might call it, responsiveness to technical demands, we can now consider the challenges and opportunities for subjective life the technical dimension of work affords.[5]

When an individual performs a concrete work task, her action is caught between two imperatives that are not necessarily easy to reconcile. On the one hand, there is the reality of the task as it has been defined, usually by someone other than the agent. This external definition of the task pre-scribes first of all the desired outcome, the product, to be achieved by the worker. In the case of waged work, this productive feature of the prescribed side of work comes from those who hired the labor of the worker and is usually defined and enforced by managers. The labor contract typically includes more or less explicit descriptions of the tasks for which the worker is hired, since these tasks are determined at least to some extent by the out-come that the worker has been hired to achieve. In the case of care work in the intimate sphere, this prescription of the outcome to be achieved is partly embraced or even defined by the agent herself, but in this case as well an external perspective comes into play through the cultural norms that determine what counts as a good outcome. Other externally imposed aspects of the prescribed task include the time frame and the deadline by which the task is to be completed, the process to be used to complete the task, the tools, the order of procedure, the feedback processes, quality con-trol, security, and so on. Such features determine from the outside what the worker needs to achieve, how she is to achieve it, by what time frame, and so on, and are partly constitutive of the technical dimension as such.

On the other hand, however, it is the worker who faces the material, technical, and ergonomic imperatives that stem from the concrete reality he is facing in trying to complete the task. In other words, the worker has to respond to the challenge posed by the technical dimension *from the inside*. The prescriptions have to be adhered to, answered to, and fulfilled, but this in turn requires a confrontation with the reality in which this is to occur, and that confrontation is the responsibility of the worker alone. This confrontation is precisely what the working activity consists in, and it is the activity of no one else but the worker herself, even if the work process is a highly collaborative one.

Now a major result of ergonomic studies is that no amount of prescrip-tion, however substantial or refined, can foresee all the possible variations in the concrete, real context in which the action is to be performed, the pre-scriptions realized.[6] There is always a gap between the prescribed task and the actual realization of the task. This gap is possibly very small in highly controlled environments. But even in environments like these, the insuffi-ciency of procedures in view of the reality of working is well established.

This gap between prescription and realization, between the task as it is defined ahead of its completion and the activity that completes the task, stems from the fact that the contexts in which working activities take place, like all real contexts of action, are affected by an inescapable contingency. This contingency is the result of the sheer complexity that reigns in working contexts and that affects working interactions more generally. Working contexts bring together human agents whose actions need to be coordinated; their work is usually controlled by other people and is addressed to other people so that communicative agreement also needs to be ensured in all those directions; they work following technical rules (and indeed other types of rules as we will see) that need to be agreed upon and interpreted and thereby introduce an inherent potentiality of conflict; and they work with tools, possibly machinery, and material resources, which themselves are inherent sources of contingency and unpredictable variability. These multiple factors present in any working context and any working interaction, which introduce an unlimited potential for contingency and indeed for breakdowns and obstacles to efficient production, make it impossible for engineers and managers to anticipate all that can get in the way of the realization of productive tasks so that in the end it is always incumbent upon the worker to complete the task herself.

In some areas of production, the contingencies that stem from complexity have been sufficiently harnessed for work to be done to varying degrees by computers or robots. But even robotized production requires supervision and intervention when the work process breaks down. And as soon as the variability in the conditions of the work context rises above a certain level, the adaptability and creativity of human agents continue to be irreplaceable. In all these cases, which continue to make up the majority of working contexts, the human worker is caught between the two imperatives of the external prescriptions, on the one side, which define the parameters of his or her activity, and the reality of the task at hand, on the other.[7]

This gap between the prescribed task and the realized task is of major consequence for the subjective life of the worker. For it means that the subjectivity of the worker must be mobilized not only on account of the effort, concentration, and physical strength required to perform a given task. In addition, there is the *extra effort* required for bridging the gap between the prescribed procedure for executing a task and the actual effective completion of it. The closure of the gap between prescription and realization is the work of subjectivity.

If we pursue our analysis of this structural gap, we realize that this extra effort, this further mobilization of subjectivity, in fact arises from two separate sides.

First, there is the side that brings with it a demand for *innovation* and *creativity*. This is because the reality of the work situation is never quite the one the prescribers of the task had anticipated. No work consists solely in the mere mechanistic application of procedures to situations fully anticipated in advance.

The need for some intervention by the working subject, some degree of innovation and creativity (of course varying across a very wide spectrum), means that the *risk of failure* is also inscribed in the technical dimension, at higher or lesser degrees of probability and with various degrees of seriousness in terms of consequences. This is another, less visible psychological burden of work in addition to the obvious burden that comes from the expenditure of mental, physical, and emotional energy. Clearly, the consequences of failure in work, and hence the psychological burden associated with it, are more serious in some occupations than others. The stakes are higher for the surgeon than the plumber. But even where the consequences of failure are not so serious, there is a job to be done and a burden to be borne by failing to do it, or failing to do it well enough. The gap between prescription and realization of the task puts pressure on the subject to succeed. We might say that an individual in a working situation is usually not allowed to fail, even though failure is always a possibility. This, incidentally, is one of the ways in which work is quite different from play.

But there is a second pressure related to the gap between prescription and realization. By definition, work procedures are prescriptive. In the cases where the work is conducted in a relationship of waged work, under an employment contract, these procedures are prescribed externally, by sources that constitute sources of strong external authority. These external sources of authority may be authoritative in the simple and direct sense of coming from above, from higher up the hierarchy. The will of the worker may be constrained by orders that are authoritative simply on account of having that source. For that reason alone, the worker is not allowed to deviate from them. This means that the worker does not have a license to ignore those prescriptions: the job has to be done, for a particular time, at a certain standard of quality, in a particular way, using particular processes, considering particular side effects (for instance health and safety principles), and so on. Such prescriptions function as imperatives it is always hazardous to ignore. In cases of work outside a labor contract, for instance in care work in the family, the authority enforcing the prescriptions is more diffuse. It is grounded in the cultural norms of what constitutes good care for a child or for an older or a sick dependent. These external norms also have the force of an imperative, even though the sanctions for not abiding by them may not be enforced in the same way.

In any case, because of the authoritative power of the external prescriptions defining the task, the worker is caught in a very specific conundrum: in order to realize the prescribed task, leading to the prescribed outcome, there is a strong likelihood that at some point in the work process he will be forced to disregard some aspects of the prescriptions, the better to adhere to them. The prescriptions must be adhered to because they are inherently linked to the outcome to be achieved. But in realizing the outcome in this particular situation, and not in the situation as it is anticipated to be in the prescription itself, the worker is forced to depart from the actual prescription. From this point of view, we can say that work is always performed, to a lesser or greater extent, *against*, or *despite*, the prescriptions. We can on this basis identify a particular perspective that can be taken on any working activity: that dimension of work we might call *real work*, which is the actual sum of efforts, cognitive, emotional, and physical, spent by the workers to realize the task and achieve the outcome *despite or against the prescriptions*.

However, it is clear that task and activity, prescription and the realization of the task, can't be opposed too starkly, because the prescriptions are *inherent in the very definition of the work*. They set the parameters defining the task. And so work, even in its technical dimension, is inherently ambiguous, complex, and, in a sense, in contradiction with itself. All work demands *cunning* from the subject, not just because of the intrinsic, technical difficulty involved in the realization of an outcome, which demands expenditure of physical force, practical intelligence, and the deployment of skills. There is also a second form of cunning demanded of the worker, a kind of cunning with the task itself the better to realize it, since part of what defines the task gets in the way of realizing it. Workers usually have to interpret the prescriptions, determine which rule they will be able to adhere to and which they will have to flaunt and possibly ignore, how literally to interpret particular guidelines, how much room there is to interpret a policy or a technical code in particular ways, how risky it might be to ignore or cheat with prescribed aspects of the process. The technical, pragmatic dimension of work thus brings into play the interpretive capacities of the worker, since some interpretation of the prescriptive framework must take place if the prescriptions themselves are to be translated into real prescribed outcomes. A substantial part of real work consists in this interpretive activity.

On the basis of this ergonomic analysis of the working activity, we can identify two extremes between which real work occurs, assuming it leads to the production of the desired output. At one end of the spectrum, one extreme is represented by modes of working in which there is total absence of interpretation and decision, full compliance with the prescription, mere procedural "rule following." This is what is referred to in particular when workers are said to "work to rule." This attitude to prescriptions is in fact highly likely to lead to the opposite of efficient performance; indeed it constitutes a most powerful way of striking, of resisting compliant work. At the other end of the spectrum, there is another extreme ideal type, namely total disregard for the prescriptions in the very name of achieving the outcome. Popular culture loves this type, the lone, anarchistic professional who "does the job," indeed "does the job well," but in total disregard for any of the rules that are not strictly tied to the quality of the outcome.[8] This is a dangerous path to follow since total disregard for prescriptions leaves the worker liable in case anything goes wrong, and such disregard is a direct affront to authority. Between those two extremes of work to rule and disregard for the rules lies the majority of workers' attitudes to the prescriptions framing their working activity: a more or less free attitude toward prescriptions that cannot nevertheless be totally ignored.

THE IMPACT OF WORK ON THE SUBJECT'S IDENTITY

We turn now to the question how the technical dimension of work, understood in terms of the concepts already introduced, impacts on the working subject. In what ways is the individual's subjective life affected by the technical demands of work? How does the structural gap between task and activity play itself out in the subjectivity of those who face it?

Before we can directly address these questions, we need to say a little more about what we mean by the terms *subject, subjectivity,* and *subjective life*, at least insofar as they feature in the model of work we are proposing. The main idea we want these terms to capture is that each individual who works is *affectively engaged* in the world around her. There is both a passive (affective) and active (engaged) aspect and an internal synthesis of these aspects within the being of the individual. In order to keep both aspects and their synthesis in view, it is crucial to see the individual as a *whole* being (a subject) with a reflexive capacity (subjectivity) whose life takes a distinctive form—subjective life. The term we use to designate the sense of self an individual develops on the basis of the many features involved in their unique subjective life is *identity*. One of our main methodological claims is that the full spectrum of the normative stakes of work only comes to view if one has realistic descriptions available of the different ways in which work impacts upon identity. Before we can delineate these impacts, we first need to outline the main features of this concept of identity.

First, let us consider reflexivity. A distinctive feature of human experience is that the individual undergoing it is somehow "in touch" with himself when having that experience. In being "in touch with oneself" the individual can be said to be "self-conscious," and the term self-consciousness, while problematic in some respects, captures the reflexivity that human consciousness or experience possesses.[9] For the most part, this "being in touch" with oneself is implicit and only rarely an object of explicit attention. In its lived, implicit, prereflective form, it is quite different from the self-objectifying distance we can take at times in relation to ourselves when we contemplate who we are, what we do, or what we believe in. We must be careful not to confuse reflexivity as such with the objectifying self-relation that reflection can easily impose. In its primary sense, reflexivity is rather a matter of a kind of presence to oneself or, as we have said, "being in touch" or "having an affinity" with oneself, and it is above all in this sense that reflexivity gives form to subjective life.

Another form-bestowing feature of subjective life is its temporality. To be a subject, or to have a subjective life, is to inhabit time in a certain way. It is to be on a life journey that stretches over time. Individual life arises at a specific time from a past that prepares it but will forever remain external to it (the material, nonalive conditions of life), and it runs its course ineluctably toward a time when it ceases to be life, when the structure of reflexivity or self-response that defines it ceases to operate and there is only brute "objective" stuff. The running its course of subjective life itself has a certain reflexivity attached to it, from a background sense of experiences being linked to each other to a more robust sense of self as continuous and evolving across experiences.[10] However this is understood exactly, a major dimension of subjective life is that it stretches over time and is constituted by its history. Past experiences can be so powerful they establish long-term, basic structures in the psyche, however articulately we are aware of them, which can shape what is possible by way of present and future experience. The work of changing the course of one's subjective life, of adapting and indeed transforming oneself in light of a deeper self-understanding, is still performed in the medium of structures that preexist. Psychic transformations do not work by wiping the slate clean, so to speak. They have to be performed through the psychic structures themselves, and so by relating to the past. Indeed, a certain conscious taking possession of the way in which one lives one's time is perhaps intrinsic to subjective life itself.[11] The meaning of one's life, the core values by which one defines one's own existence are perhaps inescapably articulated in a temporal frame.[12] If we follow Martin Heidegger's line of thought on this, the very possibility of any meaning whatsoever depends on subjective life orienting itself in its own temporality.

The temporal aspects of subjective life are linked to its *dynamic* aspect, namely the fact that subjective life (as all life, we might say) has to be sustained via the integration of complex internal processes that are essentially related to the challenges and resources afforded by the external environment. Organic life is sustained through homeostatic logics, that is, attempts at reaching forms of balance, compromise solutions between what the internal processes can sustain, what they need for their sustenance, and what the environment itself both demands and provides in terms of threats, challenges, and resources. As a direct consequence of this dynamic aspect, organic life is intrinsically fragile and vulnerable. Something similar can be said of subjective life, of the life of the human subject. The subject also has to sustain itself over time in the midst of environments, not just natural but also social environments (from the family to the school yard, from the office to the profession and the general public), that provide essential resources but also intrinsic challenges. This means that subjective life has layers of fragility and vulnerability on top of those that characterize organic life generally. Each subject is challenged not only in continuing and maintaining her organic life but also in continuing to be able to relate to herself as *this* subject of experience, as this singular form of subjective life. As a form of *life*, it is vulnerable to all sorts of injuries on account of its openness to, and dependence upon, complex internal process and external environments.

A basic form of *normativity*—in the sense of norms or standards of what it is to go well or badly—emerges from this necessity for life to sustain itself across experiences. Some forms of organic life barely manage to maintain internal and external balance in the face of the twofold difficulty of internal homeostasis and external interactions. Other forms of life become stronger as a result of the successful integration of these internal and external processes: they can take on greater challenges from the outside, they can recuperate more quickly when challenged. Health and illness, flourishing and withering, development and regression, are norms or standards that apply to organic life in general and subjective life in particular. For this reason, we can think of subjectivity, or as we also call it *identity*, as something that is vulnerable to various forms of challenge and that must struggle to maintain itself in the midst of those challenges. When things go well, it is strong and dynamic enough to meet those challenges, and in that way to "grow" and "flourish." But when things go badly, it fails in its struggle to maintain itself and becomes weak and "withered."

With this basic conception of subjective life in place, we can already give an initial response to the question of how work in its technical dimension impacts on the subject. Recall that the decisive feature of the technical dimension, the feature that summons what we called the *real* work, has to do with the gap between the prescriptions and the activity of work. Real work designates the actual efforts performed by the agent to realize what is entailed in the prescriptions despite what in the prescriptions obstructs that realization. The structure of real work activity thus has a complexity that the subjectivity of the worker has to match. The subject matches it by drawing on powers that reside in subjective life itself. It is not enough that merely physical bodily powers, or merely cognitive or affective ones, be drawn on separately for the sake of getting the real work done. Rather, these capacities must be drawn on together, in a synthetic expression of *the whole being* of the worker himself. Only an embodied being, a being with a sense of itself and of the connections between experiences over time, has the capacity to do real work, and it is only through the actualization of such capacities that real work gets done.

When work goes well, the subject is able to exercise these capacities in a way that enables the subject to flourish. The flourishing that good work in its *technical* dimension affords resembles the Aristotelian concept of *eudaimonia,* but differs from it in an important sense. *Eudaimonia* indicates an overall "doing well" of the person, which involves all the dimensions of personality, from the physical to the psychic, as well as the basic material aspects of doing well, as in being "well off." But the flourishing we are discussing here is specifically psychic, a quality of subjective life, with roots in the body. The flourishing that arises through good experiences of work with respect to its technical demands denotes a strength of the self, a capacity to withstand internal and external challenges. In a classical discussion of the normativity inherent in life, Canguilhem defined the norms of life, health and sickness, as capacity to adapt to challenges thrown up by the environment.[13] We can adapt this conception of organic life to psychic life: when work obstacles are overcome, through the trial of "real work," the self can grow in strength. The sense of identity, that is, the power of the self over itself and its internal operations, is secured and enhanced.[14]

This growth or flourishing of subjective life, or as we might also say consolidation and confirmation of identity, concerns not just the external challenges but also internal ones. And these internal challenges stem from the fact that the worker's identity is dependent on a dimension of the subject's life that is not fully under her control, namely her body. Because of its importance and complexity, this is a dimension of the worker's identity that needs to be studied in its own right. In order to see the full impact (both in the positive and the negative) that the technical dimensions of work has upon working selves, we need to look at the distinctively *embodied* dimensions of subjective life.

THE IMPACT OF WORK ON THE WORKER'S BODY

We have made the claim repeatedly that it is one and the same subject that is at stake in work experiences. This point is important first of all in a temporal sense. If work has a deep impact on subjectivity, then this impact extends beyond the working context into areas of life such as intimate life and the life of political action. This is a key point that the boundaries between disciplines always risks repressing, for instance the boundaries between psychology, sociology, and political science: the individuals involved in intimate relationships and the citizens of a polity are subjects who are working selves, and if work has such a deep impact on them then work must also play a key role in intimate relations and in politics.

But the emphasis on the unity of the subject experiencing the impact of work also points to another important dimension, namely the fact that the subjective life that is at stake in work experiences is not limited to mental representations but also includes the life of the body. Human selves are not mere consciousnesses; they are embodied consciousnesses. Stressing the unity of the subject means that we don't want to operate on dualistic premises that would hold the mental and the somatic as two separate ontological realms. At the same time, however, stressing the unity of subjective life should not lead us to make the opposite mistake, namely to ignore the body altogether, with its specific mechanisms and its specific demands. The body has its own demands, it operates on its own logic. There are good reasons why philosophers from the very beginning separated the body and the mind as two separate substances. The body and the mind are united; their unity forms the selves this book is concerned about inasmuch as they are working selves. Nevertheless, within this unity each instance has a relative autonomy: the mind can at least partially detach itself from somatic processes (if only to reflect on them, know them better) and the body has a life of its own as well.

In fact, the most plausible way to think about the unity of the body and the mind (the unity that *is* a subject) is by first distinguishing between two meanings when we refer to the embodiment of working selves.[15] The subject's body is first of all simply the organic body, the bundle of cells that make up specific organs, with their specific functions, all related to each other as the complex organism that is the human body. But this biological body is not really the subject's body. For the body becomes the subject's body through the long process of subjectivation, a large part of which consists precisely in inhabiting and domesticating that biological body, to use rough metaphors, in order to make it one's own body. Much has been written on the phylogenetic and ontogenetic importance of such basic (but in the first instance difficult) skills as crawling, then standing upright, and then walking. These very basic skills, which are such crucial foundations for any further development for the species and the individual, are not given at birth—they are not simply a gift of nature. The human subject has to master these basic skills, which give shape to his body, and this process is a long, arduous one.[16] And the same is true of all the other processes by which the human subject gradually learns to control and shape his body as his own. Indeed, this covers not just the gross and fine motor skills of the external organs but also the internal life of the body. Less apparent than gait or motor skills, but just as crucial in the process of subjectivation, is the necessity to appropriate and control, to some extent at least, the metabolic processes related to the different internal systems of the overall organism that is a human body. This view of the human body, at the intersection of psychology and anatomy, is confirmed on the side of phenomenology by the phenomenology of the "body proper" and in sociology by the sociology of habitus developed by Pierre Bourdieu. Bourdieu has shown masterfully how primary socialization already includes the acquisition of class-specific modes of behavior, which are inscribed through the entire body—in the way one walks, uses one's hands, as well as how one uses one's voice and all the expressive possibilities of the human face—as a legacy of one's positioning within the hierarchies of the social field.[17]

It is crucial to keep in view the somatic dimensions of subjective life when considering the impact of work activities on subjects, in other words, to always be reminded that working selves are embodied selves.

It matters first of all for a very basic reason, namely the fact that all work is expenditure of the subject's energies (physical, intellectual, emotional), and these energies have their material basis in bodily resources. When we look in the next chapter at the forms of social address that all work represents (the fact that work is done for someone), we will have to remember that it is subjective resources that are literally spent and given away in these addresses. For this reason it is no exaggeration to say that in the exchanges of the products of their works, members of society exchange life resources between each other. It is quite literally the "life" of the subject that is at stake in work, through the engagement of the body, which is the very expression and material support of subjective life. Acknowledgment of interdependency at this primitive level of embodied life is one of the roots of the higher-level moral and social obligations that also characterize subjective life.

Second, even after the body has been shaped into the subject's own body, it remains partly independent of the subject's powers of control.

This is true first of all in the straightforward sense that the work of domesticating the body is not done once and for all. It is ongoing, persisting more or less in the background throughout every moment of the subject's life. It may go unnoticed or it may protrude into the foreground of consciousness, as in times of illness or aging when keeping control of the body becomes a struggle. When the body is in good health, and when the mind itself is at relative peace, this process remains largely silent. It appears as a "second nature." In that case, the subject is so used to her own body that she does not even notice all the work of correction and control that goes into shaping the "first" body (the organic bundle) into a "second" body, the one that is the body of *this* person. But it doesn't take very much, a slight deregulation of metabolic processes, related to any of the great systems of the body, through accident or illness, to make that work more apparent or indeed more difficult. What this points to in the context of our discussion is that the intrinsic vulnerability of subjects in relation to their body, the fact that they rely on it totally but only control it to a limited extent, introduces a significant extra factor of vulnerability into work situations. Working selves go in to work as bodies, but these bodies cannot be taken for granted. There are many different ways in which the difficulties inherent in the working activities can disrupt the relationship between the subject and her or his body. We are no longer talking here about the burden of energy expenditure that work efforts might represent in absolute terms, the amount of subjective resources "spent" at work. Rather, the vulnerability we are focusing on now is the vulnerability of the subject's very identity, the crucial sense in which selfhood can be more or less strong, the I more or less in charge of itself and ready to face the challenges of its environment. This identity is particularly vulnerable to the extent that it is reliant on the fragile unity of body and mind, a unity that has to be worked on ceaselessly. Working subjects are particularly vulnerable to the extent that working activities can be particularly burdensome on the capacity of the self to inhabit and own his own body.

The risk that the body reassert its autonomy in relation to the self and thereby fracture the self's identity is all the more powerful if we consider that the somatic dimensions of the self produce or at least are significantly involved (depending on one's metapsychological orientations) in forms of motivation that are independent of mental powers, yet are so powerful they can significantly influence them or indeed overrule them through the fundamental affects of pleasure and pain. If we further remark that the highest form of pleasure in the human body is arguably linked to sexual functions, it is obvious that we are now talking about the unconscious dimensions of subjective life, in the specific psychological sense of the term. In the arduous process of subjectivation through which the subject shapes her body into her own body and gains control over it, the subject has to come to terms with the imperious, anarchistic force with which demands stemming from the body, looking for the release of tension or indeed for the gratification of pleasure, intrude in the psychic system and influence mental processes. The specific compromise solution found by the subject to accommodate those libidinal demands with other demands that dictate very different courses of action—such as those arising from the basic need of the self to protect itself and maintain itself in existence,[18] or from dependency on significant others or moral demands—serves to define, from a psychological point of view, the identity of *that particular* subject.

In what ways do these unconscious dimensions matter for an analysis of the impact of working activities on subjective life? A few moments ago, we focused on the way in which the burdens of work represented an inherent risk for the subject, because they risk endangering the fragile structures through which subjects establish the unity of their psychic and somatic lives. If we add the depth and power of unconscious forces over mental life to the picture, we can see how fragile indeed those structures are in the conflict-ridden, emotionally, cognitively, and physically burdensome environment that is a work environment. It is worth repeating the point with this added depth of the unconscious life of the subject in view: work is an inherently effortful, tiring psychological experience in which subjects risk their mental health, not just because they constantly have to prevent and preempt the manifold possibilities of failure (the gap between prescription and realization), and not just because they are under the judging gaze of others (see the next chapter), but also because their unique and idiosyncratic psychosomatic unity is under threat as a result of the pressures work puts on it.

However, the unconscious dimension of subjective life also matters in more positive ways. To see why, we need to recall that work represents a confrontation with the real, where the real is understood, in a simple sense, as that which resists the attempts of workers to apply the prescriptions that define the work task. One aspect of this confrontation concerns the clash between the deep, unconscious structures of subjective identity and the objective demands stemming from the real of work. Every working subject that comes to the work tasks is a bundle of fantasies and repressed urges that have been structured in such a way as to allow the subject to function well enough, within themselves, and indeed with others. The work tasks place pressure on these for sure. At the same time, however, since the real of work is an inescapable objective instance with which in the end it is impossible to cheat (you either do the job or you don't), it can also represent a bulwark against the powerful unconscious forces within the subject's soul, which the subject might struggle to contain within its subjective identity. We see here the psychological source of what Jahoda counted as one of the main benefits of employment, which she termed the "tie to reality." Early philosophers like Plato had already tried to provide formal descriptions of the human soul as engaged in a struggle, where the conscious, reflexive instances seek to keep control over the irrational urges, fears, and affects that are potentially damaging for self and other. The individual human soul left to its own devices can easily sink into its own internal world and lose touch with reality, that is, the world of objective, external facts and the social world. The working activity, as a confrontation with the hard objectivity of the facts of the situation and the independent existence of others, can act like a prick for the individual psyche: these are the facts you can't deny or disregard; these are people you can't overlook. Hegel famously claimed the fear of death is the beginning of wisdom. Jahoda has shown, with robust empirical support, that the real of work can in fact also be the beginning of wisdom.

This potential of work to help subjects maintain a "tie with reality" is not just about providing a bulwark against the tendency of the human soul to lose touch with reality because of the power of inner drives and the idiosyncratic structures of psychic constructs. It can also provide avenues for what Freudian psychoanalysis called sublimation, namely the transference of urges, notably those of sexual origin, onto nonsexual objects that act as representatives, in a socially acceptable form, of the initial objects the drives are aiming for. It is simply a fact that many individuals can find deep satisfaction in their work. One way to explain this deep satisfaction might be in terms of sublimation, in a sense that would not be reserved for exceptional artists or intellectuals but would in fact include many forms of everyday work. Again, whatever psychoanalytical model one might favor, it is plausible to argue in general that deep satisfaction for individuals is one that involves their entire being, and that being in turn includes not just conscious representations but also the affective ways in which these individuals generally find satisfaction, this in turn being the outcome of the long processes by which their psychic identity has been constituted. In some cases, work can make one happy, and this happiness can simply mean the overall well-being of the individual. Work can provide a powerful channel for realizing one's deepest, most defining, and idiosyncratic yet largely nonconscious motivational structures. This is one way to explain why some individuals appear to find genuine gratification in forms of work that to others appear intrinsically deadening or alienating, or even "dirty."

In fact, the phenomenology of professional activities shows that in some cases it might not be sublimation processes that explain the pleasure individuals take in their work but rather the fact that the pleasure taken at work, or rather through working, is directly of a bodily or, indeed, a libidinal kind. This is especially the case when confrontation with the real of work involves a confrontation with material elements: a baker kneading dough, a carpenter enjoying the smoothness of a well-polished table, a driver in perfect control of the engine.[19] In cases such as these, the work tasks entail a skilled encounter with objects and matter. The body then is involved as a direct protagonist, in all its sensitive, indeed in all its sensual, powers. The real of work that resists the achievement of the task resists materially and therefore requires a full bodily intervention, an embodied encounter, a *corps à corps* as the French language says, that is a *body to body* confrontation. And if the challenge of the real is surmounted, then it is the body in all its sensual, affective powers that has triumphed. The material, the technical object, the tool have become "second nature" themselves, they have been domesticated and integrated into the "second body." In situations such as these, the material objects and the material stuff involved in the work tasks act directly as the kinds of objects that the inner drives structuring the psyche would be aiming for. They are introjected with the kind of libidinal power that internal, fantasized objects might also be charged with in other moments of psychic life. But these objects and that matter are part of a process that is a confrontation with the real, the attempt at producing a real outcome—one that is expected by others, that will count for and be confirmed by them—thereby providing a potent "tie with reality" as we just saw. This constitutes a radical difference with mere fantasy enjoyment in which the self simply indulges in object gratification in the privacy of his psychic life. This difference in turn means that, by contrast with fantasy enjoyment in which object demand is simply granted by the subject to himself, working provides the fragile self with a channel to increase its own mastery and control over its "second body." The libidinal enjoyment at the hand of the objectual side of work is thereby the opposite of regression. The mechanism is different from sublimation but amounts to the same: a binding of the self by itself through an enjoyment of unconscious urges and desires that both gives them what they want but also maintains them under the command of the ego.

We might say that the working activity, work as *poiesis*, also offers the human soul a chance to work upon itself in the psychological sense that the term *Arbeit* takes in Freud's writings.[20] Indeed, working activity, work poiesis, is not just a way for the self to increase mastery over itself; it even offers this, as we just saw, through an increase in the body's powers of action, perception, and sensibility. Indeed, that is the main point of this way of looking at the psychological power of working: we are defining here a form of psychic flourishing, of going well or indeed of growing as a self, that is both at the same time quantitative (increase in the powers of the self) and reflexive (increase in the powers of the self over itself).

THE SUBJECTIVE INTEREST IN DOING THE JOB WELL

Drawing on Freud, we argue that the work of production (in the very broad sense in which we use the term, which as we know includes service and care work), allows the psyche to work upon itself the better to bind itself.[21] In a sense, the "I" fortifies itself and grows as a self when the task is realized (provided it is also meaningful for the subject).[22] This growth of self arises not just from the extra effort that we have seen attaches to real work (the work of bridging prescription and reality) but also from the sheer toil involved in delivering a service or product. We have seen that work is a challenge not just on account of the physical forces that must be dealt with in responding to a technical demand but also mental and emotional forces. All work needs *rest*. But when the job is done, it also brings specific subjective rewards beyond the material ones.

We can capture in a negative and in a positive way this idea of the self "growing" or "fortifying" itself through the work effort. Subjective fortification occurs through overcoming the possibility of failure, which, as we have seen, is intrinsic to all work. In any type of work, the task has to be realized, and, as we saw, it has to be realized despite, or against at least, some of the features in the context surrounding work. Expressed with a bit of pathos, we could say that in realizing the task the subject retrospectively contemplates the bridge it established over the abyss of the possible failure to do so. When cunning is involved because one has to circumvent both the difficulties inherent in the task as well as obstreperous prescriptions, the self can rightfully recognize its skills and ingenuity in the crossing of that bridge. And the difference between the expert and the novice is the confidence with which the former engages in that bridge compared with the vertigo felt by the latter toward a potentially looming disaster. More positively, subjective life is fortified through work in having tested itself in the challenge of the task and in coming out successful. As a result of going through this process, it feels itself more acutely and feels itself strengthened. This second dimension is well captured by the classical notion of *conatus*.[23] It is in virtue of conatus that the human substance as a combination of mind and body maintains itself over time. The idea of *conatus* is also associated with the idea of growth of the self, indeed, of a parallel growth in the mental and the physical aspects of the self. It is thus a useful concept for thinking about how work impacts on the subject when it goes well: success in responding to the technical demands of a task draws on the subject's *conatus* and expands it in turn.

The conative aspect of subjectivity might help to explain another point that is of fundamental importance for understanding the contemporary malaise around work: *the interest in doing a job well* that seems so deeply rooted in the subject that Thorstein Veblen could refer to the "instinct of workmanship."[24] It is clear—and evident from some of the empirical research considered in chapter 2—that workers have a desire for working well; they generally prefer to do a good job rather than a bad one, even in its specifically technical aspect. This is a difficult phenomenon to explain from the point of view of standard economic models of work,[25] but it makes perfect sense within the model of the subject at work we are presenting here. The interest in achieving the outcomes that define the particularity of the working activity, independent of the external rewards associated with successful completion of work or indeed of the punishment that might arise from the failure to perform, is explicable on account of the growth in subjective life it brings. In terms of the schematic model of subjective life we just proposed, achieving arduous work tasks means coming out victorious and strengthened from the challenges of the real. It means, at one and the same time, increasing the powers of action, perception, and sensibility of the subject, and thereby increasing the sense of psychic identity resulting from it, as mastery over one's vital powers. This also helps to explain the frustration and suffering that arise when obstacles to the performance of good work, again considered just in its technical aspect, are in place. Since the truncation of the interest in doing a job well is simultaneously a truncation of the subjectivity of the person who does it, it is not surprising that the quality of work should matter to the worker intrinsically and not solely on account of the pay package that employment provides.

As we just saw, far from being an anomaly, the intrinsic interest a subject has in performing the work tasks well, or in simply doing the job for which she is employed, is a simple expression of the subject's striving for satisfaction in a particular context. However, another key dimension also needs to be added if we are to give a full picture of the psychological impact of work, namely the symbolic dimension of meaning. Doing one's job well can also be understood as an expression of the subject's striving to find meaning in action: the expenditure of physical, cognitive, and emotional efforts requires its own internal reward, so to speak, namely the seal it receives from fulfilling the standards intrinsic to the task, which, in the case of work, makes the difference between a job well done and one not well done. On the negative side, if workers for some reason are put in a position where they are forced to not work well, where their intrinsic interest in realizing the tasks is impeded, we can expect this to have serious, deleterious subjective consequences.[26] If they continue in that work, as economic necessity may compel them to, this should not be interpreted as meaning that the interest in doing good work doesn't really matter or is only a marginal interest, a luxury. On the contrary, it might serve to heighten the lived absurdity of their situation: there is no escaping doing the task, not just because one has to do it but, even more deeply, because one actually wants to do it, and yet the task is at odds with itself by the very way in which it is set up. Such a situation is bound to be psychologically damaging in the long run. Indeed we are led to saying it would have existential impact, in the sense that it would present a challenge to features of the subject's very being. Equally, such a scenario will add to the sense of precariousness in one's very activity, since the prescriptions make it difficult to see how a core interest of the subject can be fulfilled.

Furthermore, the phenomenology of hard manual work shows that for some workers there can be an intrinsic interest in doing the job well, even in situations where the content of the job and its outcomes appear meaningless in the end, when the worker views his own life and his own activity from the outside.[27] In such extreme cases, workers shield themselves from the meaninglessness of the work as a whole by investing all their effort in the realization of the discrete steps involved in the overall task. Generally speaking, however, meaningful work means that the worker is invested in finding ways to achieve the work's outcome, in realizing the task, precisely because she thinks those outcomes are somehow meaningful, that is, useful to others in a way that makes sense to her and that fits her personality.

Just as the subjective meaning attached to the performance of a task is integral to the satisfaction of work that goes well, so the negative impact on subjective life lies behind the experience of work that goes badly. That is to say, the malaises that are felt around work have their basis, at least in part, in distortions of subjective life as it is expressed in actual work activity. We have just seen how obstacles in the way of doing good work, in the technical sense of performing a task well, contribute to the malaise around meaningless work, and how the stymying of the interest in doing a job well amounts to an inhibition on the growth of subjectivity, a block on the potential of the subject to flourish. Meaningless work is felt to be meaningless at the level of subjective life, and while, as we said earlier, there is a limit to what can be said in general terms about what makes work meaningful to someone, we can posit limiting points within which subjectivity is able to flourish and the meaning potential of the activity to be actualized and felt. In other words, while the fit between the individual and the task that is a condition of meaningful work will be a matter of the individual's personality, upbringing, education, skill levels, values, and so on, a fit between the task and the potential for the flourishing of subjective life in general must also be in place. Work that is too dull to engage the subject, for instance, or that is too onerous, or too complex, or prescribed in a way that makes it impossible to be done effectively, will fail to mobilize the subjective life of the individual. It will leave the *conatus* untouched, or indeed make it regress and wither. But that check on subjective life has a deadening effect on the whole self, the self at work and the self away from it. What we said about the temporal structure of subjectivity becomes relevant here once more. For the subjective flow of experience in and at work must be accommodated within the larger temporal flow that characterizes subjective life as a whole.

The harms that form the basis of the other zones of anxiety around work we considered in chapter 2 can be illuminated in a similar manner. That is to say, they are comprehensible in terms of damages to subjective life that result from malformations of work activity. Consider now the syndrome of concerns around stress, work intensification, and burnout. According to the model of work and subjectivity we have proposed, a technical demand of some kind is inherent to all work, and real work consists in the transformation of a prescribed task into a real outcome. We saw that in order to bring about the desired outcome workers typically need to develop a form of cunning, since they must realize the task within, yet also despite the prescriptions. It follows that the prescriptions must be flexible enough to allow adaptation to the particular task at hand. But, in cases where the prescriptions are too rigid, workers can be caught in an impossible situation, the kind of situation that systematically prevents them from satisfying their subjective interest in doing the job well. In fact, there are *many ways* in which prescriptions can actively get in the way of the realization of tasks: there can just be too many of them or not enough of them, they can contradict each other, or they can simply prevent the worker from taking the path that would most effectively realize the task. Clinical analyses of dysfunctional workplaces show that a major cause of burnout and other forms of pathology caused by the intensification of work efforts stems not only from direct exploitation of workers' position of weakness by management to increase productivity but also from failings in the task prescriptions, which make the realization of the tasks intrinsically more difficult and sometimes impossible.[28]

Up to this point we have been restricting ourselves to a consideration of the impact of technical demands on the subjectivity of the worker. We have been attending as closely as possible to the ways in which subjectivity is shaped and misshaped within what we have called the technical dimension. But the subject at work is much more than a subject responsive to and challenged by technical demands. The subject at work is a *social* subject, and it is only as a social subject that the worker has any experience of work at all. It is time now to change focus and to attend to the specific social dynamics that structure the experience of work.

Chapter Four

DYNAMICS OF RECOGNITION

The subjective life of the worker is impacted by working activities, by the technical dimension of work, inasmuch as that worker attempts to maintain her psychosomatic identity across the many practical challenges those activities represent for her. The same subjective life is also impacted by work on account of the social relations that the subject finds herself in when engaging in working activities. Contrary to the popular image of the worker as an isolated individual taken up entirely by an instrumental attitude toward an external manipulable object,[1] social relations are an inescapable feature of work as we know it and live it. This means that an account of the structure of the lived experience of work such as we are attempting here cannot rest content with a description of the technical dimension of work but must also seek to lay out the main social relations that shape and help constitute this experience. In our view, the most salient social relations at stake here are relations of *recognition*. In this chapter, we will attempt to describe the complex of recognition relationships that the subject of work is typically enmeshed in, relationships that play a crucial role in structuring and shaping the quality of the subjective life of the worker.

In taking this approach we are not proposing that *all* the social relations relevant for understanding the world of work either can be conceptualized, or are best conceptualized, as relations of recognition. If we think of social relations as relations of dependency, such that at least one of the *relata* in the relation is in some sense dependent on the other, it is an open question whether recognition or the lack of it is involved. In other words, we are not making a general claim about the structure of "the social" as such, and this limitation is an important part of our methodological self-understanding (we will return to this in chapters 5 and 6 of the book). Rather, the point of focusing on recognition is, in the first instance, the perspicuousness it may bring to the description of the lived experience of working. Furthermore, in using the concept of recognition for this purpose, we are not proposing that work is somehow a uniquely privileged locus of recognition. We are not assuming or suggesting that, of all the different ways of obtaining recognition, recognition obtained from work is the most important or the most decisive in its impact on subjectivity. And we are certainly not proposing that work is the only effective way in which subjects relate to each other through recognition and become bound by recognition relationships. To reiterate, our concern for the time being is to clarify what is going on in the contemporary experience of work, specifically in view of the malaise that surrounds this experience. What we are looking for is phenomenological adequacy, a way of talking about the experience of work, or the subjectivity of working, that is adequate to the thing itself. Our proposal is that the concept of recognition can frame descriptions that illuminate aspects of this "thing itself"—the subjective life of the worker.

Up to now our attempt at describing the impact of work on the subject has been focused on what we called the technical dimension of work. But even the technical dimension cannot be adequately described without considering the social relations that shape the meaning of the performance of a task. And this is particularly evident when one considers how the performance of the individual worker is placed in and contributes to the performance of the *work collective*. An analysis of the work collective thus provides an apt point of transition from the technical to the social dimension of work activity. After all, continuing where we left off in the previous chapter, the individual facing the challenge of real work is intrinsically related to a number of coworkers who are brought together with him by technical aspects of the tasks themselves. This defines the work collective in a technical sense. Once a description of work experience in the context of the work collective is in place, we will then be able to develop an analysis of the different kinds of recognition that also go to make up this experience. We will see in particular that there is a dynamic to recognition arising from its distinct sources: recognition by the peers, by the addressee of the worker's work efforts, by the employer, and by society at large.

THE WORK COLLECTIVE

One way to pinpoint the importance of the work collective for working subjects is to consider the following question: is the subject of work ever alone? In a qualified sense, yes: at the exact moment when the action or series of actions that will deliver the output is to be performed, the subject is by herself. This is the moment of truth in work, the moment where the bridge has to be crossed and the abyss of possible failure is faced. At the same time, though, individual activity is rarely isolated, and in its pragmatic performance it typically involves others. First, and most simply, a specific work activity makes practical sense only as part of a broader work process. The dependency on this process can be diachronically extended. This is the case when the work task requires particular outputs and resources as its material conditions and in turn produces outputs that will be used in other processes for other or larger productive outputs. Production line work is the archetypal, striking example of this. The individual work activity is also shared synchronically by all the other workers who have to perform the same or similar tasks. Typically the subject faces the challenge of real work in a work collective. The core social dimension of working activities, even as they are accomplished by individual workers, introduces complex layers to the initial challenge of real work. To begin with, the fact that most if not all workers perform their productive activities among peers adds a key structural element to real work, that is, to the actual realization of a task against or despite the prescriptions. For, if the peers are virtually present in the working activity, then the secrecy demanded by the inevitable breaches with some of the prescriptions becomes problematic. We need to roughly distinguish two possible scenarios at this level.

If the workplace operates on the basis of a certain level of *trust*, the breaches will be able to be shared, possibly discussed and debated, and collectively organized. Real work at the individual level will be made possible by real work at the collective level, through efficient cooperation. If we focus on the meaning of this scenario for subjective life, we can see that a workplace in which trust exists functions as major condition of subjective flourishing and mental health since it makes the challenge of real work structurally easier to deal with successfully. Relations of trust make it possible for cooperation to be organized collectively in an efficient way. This in turn creates a culture of work within the collective, based on the realization of technical tasks, through which each is enabled to face the challenge of work. Given all we have said, this is a highly significant feature of the work collective, given the possible challenge to identity what is hidden in the performance of work tasks and, conversely, the strong boost to identity created by successful performance.

By contrast, a workplace in which there is insufficient trust is one in which each individual worker faces the challenge of real work on their own. If they are forced to use tricks and shortcuts actually to perform the task, they cannot be open about it. Not only can they not share it; they have to keep their tricks secret since the imperative nature of prescriptions is such that they typically carry a punitive side. It is clear that the likelihood that prescriptions will get in the way of the realization of tasks is much higher in this scenario. Such a workplace will be under the constant threat that workers will go into "work-to-rule" mode, which, as we know, is the least productive mode of working. Or they will be forced to hide the routes by which they managed to achieve the outcomes, which can lead to serious dysfunctions down the track.[2]

Since work is less efficient, there is every chance that the workload increases for everyone. Indeed the work process itself can suffer as a result of a destruction of the framework in which efficient cooperation could take place. We will analyze how this can happen in some detail later in our case study (chapter 7). As we shall see, in workplaces where trust between peers has been eroded too much, in their attempts at maintaining a minimally functioning sense of identity, individuals can be tempted to engage in activities that more or less willfully undermine the efforts of others as they begin to hide mistakes or dangerous or illegal forms of work or they first ensure their position is fully protected against that of others over the efficient realization of tasks. The difficulty that work intrinsically represents for subjective life is compounded in such cases, which leads to a vicious circle: the more subjectivities feel threatened and attacked by the challenges of work, notably as a result of the absence of a supportive work collective, the more they engage in forms of behavior that undermine solidarity and cooperation, thereby further increasing the likelihood that work challenges will be more difficult to meet for everyone. In such an environment, subjective lives are much more likely to be tripped by the multiple difficulties arising from the gap between prescription and realization.

But there is not just a direct psychological cost to a workplace in which cooperation between coworkers has been damaged. The toxic aspect of dysfunctional workplaces is not merely psychological, it matters not just for what it does to the mental health of individual workers by becoming a factor for intensification of the work efforts. Further than that, when individuals face the challenge of work on their own, because the work collective no longer provides a supportive framework, that challenge can quickly lead to the development of antisocial behavior simply because the need to safeguard one's own fragile identity is every individual's deepest interest. These forms of antiethical, antisocial behavior can range from modes of obstruction or even sabotage, which only touch on the operational aspects of the work process, to the passive or even the active undermining of others, all the way to the direct sabotaging of their work and the ganging up against particular individuals that become scapegoats or sacrificial lambs. This, for us, is the fundamental context that needs to be in view if we are to understand concerns about bullying and harassment, which, as we saw in chapter 2, are some of the main elements of the current malaise around work. Bullying and harassment can be the direct product of dysfunctional workplaces, not just of pathological individual personalities, if they have removed the possibility for individuals to rely on supportive networks internal to the work collective and instead have created a toxic culture of each against everyone else.

In chapter 8 we will describe a real case that we believe powerfully illustrates this capacity of work collectives to either "make or break" subjective life, notably through the constitutive role of work collectives. But, for now, let us move on from the theme of the work collective to the recognition relations that mediate the subjectivity of the individual worker.

MEANINGS OF RECOGNITION

When we looked at the varieties of disrespect that are widely experienced in the context of work, we noted that the concept of recognition could serve to clarify the content of the experience and the social relations that structure it. Let us now look at this concept in a little more detail.

In the sense in which we will use the concept, recognition designates the process of acknowledgment and confirmation that is afforded from an external perspective in response to a claim, a demand, a performance, or a statement of identity made by an individual (or a group of individuals for collective claims) from an internal perspective. The concept figures prominently in the Hegelian philosophical tradition, where it is bound up with the concept of freedom. The general idea is that my freedom requires recognition by others to become effective both in itself, in reality, and for myself. I am truly free only if the inner certainty with which I regard my capacity for free action is confirmed outside. This in turn requires and is made real by acknowledgment from others. Recognition in this sense is like the seal of approval granted by the outside to normative demands and expectations stemming from individuals, a seal of approval that lends them substance. This substance is at the same time social and subjective: through recognition some normative status is granted that has reality both for the subject enjoying it and in the eyes of the community to which the subject belongs.

This logic of recognition structures the reproduction of modern societies. As Axel Honneth has famously shown, in modern society, social interactions are driven by general expectations of recognition of myself as a person (expressed by notions such as dignity and respect), which ensure the reality of my equal moral status with others.[3] Social interactions are driven also by more specific expectations of recognition related to specific social roles, in which my particular social status can also be confirmed. In particular, as Hegel observed, professional status, or standing as a contributor to what he called the system of need—the system of production and consumption through which the gamut of needs are satisfied—is fundamental to the form social recognition takes in modern societies.[4] To lack this status, to be without recognition in one's capacity as a contributing member of society, is in a more than metaphorical sense to lack reality, to lack social existence. Similarly, yet in a way still directly related to employment, if one also lacks the means to participate in society as a consumer, if one's access to the system of need is constrained by poverty, then one's lack of social reality is entrenched further. Viewed from this perspective, Bourdieu's remark that the unemployed of Marienthal suffered a "social death" thus captures a profound truth about the meaning of unemployment and the distinctive form of suffering the nonworking poor endure.[5]

But the logic of recognition functions not just in social interactions generally, at the level of society, but also within the working experience itself.

Of course, one's dependence on recognition will vary with the place one occupies within a work organization: the demand to be recognized in one's equal dignity, for example, is likely to matter more for those at the bottom of the work hierarchy more than those at the top. Furthermore, working interactions are structured by expectations associated with social roles and by expectations of being recognized as playing my role in conformity with the expected standards. A problem defining what Everett Hughes termed the "social drama of work" is that, in contrast with ordinary interactions, there could be strong disagreements in the definition of the correct manner of playing the various roles involved in the social activity of work: between workers and management, as well as between service workers and their clients, there are structural sources of disagreements about what counts as good work.[6] Finally, the social relations that characterize work as a social activity, such as relations with colleagues who have a similar standing in the organizational hierarchy and those with others higher up, have their own form of recognition. As we will see, each of these social relations gives rise to particular recognitive expectations, and these expectations play a role at the very level of the working activity inasmuch as they impact deeply on the working subject.

PEER RECOGNITION

Given the importance of taking part in a working culture for the individual, for the reasons highlighted in the previous section, a *first stake in recognition* arises at this local level of social interactions within the work collective. A condition of psychic identity is *recognition by peers around real work*. This initial form of recognition at work is itself multifaceted.

As we just saw, the very structure of working activity means that the challenges it presents cannot be faced in isolation over a period of time, for basic ergonomic or pragmatic reasons. Trust is required at this pragmatic level, as a necessary condition shared between the individuals involved in the group so that effective cooperation can emerge, making it possible for all those involved to face the challenge of inadequate prescriptions. The need for recognition adds a new element to this dimension of trust. Recognition is required at an individual psychological level to give the seal of approval required by the subject to confirm that her efforts at bridging the gap between the prescribed and the real are indeed valid. Recognition by peers acknowledges the contribution of the individual worker to the collective's effort at performing real work. As can be seen, from the perspective of the collective, and like trust, this recognition is also a necessary condition of effective cooperation since without it, by definition, there can be no effective coordination of individual efforts, as some of them would simply be discounted. From the individual's perspective, recognition of the contribution to the collective work effort settles part of the intrinsic insecurity that is inherent in real work in the form of the possibility of failure.

This kind of recognition has two interrelated aspects. First, it involves the acknowledgment of the *efforts* undertaken by the individual to solve tasks that impact on the collective or, indeed, are part of a collective work effort. This is the recognition one expects for making an effortful contribution. In work especially, free riders are not acceptable; actual, positive contribution is a basic element of fairness. And, second, this recognition involves acknowledgment of the *technical value* of the work done. The gap between prescribed tasks and actual outcomes means that *only those* who are actually engaged in the effort, those who are in the nitty-gritty of having to bridge that particular gap, are able to say what physical, mental, and emotional effort, what manual, intellectual, emotional skills went into the performance of the real work. In turn, this means that the recognition requested and afforded at this level can only be granted by a very specific group of people, namely those who are acquainted with the activity itself, who have to perform the same tasks under similar constraints. All professions are elitist and exclusive in this sense, to the extent that only those who have undergone the specific challenges involved in that work can know exactly what it takes to perform that work. Even adjacent workers in work organizations who nevertheless perform different activities lack this knowledge. For instance, university administrators who work in the same building as university lecturers cannot really know what it means to lecture in specific circumstances. Equally, older workers who used to be in a particular industry but have moved on or retired quickly lose touch with the present, living reality of that particular work. Their old memories of living work no longer quite correspond to the living work of the present.

The technical recognition structuring workplaces draws on the *working culture* we already encountered, whose heart is a set of commitments toward ways of doing things. These are for the most part matters of technical know-how, but they extend more broadly than that. As the historical example of the old corporations shows us, professions usually display allegiance to moral, political, and sometimes even "spiritual" values; they can have specific moral or political leanings. The continued existence of these cultural realms, which are based on *shared experiences of living work,* should not be forgotten, nor their significance underestimated, despite the co-called hyperflexible character of contemporary societies. Individuals taking part in these cultures can receive rich forms of recognition that can play a major role in securing psychic identity. When this happens, we can see that work is directly capable of providing support for subjective life. *Professional identity,* as noted, can play a big part in structuring and making sense of the life of the subject. To lack the opportunity to develop such an identity adds to the negative experience both of unemployment and precarious employment. Conversely, professional identity and the belonging to a particular working culture can in some cases offset the negative impact of precarious conditions of employment, as in the creative industries or in academia where many professionals find it hard to achieve long-term employment security but are strongly committed to the particular ethos and culture of their chosen profession. Here, we have a clear case where the positive impact of the working activity is largely separate from the conditions of employment.

VERTICAL RECOGNITION: WORKING FOR THE BOSS

The subject engaged in a work task faces the risk of failure that is inherent in every task. For the expert, the risk is minimal and only arises upon sudden unplanned occurrence. It's not that the risk of failure is nonexistent for the expert, but rather that the expert can face it with a much broader scope for intervention and, as a result, with more confidence and lack of concern. In situations where there is almost no risk of failure because the task is very basic, the threat is that of meaninglessness or boredom and drudgery, another challenge that workers have to deal with.[7] And as we noted previously, many jobs might seem low-risk and yet entail hidden challenges that only the workers know about. In this sense, therefore, and despite appearances to the contrary, all work involves the risk of failure. And with the technical failure comes a raft of other negative consequences: being looked down upon by one's peers; being admonished or even retrenched by the employer; losing respect in one's own eyes or in the eyes of relevant others, notably those sharing the same culture of work. Because work always involves the possibility of failure, it is never psychologically neutral.

We have seen how, in responding to technical demands, the subject "spends" his mental, emotional and cognitive forces. But the full meaning and extent of this subjective expenditure only comes into view when we place the technical demands that confront the subject at work in a social context. To view the activity of work in its social context is fundamentally to see it as *addressed*. We have just considered one of work's addressees: the peers and the work collective to which worker and peer belong. When addressed in this way, certain forms of recognition can be assigned to it. But there are other addressees of work, and work addressed to them brings its own forms of recognition, which in turn have their own distinctive consequences for subjective life.

The most obvious series of others to whom work is addressed, in the case of waged work at least, are those who pay the wages: the hierarchy, management, and, in private industry, the owners of the means of production. But in what sense exactly is work addressed to them? Workers engaged in waged work don't work *for* their boss; they work for themselves, first and foremost to extract the means of subsistence from the wages paid to them as a result of their work. Only because the owners own the means through which the work is performed, and because the managers are granted a form of authority based on the work process, is work *under* their command. This is the key difference between abstract labor that is characteristic of modern societies, in which the work relation is mediated by money, as opposed to work in premodern societies in which working relations are more directly personal, and many workers do indeed work directly *for* their superior, in the literal personal sense of the term.[8] While there has to be a substantive addressing of personal efforts to others at the level of the work collective, it is actually debatable whether the same can be said of the hierarchy in the work organization. How can we say that the worker's actions are "addressed" to the managers, or indeed the owners, given that these actions are performed under conditions that take authority away from the worker to define many if not all the conditions of the working activity: the outcome to be produced, the timeline in which it is to be produced, the means by which it is to be produced, the measures by which the work efforts will be remunerated, and so on?

A form of address in fact has to exist since a common form of suffering among workers relates to the lack of recognition they experience when their work efforts go unnoticed or, indeed, when their dedication to the prescriptions issued by management remain unacknowledged. One of the bitterest aspects of being retrenched, or of retiring without acknowledgment from an organization of one's contribution to it, is the sense of "having given your life" for the organization with no thanks in return. "Recognition for good work," "acknowledgment of effort" is a universal demand across all professions. If that is the case, though, then clearly the relationship of employees to managers and owners of capital cannot merely be one of instrumental financial interest. Somehow, however reluctantly or ambiguously, and despite the relation of domination that wage work inherently consists in, work is also addressed to the superiors.

This demand by workers to be shown recognition for their contribution to the organization has several aspects. For example, there is a demand for a form of recognition that renders the efforts made by the worker visible to all, and there is an expectation that the technical value of the effort, its role in achieving the prescribed task, will be properly acknowledged. Thankfulness is the kind of recognition one might expect for this.[9] Vertical work relations between workers and management are thus intrinsically ambiguous since they are by definition asymmetrical, with one group exerting authority and power over the other—a power the exercise of which can have devastating consequences for the subordinate party—and yet also carry strong normative demands, all the way to something like a need to be shown gratitude for the expenditure of one's subjective resources. Yet this combination of claims for equal recognition and unequal access to power is consistent with the phenomenon of real work. As we have seen, the gap between prescribed work and real work is an inherently complex one since the activity of work has to take on board at least some of the prescribed elements. Indeed, there is no task to perform "for real" without a definition of it, and in situations of capitalistic work a substantial part of that definition comes from management, not just on the economic side but also on the technical and the ergonomic sides. Therefore, even if a worker engages in her work on purely instrumental grounds, merely for the pay package and to be able to pay the bills, the fact that she engages in real work and has to perform living work entails a form of address to the managers and the boss simply because real work requires of the worker that she subjectively engages with the external, prescriptive side of the work. This is why a most powerful form of psychic sealing of work efforts for the subject is the acknowledgment by the hierarchy of the efforts made. In the capitalistic context, this form of reciprocal address represents a fascinating social relation, since a form of positive acknowledgment of the other is carried by what is also an antagonistic relation. Workers demand and in normal cases receive a form of appreciation from someone who holds them in relative subjection. Once again, we see that work is structured by highly complex and ambiguous forms of social relations.

VERTICAL RECOGNITION: WORKING FOR THE CUSTOMER

A second form of "vertical recognition" is the one the worker demands of and hopefully receives from the ones to whom the "product" of work—which, as said, can be a service or a type of care—is addressed. In the capitalistic context, these are the customers; though in other contexts, such as a patient at a public hospital, the addressee and beneficiary need not be making a payment. Especially in those cases where a payment is made, this is an intrinsically ambiguous relationship of recognition since, as Adam Smith observed, the economic relationship is at first purely utilitarian.[10] And yet the producer-consumer/user relationship can be more complex than that. So much of the worker's identity is mobilized in the work effort that a rejection of the quality or suitability of the work produced can have effects on the psyche comparable to an absence of recognition from the hierarchy. In fact the judgment of quality, which finds its roots in the expert knowledge shared by those who partake in a particular work culture, finds its ultimate test in the satisfaction of the client, since the latter has no insight into the technical difficulties of the work and is interested only in its outcome. The customer's satisfaction with the outcome therefore is untainted by any consideration outside the purely self-interested one of whether the job was well done or not. The peers can appreciate the intricacies of the technical skills that had to be deployed to arrive at the outcome, but the outcome is ultimately measured by this addressee of the work efforts. In turn, when the "customer is happy," or the client satisfied, a powerful seal of recognition is put on the work effort. Indeed, one of the pleasures of work lies in the gap between the two forms of recognition: knowing as an expert how much effort, skill, and experience had to go into a work process and receiving peer recognition for it, but keeping this whole world of technical effort and knowledge hidden from the nonexpert and enjoying their unlearned, ignorant gratitude for the sheer achievement of the sought-after outcomes.

The psychic significance of this moment is such that it shines through in a number of well-observed phenomena of work. It is probably the psychic premium afforded by the addressee's recognition and thanks for a job well done that explains the oft-noted tendency of many workers to go "beyond the call of duty," that is, to actually perform more work than their contract stipulates. It is not so often remarked that long work hours, about which, as we have seen, so much anxiety is expressed, might have a source in this psychic satisfaction and not just the financial rewards they bring. This might help to explain the conundrum, noted in chapter 2, of the discrepancy between the reduction in average number of hours spent in employment and the rise in concerns about work-life balance. The intrinsic as well as the recognitive rewards of work might actually make many workers go well beyond the official number of hours stipulated in their contracts. This would be one insufficiently noted aspect of the work-life balance debate: namely the fact that part of the problem lies with workers themselves and their own tendency to let work intrude the other spheres of their life. The deep satisfaction work can provide, both intrinsically and through forms of recognition, would thereby be an ambiguous phenomenon: positive on one side as subjects draw subjective rewards from it; but negative for its impact on other sides. We can note that this is not the only ambiguity of work in terms of its subjective implications: as we shall discuss later, because work can mobilize individual souls so powerfully, it can be put in the service of causes whose aims are destructive.

In any case, when recognition is not granted, for instance, when an unfair complaint is made by the addressees against a technically valid outcome, workers can find support in their technical knowledge and the work collective and on that basis reject the complaint. The situation becomes more damaging for workers when management takes the side of the customer (for instance on the principle that "the customer is always right"). In this case, the relation of authority and subjection means that technical knowledge suddenly counts for nothing. It is not unreasonable to suppose that all these scenarios contribute to the burnout syndrome, when workers either willingly, or through more or less direct forms of compulsion, are forced to go beyond the terms of the work contract, either extensively, in terms of longer working hours, or intensively, in terms of the personal sacrifices they are asked to make in order to keep the customer or the manager happy.

So far we have been considering the social relation between worker and the addressee as an *interpersonal* one: the worker is a person concretely addressing their efforts and the outcome of their efforts to concrete other persons. Even on the production line the worker's gestures are addressed to the anonymous singular person who will be using the product the worker is contributing to produce. We encounter here the ethical import of the work collective, which we will discuss at more length in the parts 3 and 4 of the book. Supportive work collectives encourage a respectful attitude toward external as well as internal addressees, to the real yet anonymous other to whom my work is addressed as well as peers. In other words, the respect of others that work solidarity can teach can also be extended to solidarity with peers outside work, by providing them with a product or a service of good technical quality.[11] By contrast, dysfunctional work organizations will tend to produce damaged goods. This happens even if, and, indeed, sometimes precisely because, management introduces constraining methods to enforce "total quality" in outputs.[12] If we turn to the worker placed in the kind of dysfunctional collective workplace we have already described, and if we think about his attitude toward the anonymous, real other to whom his work is addressed, we will find an illustration of the rule according to which the moral nature of work interactions spreads beyond workplaces into social life more generally. Disrespect learned at work will spread to disrespect for the customer in the form of indifference to below-par work outputs.

This relationship is also social in a broader sense, or, we might also say, it is a "vertical" social relation in a way that is different from the vertical relation of subjection to management and the owners of the means of production. What we mean by this becomes clear if we focus on the negative experiences related to this dimension, namely in this case the lack of recognition felt by members of a profession by society at large. This lack of recognition is often linked to dissatisfaction regarding the level of remuneration: complaints about underpay, for example, are often expressions of indignation, as if the actual work done within a profession could be worth so little. In cases such as these, the demand for salary increase is equally a demand for better recognition. They indicate that the act of working is *also addressed to society at large*. In working, the subject takes part in the general order of cooperation that underpins society. Living work is addressed simultaneously to an anonymous real other whose specific need will be fulfilled by the outcome of my work and to society at large. The latter is my contribution to the division of labor.

The type of recognition this social relation carries is the one that has been discussed the most in the philosophical literature on recognition.[13] It refers to the values and norms making up the broad social-cultural background within which technical and economic tasks are performed. This background contains symbolic hierarchies and normative judgments ranking types of tasks, but also the usage of particular instruments, tools, and machines, the ranking of professions, which all impact on the individual's capacity to give meaning to their work and integrate it in their identity. Some forms of work can be poorly paid but have high social prestige, and this can be sufficient for individuals to offset the lower financial reward. Other forms of work can be well paid but lack prestige (truck drivers in the Australian mining wild west). Others again lack social prestige, for instance because they are feminized professions and receive low remunerations to go with it. Even in such professions, however, it can be that strong work collectives, strong working cultures and ethos, can provide strong defenses against a broad social depreciation. In any case, it is clear that specific struggles for recognition will be constantly waged within modern societies, to challenge depreciative social judgements over any aspect of an occupational culture and to claim a better acknowledgment of that occupation's contribution to the common good and, by way of consequence, of the value of the individual contributions made by the workers in those occupations. These remarks point forward to the next part of our study, which is concerned with the political dimensions of the organization of work in contemporary societies and the methodological tools that ought to be used to critically evaluate them.

With the consideration of the general judgments that social groups reciprocally apply to each other in relation to specific kinds of work tasks and occupations, we have completed our analysis of the large spectrum of recognition demands that structure working experiences. Looking back at this full spectrum, the beginning of which, to recall, was the recognition by immediate peers within the technically defined work collective, some important general conclusions seem worth highlighting.

The first concerns the sheer *complexity* of work experiences from the point of view of their impact on subjective identities. Indeed, work experiences are complex in a number of ways. This complexity is, first, linked, as we saw earlier in this chapter, to the fact that working is at the intersection of different forms of social interaction, which bring the subject into contact with different kinds of social partners. In each case, the expectations workers express toward these interaction partners can be brought under the umbrella concept of recognition, but there are as many different kinds of recognition as there are social interaction converging in the working activity. As we consistently highlighted, there are multiple ways in which these varied logics of recognition can complement or contradict each other.

A second aspect of the complexity arises from the nesting of recognitive demands within the technical dimension of working activities, which we considered in the previous chapter. It is clear that an analysis of the different subjective stakes of work experience must remain incomplete without a fine-grained, ergonomically realistic account of working activities. Indeed, an ergonomic perspective must be brought to bear on the lived experience of work if we are to understand the depth and extent of what is at stake for the subject in the activity of working. To designate working activity as merely instrumental action that has no intrinsic bearing on subjectivity at all—a designation that is all too common in critical social theory—is clearly inadequate in the light of our analysis.

Third, our analysis has brought out the normative *ambiguity* of work experiences. The ergonomic perspective we took up in the previous chapter, and the social perspective adopted in this one, show up the reality of the lived experience of work in a mixed light. The activity of working impacts on subjects both positively and negatively, for better and for worse, in both its technical and social dimensions. This makes it impossible to say of work activity, without further qualification in regard to how the technical and social dimensions of it are organized, that it is good or bad for the subject. On the other hand, given the seriousness of what is at stake for the subject in relation to work—a seriousness we are better able to appreciate as a result of the preceding analyses—it must strike us as all the more important that work is organized *well*. But what exactly does it mean to say that things are well with work? What are the normative standards against which the worth of work, or the worth of the social and political organization of work, is to be judged? What are the norms that guide our thinking about how work ought to be? And what kind of politics would be commensurate with the proper instantiation of those norms? To these questions we now turn.

PART III
A Critical Conception of Work

Chapter Five

JUSTICE AND AUTONOMY AS
NORMS OF WORK

In part 1 we examined a series of worries that currently surround work in our societies. Contained in these worries is a more or less explicitly articulated sense that all is not well with work, that work is not as it should be, not just in minor or trivial ways, which are easy to shrug off, but in ways that have a big and lasting impact on those affected by them. In other words, they correspond to negative experiences of work that are highly consequential for individuals, families, groups, and society at large. In part 2 we proposed a model of work that could account for this significance. We analyzed what is at play in the experience of working in general so as to elaborate a theoretical framework that enables us to make sense of the varieties of negative experience associated with contemporary work for many individuals, be they unemployed or employed. From the perspective of the framework that emerged from our discussion, the ways in which the malaises around work are articulated remain superficial insofar as they neither make explicit the specific social relations that structure the work experience nor identify the psychic stakes that explain why the negative experiences of work matter so much for the individuals concerned. We have also seen that the problems met with at work have the power of negatively affecting not only social life (both at work and outside of work) but also private, intimate life, and that they can also deeply impact negatively on mental health, or as we put it in chapters 3 and 4, *subjective life*. Conversely, having an opportunity to work and working in situations that provide the individual with ties to reality, with the opportunity to participate in social interactions aimed at producing socially useful products and to get recognition for one's individual capacities and social standing through one's own activity, all this conditions the possibility of having a social and private life that is of value. Both on account of this negative sense (because the problems arising from work affect our lives so badly) and in this positive sense (because work provides some of the requisites of a satisfying life), it makes sense to say that there is a *centrality* to work.

But the idea of a centrality of work has been widely repudiated. A major reason for this has been the popularity of the "end of work" scenario among social theorists, philosophers, and social commentators generally, which we discussed in our introduction. According to this scenario, just as the activity of productive work is on the wane, so the malaises around work shouldn't be taken too seriously. They shouldn't be taken too seriously partly because, according to this line of thought, people will eventually come to realize (if they have not done so already) that their existence would be more satisfying if it was centered not on work but on their life outside of work. Another reason for downplaying the significance of the malaise around work is that, fundamentally, nothing can be done about the way things are with work. The old expectation that working conditions could be radically transformed so as to make work a central vehicle for self-realization eventually revealed itself as the empty hope it was, since it was simply not compatible with the contemporary economic organization of work, if not with work as such.[1] From this point of view, the only possible progressive responses to the malaises around work would then be, on the one hand, to struggle against the cultural centrality of work, in order that people learn to achieve self-realization outside of work, and, on the other hand, to reduce the quantity of time spent at work, as well as the material dependence on work, in order that people suffer less from the necessary evils of work. But the account of the subject at work we provided in part 2 opens up another kind of response. For we have seen that work is not only a source of suffering but also of satisfaction, and that, depending on its social organization, it could provide individuals with opportunities for self-development from a social as well as from a personal point of view. It has also been shown that the centrality of work is not only *cultural*—a value that may or may not be endorsed depending on one's culture—but *anthropologically deep-rooted*, with specific socializing effects through its dynamics of recognition and structuring effects on the psyche through the "ties to reality" it provides. If the model we have proposed is on the right lines, then far from brushing off the negative experiences that are characteristic of the contemporary organization of work, we should be taking them very seriously indeed.

Since these negative experiences belong to what many workers and unemployed people *themselves* consider as the main problems of their life, a critical model should be elaborated to help analyze what exactly is going wrong and how it could be tackled. And since these negative experiences are structured by specific social relations, such a critical model should not only deal with the best ways for individuals to *adapt* to the flow of problematic situations but should also be oriented at *transforming* those social relations that are responsible for the negative experiences. The model should be informing and guiding political discussions about how to make social life better. In other words, what is required is a *critical conception of work* that would consist in a model of social critique attuned to the various negative experiences corresponding to the worries about work we analyzed in part 1 and taking into account the subjective stakes of work analyzed in part 2. Our task in part 3 is to spell out in more detail the shape such a model should take.

Articulating a conception of critique is typically a job for the philosopher. But it is simply a fact that contemporary philosophy offers little by way of systematic discussion or analysis of what is going wrong with work and how things could be changed.[2] Just as social theorists and social commentators have neglected this issue in the last decades, notably because they have taken for granted the end of work diagnosis, philosophers have generally remained silent about work, and this for reasons we also foreshadowed in the introduction. The first main reason is methodological: the whole contemporary discussion about the tasks of a critical theory of society and the foundations of social critique has been premised on the presupposition that what is required is a *general* model of social critique. It has largely been assumed that the more general a model of social critique is, the better it is. We will look at this idea more closely, and the alternative we want to present to it, in the next chapter. Suffice it to say for the moment that in contrast to a model of critique that applies generally to all contexts of social criticism, the model we favor is particularized, aimed in this instance at negative experiences of work. The second main reason why philosophers have been reluctant to tackle the issue of the critique of the organization of work has to do with their anthropological and sociological prejudices: either work is presumed to comprise one of the lowest forms of human existence (inferior to political action and deliberation for instance) or it is presumed to be of contingent significance, one source of identity among many, with its own set of goods, which individuals may or may not opt for depending on their preferences or particular value horizon.[3] If the argument presented so far in this book is sound, then the latter presumption is false and work plays a central (though by no means always positive) role in the life of a subject.[4] Since the subject is always a subject among other subjects—since, as most philosophers now acknowledge, the self is inherently a *social* self—another way of putting this is to say that the *social* self is also a *working* self. But philosophers have been reluctant to acknowledge that the self might be *at once* a social self and a working self, and this not just on account of the quality of the arguments on offer but because of long-standing prejudices about the reality and value of selves that work.

In order to articulate the critical conception of work we are looking for, we will try in the remainder of this chapter to make explicit the normative expectations that are embedded in contemporary worries about work and their corresponding negative social experiences. We shall deal mainly with standards of *justice* that reveal themselves in expectations that subjects have about *employment* relations and work *activity*, though we shall also consider standards of *autonomy* separately from these. Our task here is to describe the often merely implicit demands for justice and autonomy that subjects make regarding the availability and terms of employment, on the one hand, and the kind of activity performed at work, on the other. In the next chapter we will consider the philosophical relevance of such a description and the contribution it makes to a critical conception of work (the conception we need for effective critique of work).

EXPECTATIONS OF JUSTICE AND AUTONOMY IN EMPLOYMENT

As we have seen, current worries about unemployment, precariousness, work-life imbalance and work overload, disrespect at work and meaningless work correspond to shared negative social experiences in which general expectations about work remain unsatisfied. By analyzing these experiences, we can hope to spell out some widely held normative expectations about work, that is, expectations about the standards that work ought to meet but does not. It is precisely through this negativist approach that we will try to articulate the types of normative problems that should be tackled by a critical conception of work. These problems turn out to be centred on justice and autonomy.[5] Workers typically articulate their negative work experience in terms of injustice and lack of autonomy, and their negative experience reflects a positive desire to be treated in a way that is more respectful of their autonomy and that recognizes their rights and the value and reality of their actual work.[6] The claims for more autonomy and justice are certainly not *restricted* to work. But the normative problems of autonomy and justice do take specific forms when they arise in the context of work. Indeed, one of the main challenges facing the critical conception of work we are looking for is to be able to take into account the full range of these specific forms.

To begin with, let us consider the malaises related to unemployment, underemployment, and precariousness. The corresponding negative social experiences concern forms of work *deprivation*: complete deprivation in unemployment, quantitatively incomplete deprivation for those who would like to have more than a part-time job (quantitative underemployment), qualitatively incomplete deprivation for those who would like their working experience to be less affected by uncertainty and instability. A fourth type of negative experience needs to be added to this series. It could also be described in terms of underemployment—as "qualitative" underemployment. This is the experience of those who are overqualified for the job they do or more precisely, of those who find themselves doing work that falls short of the kind of work they feel they ought to be doing given their professional or educational background.[7] These latter experiences are all the more pervasive in those countries where the general educational level is rising without corresponding rises in the level of employment. They are also very common among qualified migrants.[8]

In what sense are expectations of justice at stake in these experiences? The most obvious sense refers to the *distribution of the goods* the deprivation of which is constitutive for the experiences in question. In other words, the normative expectation is one of having fair and equal access to the goods associated with employment, that the goods be distributed fairly or in accordance with principles of distributive justice. Conversely, the *demand* implicit in those experiences is that of a *redistribution* of those goods; it is through such redistribution that the normative expectation implicit in the experience would be met. It is above all in this sense that unemployment is discussed as a normative problem in mainstream political discourses as well as in political theory. Most would agree that it is unjust to be arbitrarily excluded from a vital good—an income and the other benefits of employment we looked at earlier—and most would also agree that the cause of unemployment is in most cases an arbitrary matter, at least in the sense that it is beyond the control of the individual affected. Layoffs are typically the result of changes in the labor market, be it internal or external, rather than choices an individual makes or behaviors he is responsible for. And the experience of unemployment does typically come with a sense of being unfairly treated, either directly by the employer who has suddenly laid one off or indirectly by those in political power for failing to create the conditions in which employment is generally available to anyone who genuinely seeks it and needs it, or, indeed, when these political leaders enforce policies that facilitate the laying off of workers simply to increase returns on investment. In our societies, wages remain the main form of wealth distribution, and the loss of wages that is subsequent to unemployment also raises issues of social inequality related to income. This sheds light on a general normative expectation about work whose implications should be articulated in terms of justice and injustice: the expectation of receiving an income that enables one to survive and support one's dependants as well as to enjoy a decently resourced life as defined by prevailing social standards. Wages are one means of receiving such an income, and they are more valued than the various other means available (we will see why later on). This is the first way in which the issue of distributive justice intersects with that of wages, and it is undeniable that the loss of wages that results from unemployment is typically experienced by those who suffer it as an injustice.

But wages could also produce another type of distributive injustice which also relates to general expectations. Among the general expectations about work, one should also count the expectation of being paid *in proportion to the efforts spent* or in proportion to the contribution made to the firm or organization that pays the wage. If access to *some* wage, to some employment, is the most obvious requirement of justice from the point of view of those without employment, then provision of a wage that is proportionate to contribution—a *fair* wage—is the most obvious normative expectation from the point of view of those with employment. In a time of rising inequalities in terms of income and wages,[9] the remuneration of work has become a particularly acute and widespread source of feelings of injustice. Wage freezes and cuts to pensions imposed on large swathes of public sector workers in the advanced economies in the wake of the financial crisis of 2008—not to mention all the layoffss—have provoked moral outrage not just because of disappointed expectations of rising standards of living but because of the sheer injustice of it all. The sense of injustice here relates to inequalities that arise both from disproportionately low remunerative rewards for the work of some and disproportionately high remunerative rewards for the work of others.[10]

Furthermore, these two types of distributive injustice—the injustice of being arbitrarily excluded from the manifest goods of employment (a living wage) and that of receiving less than one's due of that good (less than the effort or contribution made through one's employment entitles one to)—can compound each other. This is the case for those in precarious work who receive low levels of income for short-term contracted labor, contracts entered into not out of choice, but for want of secure, well-paid employment. This combination of distributive injustices is characteristic of what has been termed the "social question" and "pauperism" in the nineteenth century: at the beginning of the capitalist era, the working class was suffering from both low wages and periodic unemployment. Due to the contemporary pressures on wages, and to the development of quantitative underemployment and precariousness, one can wonder if some kind of "return of the social question" in its original form is now taking place.[11] Certainly, the experience of the contemporary working poor and the impoverished precariat would be inadequately described as one merely of hardship due to bad luck. That would leave out something essential: the sense of injustice coloring the experience.

We also saw in chapter 1 that, for the individual concerned, the experience of unemployment is problematic not only because it implies poverty or reduction of income but also because it implies deep transformations of one's whole social experience. What is at stake in these transformations depends notably on the fact that the loss of a job is not only a material deprivation but also a loss of *social status*. It is indisputable that unemployment is generally experienced as an injustice on account of the loss of social status that comes with having a job. To contribute with one's own professional activity to the life of society means having a social function and a social status to go with it. Conversely, unemployment means a deprivation of social function and status.

We could call this lack of status an injustice of *misrecognition*, or an inequality of recognition, to be contrasted with distributive injustice, or an injustice of *maldistribution*.[12] Inequalities in recognition that are independent of inequalities in income distribution can take various forms. Some of them relate to the fact that not all individuals have the chance to get the social status they need through their professional activity. It is partly because this type of recognition matters so much to them that their experience of unemployment is so bitter. This explains why any attempt to compensate the income reduction with social welfare, although necessary, will always remain insufficient—not to mention the fact that poverty and social welfare usually go with a devalorizing social recognition that is all the more painful.[13] This also explains why the distribution of income through wages is more valued than any other mode of distribution.

Another injustice related to recognition concerns the fact that there is a hierarchy of social status among the professions and that this hierarchy condemns groups of individuals engaged in poorly valued professions to be recognized through inferior social status. By way of illustration of such injustice related to inequality of status, one could mention the injustice typically felt by nurses in hospitals where, at least in some countries, they receive not only the lowest wages but also the lowest social status. They experience a structural denial of recognition of the value of their contribution to the functioning of the hospital as well as to social life in general.[14] The injustice felt by those who experience underemployment in its qualitative sense (getting a job inferior to one's qualification or professional background) compounds these two types of injustice linked with social status.

What follows from these remarks is that two types of normative expectations about status, and so a certain kind of recognition, have to be counted as general normative expectations about work. First, we have seen that what remains unsatisfied in the experience of unemployment is the general expectation to benefit from the opportunity to get social recognition through a profession. It means that something like a right to work should be recognized. Second, what remains unsatisfied in the experience of workers at the bottom of the status hierarchy is the expectation that each social function be recognized for the value of its contribution to social life and not only for its cultural prestige depending on social prejudices rooted in class, gender, or ethnoracial distinctions. The conception of justice that is implicit here is that it is a form of disrespect, and in that sense unjust, not to be recognized as a member of a profession that is socially useful,[15] and, conversely, that it is just to struggle for more equal recognition between professions. It also implies that a just social division of labor should reduce, if not equalize, the hierarchy of social prestige among professions.

The experience of unemployment also raises the issue of autonomy. Just like justice, autonomy could be taken in many senses, but its broadest meaning concerns the ability to conduct one's own life. It is precisely the lack of autonomy in this broad sense that shapes the experience of unemployment, and, as we saw in chapter 1, it is plausible to suppose that this lack or loss of autonomy is at the root of the psychological harms of unemployment. Whereas employment means being able to depend on one's self in terms of income and possibilities of meeting the material conditions of one's personal projects, unemployment means having to depend on social welfare and a material inability to engage oneself in long-term personal projects. Here again, unemployment has similarities with precariousness since the latter also undermines horizons of expectation as well as the conditions that fuel the feeling of being capable of leading one's own life. In the negative experiences of unemployment and precariousness, a general normative expectation is at play that one's relation to work shouldn't prevent one from leading one's own life. This expectation concerns work as employment, since being employed is one of the material preconditions for leading one's own life. But what is expected is equally not just to be employed in any kind of labor contract. In the experience of precariousness, as already mentioned, the capacity of engaging in long-term projects is undermined: the sphere of autonomy is restricted to short-term projects and choice of the best means to cope with uncertainty.

Indeed, for reasons we discussed in the previous chapter, employment is characterized by a loss of autonomy too. The labor contract implies that the worker will have to obey orders and prescriptions in the workplace and that she will therefore partly renounce her own capacity to conduct her own actions. In other words, waged work is subjected to a structural domination. In which sense, then, should unemployment be considered as a loss of autonomy? Shouldn't it be considered, rather, as a gain in autonomy, since it frees one from the relations of subordination that characterize waged work? Isn't such a gain too significant to be canceled by the loss of autonomy that results from depending on social welfare? There is no doubt that some individuals feel more autonomous in unemployment than in waged work and that others (sometimes called the "Freeters") consider precariousness as an opportunity for getting loose from the ties of subordination to the employer and his representative.[16] But, for many others, unemployment is clearly experienced as a loss of autonomy. And if this loss of autonomy is not simply compensated by the gain of autonomy that results from exiting a labor contract, it is mainly because unemployment and waged work amount to two different kinds of loss of autonomy. In waged work, loss of autonomy means having to obey: in other words, it is an experience of domination. In unemployment, loss of autonomy means losing control of the organization of one's life and finding oneself in situations that don't make sense and in which one is becoming a stranger to oneself: in other words, it is an experience of failure of appropriation of one's own existence or of alienation.[17] Indeed, waged labor also could generate experiences of alienation, but they depend on specific working conditions and the work organization. Conversely, the material insecurities that accompany unemployment imply various type of vulnerability to domination. But it remains true that the loss of autonomy experienced by waged workers and the unemployed are structurally different.

EXPECTATIONS OF JUSTICE AND AUTONOMY IN WORK ACTIVITY

Up to now we have characterized some general normative expectations that concern work as employment and that consist in expectations of justice and autonomy. But what is problematic in these negative social experiences does not solely relate to employment as distinct from work as activity. For instance, to return once more to Marie Jahoda's formulation, the experience of unemployment brings with it deprivations of "latent" goods such as "ties to reality" and possibilities of recognition working activity provides, in addition to the manifest material benefits that come from employment. These latent goods extend to other forms of affirmation or recognition, or promises of recognition, embedded in past or future working activities in the workplace of the kind discussed in the previous chapter. The fact that these goods bound up with activity are no longer at the disposal of the unemployed contributes to the moral injuries suffered in unemployment, and it could also be considered as a specific form of injustice (as arbitrary inequality concerning the possibility of benefiting from ties to reality and recognition in the workplace). In other words, the sources of feelings of injustice associated with unemployment extend from unfair financial deprivations to less obvious ones in relation to the kinds of activity at their disposal. We will suggest that something similar holds for experiences of the loss of autonomy: they too arise in relation to the activity of working as well as from exclusion from the financial benefits of employment or inadequate access to them in the case of badly paid employees.

Let us first look more closely at expectations concerning justice with respect to work as activity. It is a fact, demonstrable through the kind of social research we considered in part 1, that *within* workplaces the worker can be confronted with various feelings of injustice. Some of these feelings depend on the sense that each worker has of being a singular individual, irreducible to a workforce, who has rights that ought to be recognized. At a minimal level, workers expect their rights as persons to be respected, that is, to have their basic human dignity upheld in the workplace. This ought to protect them from being treated merely as cogs in the machine or as the property of the person paying the wage—as mere means to someone else's chosen ends. If a worker finds herself without such protection, as a mere appendage to the productive process or a slave at the mercy of a master, she is bound to have her sense of justice tested. No one expects to have to forfeit their basic human rights when they are at work. They expect to be able to retain their basic moral status as a "person" and to be treated with the respect owing to all persons.

But there is another level at which they expect basic respect to be shown. This relates not so much to being treated as an end and not just a means, to having their status as a person with basic human rights upheld, but to being shown the respect owed to someone *contributing to a collective action*. As participants in the collective action of the work process, workers generally expect the workplace to be organized not only according to technical rules, the private interests of shareholders, and arbitrary decisions of management, but also according to rules that are *reasonable*. A rule may be deemed reasonable or not on many counts, but a crucial one has to do with its capacity for correction by the people whose actions are regulated by it. For this reason, a strong normative expectation arises that workers be treated not just as "persons" but as "citizens" within the workplace, that is, as agents with a "voice" that ought to count for something, as well as persons with a basic dignity that should be respected (without dropping the expectation that they will be treated as "human resources" too, with productive powers to be exploited). While this normative expectation may not be explicitly formulated, and may be variable in force across working populations, there is plenty of evidence to suggest it remains important in shaping the experience of work. We mentioned the recent British Workplace Behaviour Survey in chapter 2, with its finding of widespread grievances about unreasonable management among British workers on account (in part) of having their views and opinions ignored. Many other sociological and ethnographical studies of workplaces confirm that there is a general expectation among people who work that they be recognized as having the right to have their say about the work organization and that this expectation is a constitutive, not adventitious, element of dignity at work.[18]

This expectation, that could give rise to feelings of injustice when it remains unsatisfied, might seem too utopian to be taken into consideration in a critical conception of work. Is it not unrealistic, especially nowadays, to expect workplaces to be subjected to the norms of citizenship? Must we not concede that technical and economic constraints are bound to predominate in work organizations? But the normative expectation of something like citizen status among the people who work in an organization is not as far from reality as these questions suggest. At least two reasons show that they have to be taken seriously. First, throughout the twentieth century, various forms of firm citizenship have been implemented, from the simple legalization of trade unions to different forms of worker control. In countries such as Germany, strong unions still play a decisive role in the strategic choices of firms. Second, as discussed in the previous chapter, a public space internal to the work collectives plays a role at the very level of the work activity. For a worker, working doesn't simply mean obeying prescriptions in conformity with technical constraints. It also involves trying to find collective solutions to the problems at hand in order to meet the objectives. To find such solutions, discussions inside the work collective are required. It may be that contemporary work organizations have tended to undermine the traditional forms of firm citizenship and that even the work collectives and their internal public spaces have been weakened (we will describe these trends more precisely in chapter 7).[19] But this also contributes to the contemporary worries that surround work as well as to negative social experiences outside work. As suggested already, the malaise around "bullying" has to do at least in part with the lack of protection available to individuals from networks of solidarity between colleagues and from political engagement in the workplace. This heightened vulnerability thus provides a supplementary argument to take seriously the specific types of feelings of injustice that result from the experience of not being recognized as having the right to a say.

Another general expectation concerns the right to be treated not only as a person, and as a citizen, but also as an *individual* having a life *outside* of work. The labor contract implies subordination during the working day, but it is supposed to leave room for the free enjoyment of life once work is finished. There is a general expectation that firms respect specific constraints regarding life outside of work, notably when they are related to family life and intimacy. If it is a right to pursue the happiness of being a parent, or more generally to have a private life, then it is legitimate to expect that the working activity should be organized in such a way that it does not become incompatible with this life after hours. Hence the feelings of injustice when somebody is sanctioned because the needs of her private life collide with what is supposed to be a requirement of her work. There is no doubt that the "blurring" trend that is specific to the present times and the subsequent problems concerning the work-life balance make these feelings of injustice highly significant. This provides a sufficient argument to introduce a reference to the general expectation of being recognized as an individual having specific needs in our critical conception of work. But the expectations of such recognition also relate to other negative social experiences at work. They are also at play when workers are pushed to their limits and when their need to rest, or to slow down, is not taken into consideration. Specific experiences of injustice, or loss of dignity, concern the fact that it is not legitimate that people are confronted with the choice either of being sacked or of being worn down. In the general expectation of being recognized as an individual having specific needs, a specific conception of justice is implicit that enables us to capture normative aspects of the experiences of work-life imbalance, overwork, and burnout.[20]

Other types of experience of injustice within the workplace refer more specifically to the working activity itself. The last chapter showed that recognition plays a crucial role in the experience of working. Workers generally expect from management that it recognize the reality of the effort spent and the value of the contribution to the firm or organization they work for. They also expect from the work collective recognition of the quality of the solutions they find to technical problems and to meet objectives in terms of productivity. It is mainly the first of these two types of expectation that gives rise to feelings of injustice: feelings that the amount of effort spent is underestimated, or that the difficulties of the work are not really taken into account, feelings that the value of the contribution to the firm or the organization is not properly appreciated. Various reasons explain why these experiences of injustice are so pervasive nowadays: the development of forms of management based purely on the achievement of numerical goals and disconnected from knowledge of the working activity itself, the development of forms of evaluation of performance that are purely individualized and used as a means to increase the competition among workers—all this contributes to denial of recognition of the reality and utility of work. And this denial of recognition is all the more bitter when workers are not compensated for it by recognition coming from work collectives that have been undermined by internal competition or when they have to pay the price of their bad evaluations, either through a loss of income or through relegation into less interesting activities or lower professional positions. We will analyze some of the reasons for these developments and how they concretely play out later. For the time being, suffice it to note that experiences of injustice are at stake of a kind significant enough to merit a place in a critical conception of work.

One further remark should be made about expectations of justice in regard to activity, one that links them back to expectations of justice in regard to employment. We have seen that distinctive forms of normative expectation attach to the sense one has of oneself as a person, a citizen, and as an individual. But we must now add to this list the sense one has of oneself as a *producer* and the distinctive claims that arise within the experience of working from that self-understanding (however implicit it may be). These claims relate not so much to expectations of having a certain share (a fair share) of goods and services—that is to say, access to goods of consumption—but to expectations of participating in productive activity itself and of obtaining due recognition for that contribution both at the level of work organization and society at large. We might call these "goods of production," exclusion from which elicits demands for redistribution, or we could call them "statuses," exclusion from which elicits demands for recognition. Or we might say that what is at stake here is a different kind of justice claim again, a claim distinctive to the experience of work qua work or to the experience attached to those activities that contribute to collective action within the work organization and beyond it, thereby contributing to social wealth. The term *contributive justice* is apposite for this.[21]

Let us finally consider the various forms of restriction of *autonomy* that workers experience in workplaces.

The first concerns the relation of subordination that is embedded in the labor contract. Being employed as a wage worker means having to obey orders and to organize one's activity along the prescriptions of management. In this respect, the working activity is structurally a dominated one. But, as we have already shown, in the very working activity there is also structural room for autonomy. Real work is always different from prescribed work, and this is true at the individual and collective level. At the individual level, at least some degree of personal involvement, of interpretation, and of adaptation is always required to transform a prescribed task into working activity. At a collective level, where individual activities depart from the tasks prescribed, the prescribed coordination may be inadequate for organizing the collaborative work. Some readjustment of the prescriptions in relation to the individual activities has to happen within the work collective. Its internal public space is the main medium to achieve this transformation of prescribed coordination into efficient collaboration.

Now, in the power relations within the workplace, what is at stake is precisely the relation between this structural domination and this structural room left for autonomy. On the one hand, since Frederick Taylor's time-motion studies it has always been an objective, on the part of the managers, to reduce as much as possible the autonomy of workers concerning the way they could organize their activity, adapt and readjust the prescriptions. In fact, the scientific organization of work promoted by Taylor was precisely intended to dispossess the worker of the professional knowledge that gave him authority to organize his working activity as he wished. In some industrial sectors, Taylorist principles are still applied. What might be called neo-Taylorist organization of work has taken hold in other sectors: service work through scripts (as in call centers, where the workers have to strictly follow written instructions during the discussion with the client) or the normalization procedures (such as prescribed by the *International Organization for Standardization*, which require the worker to write down everything he does and to do only what has been written down) are renewed forms of the old attempt to reduce as much as possible the room for autonomy in order to increase productivity. The development of new methods of management, such as "reengineering" or organiszation and control via computerization (notably via programs of *Enterprise Resource Planning*) are using comparable means to reach comparable goals. But, as we have also seen, the space for autonomy cannot be fully eradicated. Many empirical studies have shown that the normalization systems and the *Enterprise Resource Planning* programs become counterproductive if they are applied too strictly. To be properly implemented in the working activities, they have to be *appropriated* by the workers, that is, interpreted and adapted.[22] At the individual level as well as at the collective level, the room left for autonomy is a matter of confrontations and of compromises, as empirical studies have also shown.[23] It is often from the point of view of the defense of their spaces of autonomy at work that workers criticize the work organization, and it is often from the point of view of the knowledge acquired in exerting this practical autonomy that they want to have their say about the work organization. There is no doubt that this specific type of expectation of autonomy should also be taken into account in a critical model of work.

The formal, structural space for autonomy that is located between prescribed work and real work does not concern the content of the working activity. The transformation of prescribed task into real activity has to be performed whatever the activity is about and, in particular, whatever the worker's attitude to the worth of the activity. But there are other types of restriction of autonomy in workplaces that are specifically linked with the content of the activity and with how the worth of that activity is judged by the agent. On the one hand, there may be activities that are so menial, routine, and repetitive that they fail to engage the subjectivity of the worker at anything more than the minimal level required to realize the task. If the tasks are designed in a way that prevents the worker from expressing and developing his problem-solving practical capacities, if they provide little opportunity for the development and maturation of those capacities, then the worker will find it difficult, certainly in the long run, to appropriate those activities, to see them as properly *his*. But in not being able to take ownership of his activities in this way, the worker experiences a lack of autonomy: it is impossible to be self-directing (autonomous) in activity one fails to identify with or to see as an expression of one's own distinctive powers of agency. On the other hand, there may be activities that do engage the productive powers of the worker, but which the worker nevertheless judges to be incompatible with the good life *for him*. In this case, it is not so much the design of the tasks that present obstacles to subjective appropriation, but the fit between the content of the tasks and the subject's conception of a well-led life. In these two ways the malaise of meaningless work is rooted in expectations regarding autonomy: on the one hand, expectations regarding the quality of the activity to be appropriated (it should be complex enough to count as meaningful activity I can count as *mine*) and, on the other hand, expectations regarding the place of the activity in the course of a meaningful life (I should not have to do it if it is incompatible with my conception of a well-led life). Another way of saying this is that in the negativity of the experience of meaningless work the subject's expectations of autonomy in regard to the activity of working are disappointed.

This brings to a close our analysis of the normative content of work insofar as it is revealed in the negativity of the contemporary experience of work. We have focused on the ways in which norms of justice and autonomy are at stake in this experience, in regard both to work as employment and work as activity. The aim has not been to offer a comprehensive account of what these norms mean in the context of work, or how they ought to be applied in that context, still less of what justice and autonomy might consist in in general. Rather, the aim has been to indicate the main ways in which these norms shape the experience of work, insofar as that experience is reflected in empirically grounded worries about work. In this respect, our goal has been philosophically modest. Nonetheless, our approach to problems of justice and autonomy may be taken as philosophically objectionable and certainly departs from the one to be found in mainstream political philosophy and critical theory. In the next chapter we will defend our approach from some of these objections.

Chapter Six

TWO MODELS OF CRITIQUE

We are seeking to articulate a critical conception of work that can clarify how it is that the contemporary organization of work goes wrong and suggest ways of putting it right. Our method has been to analyze negative experiences of work (including lack of work) using empirically established zones of anxiety and discontent around work as our guide, interpreted through a conception of the structure of working activity. Our analysis in the previous chapter showed that these negative experiences are negative in large part on account of the injustices and loss of autonomy they are taken to involve. Another way of putting this is to say that the experiences are responses to work situations that are not as they ought to be in regard to generally held expectations of justice and autonomy: the experiences have a normative content given by a discrepancy between the standards of justice and autonomy that are generally expected to prevail in the circumstances and the standards that actually prevail. Having clarified what these general normative expectations regarding work are, as revealed in the negativity of the work experience, we have laid the basis for the critical conception of work we seek, which is to say the conception best suited for critical theoretical reflection on the major social and political problems of work and their solutions.

But as we foreshadowed in the previous chapter and earlier in the book, it might be argued that this whole way of proceeding is wrongheaded. If we are to be genuinely critical in our reflections about social and political issues, the objection runs, it is no use beginning with the experiences people have, or report as having. Various reasons might be given for this. First, most generally, it might be said that one does not discover how things ought to be from how things are. The mere fact that certain feelings and expectations circulate in a population, for example, tells us nothing about the standards that ought to guide behavior. Or if they do tell us something, it is sheer coincidence, arising from an accidental convergence between the standards that people happen to expect to apply and those that really ought to apply. For example, the mere fact that a population generally expects women to be subordinate to men tells us nothing about the gender relations they ought to have, and if the general expectation is for equality, that does not tell us why it is right. This brings us to a second objection to our approach. For if the congruence between empirical psychological fact (the existence of an expectation or disappointment) and normatively valid standard is accidental, and certainly cannot simply be assumed, then this can be explained by a process of *reasoning* or *justification* that standards, but not facts, can possess. Without an anchoring in such rational standards, or procedures of justification, the objection might continue, social and political critique would be all at sea. It would be incapable of distinguishing the valid normative expectations from the invalid ones. It would be at the mercy of sexists and xenophobes who happen not to like progressive political developments and social change. In order to be genuinely critical, the objection continues, a critical social theory must therefore have recourse to some *independent measure* of the validity of normative expectations. Indeed, the construction of such a measure, or procedure of justification, can be seen as the first—and perhaps even the last—task of critical theory. The superiority of this method might be sealed in the following thought: in societies where there is reasonable disagreement about how best to lead a life, or how best to arrange political and social institutions, the appropriate standpoint of criticism is that of *impartiality*. For it is by assuming a standpoint of impartiality, or an *objective* standpoint, that we come to see things at once from a standpoint independent of the contingent psychological dispositions of individuals and from the standpoint of justice. Ideally this should also be a unified theoretical standpoint from which *all* injustices can come into view, not merely injustices of this or that particular type.

Now this model of critique, or in other words this conception of how critical social and political theory becomes critical (and, for that matter, political), is by far the dominant one in contemporary social and political philosophy. Clearly, it represents a rival model, with competing methodological strictures, to the one we are proposing here. By making explicit the contrast between this standard model and the one we are proposing, the significance of the critical conception of work we are after might become clearer. We will first say a little more about the motivation behind this model before turning to the conceptions of justice and autonomy it frames specifically in relation to work. Our argument will be that in comparison to the picture of justice and autonomy that emerged from the analysis of the negativity of the experience of work presented in the previous chapter, the conception of justice and autonomy in work available within this frame is narrow and lacks traction with aspects of social reality a critical conception of work ought to be engaged with. As the alternative model of critique we propose includes a broad and differentiated conception of these norms and is explicitly engaged with the real experience of work, so we argue, it is better suited to the tasks of the critique of contemporary work.

THE OBJECTIVIST MODEL

Since the standpoint apt for social criticism, according the standard model, is that of objectivity, because it strives above all to provide an objective basis for its criticism, we can label this model the "objectivist" model of critique. We can characterize it along the following lines. First, it is *general* in its orientation. By this we mean that, according to this model, social critique requires a set of norms that could decide whether or not a social practice or institution has legitimacy, whatever its context. It should not matter, as far as the basic norms of social criticism are concerned, which society or social sphere the institution or social practice targeted for critique belongs to or whatever local justifications it could have in those specific contexts. The basic idea is that in order to decide whether a social practice or institution should be preserved from transformation or transformed, the people involved should be able to refer to norms that are generally understood and understood to apply equally to all cases.

But these norms should also apply univocally. This means that they should not be prescribing or justifying different and competing outcomes.

For this reason the standard model could be described as *unitary* in character. If the people involved in deciding whether or not a social practice has legitimacy have two or more different sets of norms at their disposal, they could be confronted with conflicting and contradictory conclusions and, therefore, paralyzing political indecision. This is not to say that the model cannot accommodate more than one type of valid norm, but if there is a plurality of norms there must be some hierarchical order to them, and one must have priority over the others. Otherwise there would be no way to avoid ambiguity in the application of the model, and the introduction of such ambiguity would fatally weaken (according to its defenders) its critical force.

But indeed, in order to avoid political indecision, both the norms and their hierarchical ordering should be considered as legitimate by all those who participate in discussions about the legitimacy of the social practices, whoever they may be. This means that social critique has to be grounded in principles that could be considered as *justified by all* or, in other words, that could resist the test of rational discussions in which all those involved can participate. In this sense, the model is *rationalist*. It is a reflection of the rationalist character of the standard model that much of it is devoted to a determination of the procedure by which a norm and its application properly count as rational. Much of the conceptual armory of the model is designed to defend it from skeptical attack, that is, to answer questions posed by the skeptic about the rational status or claim to validity of any given moral norm or principle. But whether the procedure of justification is conceptualized formally through a theory of rational choice or informally through a notion of public reason, it still provides the center of theoretical gravity for the model of critique.

The objectivist model of critique thus has these three key features: it is general, unitary, and rationalist. In contemporary political philosophy, John Rawls's *A Theory of Justice* still provides the paradigm of such a general, unitary, and rationalist model of social critique: it is based on a procedure of rational justification, it consists in a set of formal principles that could be applied to all basic social settings, and one important part of its appeal stems from the strict "lexical priority" it establishes between the different norms.[1] But the model informs other theories too. Rawls's later theory of political liberalism also shares some of its key features, as does Habermas's discourse theory of justice, even though they both repudiate the formalism and to some extent the unitary character of Rawls's earlier liberal theory of justice.[2] While there is of course much more to these theories than the schematic model we are considering here, and while any given theory of justice or critical theory of society will approximate to the model to various degrees and in different respects, the model nonetheless represents in simple form an approach to social critique that appeals to many theorists.

When we consider now how the objectivist model might frame the social critique of work, we get something like the following requirements. First, the norms the model draws on should apply to society (through its basic institutions) as a whole. They would have general application across society including work if the critique is to be valid, but the norms would not be conceptualized specific to work as such. Second, public justification and not general expectations manifest in negative experiences should define the relevant norms of social critique. A hypothetical or idealized testing procedure might also be invoked, but the point is to establish norms that pass the test of rationality (universalization) and base critique on them. Third, rather than trying to make explicit the various dimensions of the normative problems at stake in negative working experiences, the focus of the model should be on the hierarchical ordering of the norms.

Now the first point to make about this model is that its appropriateness for a critique of the social and political dimensions of work is by no means obvious. If we are oriented by the constraint of generality, we run the risk of screening out those particular wrongs that are specific to the needs and contexts of work. We have seen that work has its own psychic dynamics, social relations, and relations of domination, which are in danger of being obscured or missed altogether once we adopt the perspective of a critical theorist of society in general. In being oriented by the constraint of univocity, we run this risk further, since our attention is directed at the coherence or internal consistency of the critical stance, and the vocabulary that articulates it, to the potential detriment of our descriptions of the social phenomena themselves. The unitary nature of the phenomena, their unity insofar as they reveal legitimate justice claims, should not be prejudged, or, rather, we presume their unity only at the risk of distorting their specific content as justice claims. And if we are oriented exclusively by the rationalist requirement that the reasons that justify normative claims in relation to work must be valid for everyone concerned to be valid at all, that they must be objectively valid or valid for anyone to serve the purposes of genuine social critique, then our attention is deflected from those locally applicable norms, norms that apply only to specific groups or in the context of specific activities, which nevertheless matter enormously to the participants themselves, who can feel deeply wronged when they are not satisfied.

To make these general reservations more concrete, we shall look at the specific norms available to the objectivist model for the social and political critique of work. These are the same norms as those we analyzed in the previous chapter using the negativist and inductive method at the disposal of our rival model: justice and autonomy. But the sense in which justice and autonomy are at stake is conceptualized differently in the two models. In the objectivist model, justice is conceptualized primarily as "social justice" and is seen predominantly from what we call a "sideways on" perspective. The objectivist model also has a conception of autonomy in relation to work limited to the capacity for choice of the individual agent. With respect both to justice and autonomy, we argue, the objectivist conception is too narrow, and so ill-equipped for the variety of tasks presented to critique, by comparison with the conceptions that emerged from the analysis of these norms undertaken in the previous chapter (the conception tied to the rival model of critique we are proposing).

Let us consider how this narrowness of perspective arises first in relation to justice. With its focus on objectivity, impartiality, and generality, the objectivist approach is well-positioned to capture one crucial set of normative requirements in relation to work: justice secured through *labor law*. And it is perhaps the most obvious way of thinking about how the norm of justice applies to work to consider work as a fit object of legal regulation. It is evident that work is widely regulated by a set of legal rules, which mainly serve to define the conditions under which a labor contract can be established and fulfilled. The regulation of the relationships between employers and employees by labor laws can be captured as a constitutive dimension of the very idea of social justice within the objectivist model. The model can present the justification of such labor law in terms the basic rights of workers, rights they can exercise when they establish contracts with their employers and when they are asked to obey their bosses within the workplace. But it must also acknowledge the fundamental asymmetry in the relation between the employer and the employee, an asymmetry that actual labor laws generally acknowledge, which arises from a relation of dependence (the employees depend on their employer for their wages) and subordination (they have to obey orders and prescriptions). It is for this reason that workers need special legal protection. It is worth emphasizing that actual labor laws regulate not only the ways in which labor contracts can be established or broken but also the ways in which these contracts are fulfilled within workplaces. In other words, it is not only work as employment but also work as activity that is legally regulated. Nevertheless, from the perspective of labor law, the workplace is considered only as a sphere where basic rights (such as protection from injuries, diseases, ill-treatments, misconduct) could be respected or not. There is nothing at the normative level of labor law about specific norms that would be tied to the work activity, nor about the specificity of the activity of working.

In this respect labor law takes a "sideways on" view of justice within the workplace. While there is no denying the legitimacy and importance of this perspective, it is also important to see its limits. Unfortunately, the objectivist model is ill-positioned to do this. Within the framework of this model, work may be conceived of as one of the fundamental liberties, and thus the freedom to work conceived as a right and the conditions of work subjected to just legal regulation. This makes possible a social critique of situations where individuals are forced to work without any contractual agreement (modern slavery or "forced labor"), where individuals are forced to work in a way that is not compatible with the terms of the contract between the employers and the employees, or where workers cannot be considered as free and responsible contract makers (child labor, for instance). The principle of freedom to work could also be used to justify the claim that there is a right of open access to social and economic positions. And such a right could be used to ground a critique of all forms of discrimination in regard to employment. But while these criticisms are important, they do not exhaust the terrain, since they remain at the level of employment opportunity and working conditions without getting into the activity of working itself. We could say that when work is discussed within the objectivist model in terms of social justice, either the worker is considered as a consumer who needs to get enough money to satisfy her needs or she is considered as a citizen whose rights have to be respected. She is not yet conceived of as a producer having special claims arising from the fact that her activity is one of producing goods or services for others. In other words, the model remains at the level of *distributive* justice (where at issue is the distribution of one particular kind of good—employment and the rights associated with it), without yet having touched on matters of what we called *contributive* justice (justice that pertains not to the distribution of the consequences of productive action but to participation in productive activity itself).

Once we reach the level of the norms that apply to production, the question of justice in the division of labor arises. Relations of mutual recognition are of particular pertinence here. Honneth has argued convincingly that legitimate demands for a just division of labor follow from the fact that work is a crucial source of social recognition, which in turn is a condition of real freedom.[3] By a just division of labor, he meant, on the one hand, a division of labor that could give to everyone the same opportunity to participate in the process of the production of goods and services (the productive side of "the system of needs," as Hegel called it)[4] and, on the other hand, a transformation of the hierarchy of status associated with the professions in order that the various types of socially useful production could get positive social recognition. But in Honneth, again, the relation between work and recognition concerns mainly work as employment: work as being employed in a particular branch of the social division of labor and as having the particular social status that is associated with a particular profession. While there is much in Honneth's approach that departs from the objectivist model (and indeed his theoretical framework is a major source of the model we oppose to it), in a different way this is also a sideways on view, and normative problems linked with the ways in which recognition is at stake within workplaces are not really addressed. As shown in chapter 4, the issue of recognition at work has many other dimensions, and as shown in chapter 5, they also intersect with experiences of injustice at work.

If we are to escape the limitations of the "sideways on" view of the norms applicable to work, if we are to see beyond the normative issues of social justice clustered around the redistribution of goods, on the one hand, and social recognition within the division of labor, on the other, we need to probe further into the norms that apply to working activity itself. Here the norm of autonomy becomes especially relevant. But the conception of autonomy available to the objectivist model is again not well suited for this purpose. Let us briefly consider why.

Within the objectivist model, autonomy can provide the crucial norm in relation to work on account of it being a capacity for choice that is independent of particular conceptions of the good life and therefore something the state can support without compromising its impartiality or "neutrality" in regard to those conceptions, about which there is reasonable disagreement among the citizens of a liberal democracy. The basic idea is that each citizen should remain free to orient his existence according to the particular conception of the good life he endorses. For some citizens, but not all, work is a major component of their conception of the good life. Some are committed to a work ethic, to personal advancement through a career, to self-realization through professional achievement, all at no cost to their autonomy. But others reasonably reject that conception of the good life; they see gainful employment as a sacrifice of their autonomy and would prefer to exercise their capacity for autonomy in other ways—say, to use the celebrated example, surfing at Malibu.[5] According to this line of thought, it is not for the philosopher, or anyone else, to pronounce upon the superiority of one conception of the good—work or surf—over another. Given the lack of *univocity* over the good life, given the difficulty if not impossibility of establishing *general validity* for conceptions of the good (conceptions that can be justified by the agreement of all), justice must be conceived to require only that each citizen be granted the *autonomy to choose* that conception of the good that suits her—a busy life of meaningful work, say, or one more laid back and attuned to nature. Within this model, the principle of autonomy, insofar as it applies to work, *is just* this capacity for choice. Work is a matter of justice only in the sense that it is one option an individual might choose as part of her life project to realize the good for her. This is premised on the assumption that justice is a universal norm that, to have any legitimate application at all, must apply to everyone. While there are social conditions of autonomy that everyone has an interest in and are therefore also matters of justice, the objectivist model regards only the "value-neutral" remuneration obtained from work, which can of course be distributed independently of work (for example, through a basic income), and not the work itself, as such a condition.

This argument actually constitutes one of the main objections against the inductive and negativist method of the previous chapter: what we have described as normative expectations of justice and autonomy about and in work are not universal enough to be counted as legitimate components of justice claims in a strict objective sense. The argument, however, rests upon a twofold fallacy. Firstly, it relies on examples that are too particular and decontextualized to do the argumentative work required of them. The surfer in Malibu is a very specific type of person: he has a passion and tries to center his whole life around this passion. Every individual could have a passion and decide to devote his whole life to it, at whatever cost, and whatever the passion: love, sex, gambling, sports, arts. Such a decision is a decision to break with the rhythm of ordinary life, and with the ordinary condition of men and women. But social and political arguments are aimed in the first place at that ordinary condition. The question at issue for us is not whether everyone should have a passion for work rather than a passion for surfing, but what is commonly at stake in the work experience such that a normative content can be extracted from it. Second, the argument falls foul of a naturalistic fallacy, that is, in a confusion between the *is* and the *ought*. It is grounded on a fact: some people *do have* a merely instrumental relation to their work; they see it merely as a means to do something else which they really value. And it transforms this fact into a norm: this is *legitimate* since there are no good grounds to criticize them for that. But the question at issue is not whether such individuals ought to be criticized or not. It is whether the social conditions that make work meaningless in the first place, and the relation to work merely instrumental, could be changed, and, if that were the case, whether such change would be in conformity with norms of justice and expectations oriented toward more autonomy or more valuable forms of autonomy.

The relation between work and autonomy need not be construed in such a narrow way. Rawls himself has contended that in a well-ordered society "no one need be servilely dependent on others and made to choose between monotonous and routine occupations which are deadening to human thought and sensibility," and he inveighs against "monotonous and routine occupations which are deadening to human thought and sensibility."[6] This line of thought has been fruitfully developed in discussions about the relations between autonomy, identity, and the formative character of work. The main argument goes as follows: work can have formative effects on identity that can hinder full personal autonomy. Since full personal autonomy is to be considered as a fundamental ethical and political norm, work has to be organized in such a way that its formative effects remain or become compatible with full personal autonomy. Adina Schwartz has argued that the formative effects of work can become an obstacle to autonomy in two ways.[7] Firstly, routine jobs or mechanical activities "hinder [individuals] from developing the intellectual abilities that they must have if they are rationally to frame, adjust, and pursue their own plans during the rest of their time."[8] Second, the very idea of autonomy implies a kind of unification of personal identity whereas meaningless work and lack of autonomy at work imply a kind of split identity with subsequent limitations of self-reflection. This general argument marks a move away from the objectivist approach because it promotes a type of social critique of work that is no longer general but *particular* insofar as it focuses on the specific forms of autonomy and restriction of autonomy at work. It also suggests that the *social self*, in its endeavor to integrate the various dimensions of its social life, is also a *working self* and that work plays a decisive role in the possibility of such an integration.[9] But even here the conception of work as activity remains too general to capture fully how autonomy is at stake in actual working experience. On the one hand, autonomy is still understood from the point of view of an ideal conception of full autonomy defined independently of work. As a result, there is no impetus to investigate the specific forms of autonomy at stake in working. On the other hand, the criticism targets mainly working conditions incompatible with any kind of autonomy, ignoring the possibility that a minimal degree of formal autonomy is a structural condition of working activity that must also be taken into account.

It is a characteristic of the objectivist model of critique to think of autonomy in relation to work in terms of either/or rather than in terms of degree, in unitary terms rather than in terms of a pluralized conception of autonomy, and in positive terms rather than in terms of an experience of autonomy that is interconnected with attempts to protect a precarious good. Unless these other expressions of autonomy are taken into account, the model is bound to remain one-sided in its critical approach to work. And while, as we saw, the approach can be developed to take into account the formative effects of work and their implications for autonomy, these formative effects could hardly be analyzed accurately without taking into consideration the specific psychic stakes of work. The formative effects of work do not depend merely on the ways in which autonomy is exerted at work. They also depend on our capacities to transform suffering into satisfaction, whether the work context allows us to "bind" ourselves or not, as we discussed, and also on our capacity to find other solutions to structural domination than voluntary servitude. These formative effects do not depend only on the fact that work has to remain compatible with autonomy in order to avoid overly burdening subjective lives and thus splitting identities. The specific defenses against suffering at work, at the individual as well as the collective level, can produce strong distortions of identity and, more generally, can affect our sense of justice as well as our desire for autonomy. In fact, suppression, in the Freudian sense of the term, of our suffering at work could impact our capacity for compassion and also the trust we have in our moral feelings and ethical principles. The experience of working can obstruct the development or exercise of subjective capacities not only negatively—because it doesn't develop capacities of self-reflection or lead to their atrophy—but it can also provide positive obstacles by creating individual and collective defenses against suffering that involves restrictions of capacities of reflective thought. These subjective dimensions of the negative experience of work also deserve consideration if one wants to spell out the ways in which work can hinder autonomy in general.

THE EXPERIENTIALIST MODEL

The objectivist model is a general model of critique, which aspires to be grounded on universal principles that can be applied with equal legitimacy to any social context or institutional setting. We have argued that the constraints imposed by this model are responsible for the restriction to what we called the "sideways on" perspective on work that characterizes much contemporary philosophical discussion of work. The principles of justice and autonomy invoked are by no means specific to work, but are regarded as generally valid principles that can be applied to work, among other things. The result is a neglect of meanings of justice and autonomy that are specific to work. In addition, the model has difficulty incorporating the normative content of work as activity. This is because it is more difficult to extract a universal claim to justice and autonomy from the activity of working itself than it is, for instance, from the employment relation or the rights one has as a consumer or a citizen.

Our discussion of justice and autonomy at work thus strengthens our methodological conviction that if we are to elaborate a critical conception of work that could tackle the challenges of the new malaises around work, we should replace the objectivist model—which as we have seen is general, unitary, and rationalist—with a model of social critique that is *particular* (particular to the working experience), *pluralist* (taking the variety of what is normatively at stake in the work experience into account), and *pragmatist* (oriented by the practical demands presented by the problematic situations of work, including demands for transformation). The methodological alternative is between an immanent critique of work that draws on the normative content of work experience and a critique of work that seeks to transcend that content, that is, the particular expectations and specific social settings that structure the work experience. Since the experience of work provides the source of orientation for this model of critique, we can call it the *experientialist* model. To be more explicit about the critique of work that we urge, we will now answer the following two questions: in addressing injustices concerning work, why do we start from the experience of working rather than from universal norms? And why do we distinguish the norms of justice and autonomy rather than bringing them together in a unitary theory of justice?

Starting from the experience of working means giving methodological primacy to experience, and to particular experiences thought of in their specific social contexts as well as in their social and subjective dimensions. This methodological primacy has a threefold justification: it has a *phenomenological, sociological,* and *political* accuracy.

By *phenomenological* accuracy we mean the capacity of our critical conception of work to capture what is at stake in experiences of work. These experiences of work could be either positive or negative. In the positive experiences of work in which individuals manage to transform suffering at work into satisfaction, even when the activity is not meaningful, the various expectations that underpin the working activity usually remain tacit. It is only in negative social experiences that they become explicit. They become explicit in particular in attempts made by individuals and groups to disclose what is at stake in these experiences, what they expect from work, and which kind of solution they prefer. That is why we give these negative experiences a methodological primacy: they reveal which normative content (or implicit definition of what is of value) structures positive as well as negative working experiences. A theory of the general expectations of working experience is required if one wants to make sense of the ways in which positive experiences are lived and if one wants to capture what is at stake for those who suffer from negative social experiences of work.

By *sociological* accuracy, we mean the capacity of a model to give accurate descriptions of the social and subjective dynamics to which the general expectations about work contribute. These expectations not only underpin working experience, making it satisfactory or unsatisfactory if they are met or not. They also interact with a social environment, producing effects on this environment that react on the subject experiencing this environment. For instance, these expectations could also be instrumentalized in managerial techniques or strategies. It would be difficult to understand the motivational force of the managerial discourse about autonomy,[10] or recognition,[11] if the ways in which autonomy or recognition are at stake in working experience were not taken into account. Furthermore, it would be impossible to criticize these instrumentalizations of autonomy or recognition without a consistent conception of the ways in which expectations concerning autonomy and recognition could be better satisfied in the specific social context of work experience. By sociological accuracy, we also mean that a conception of the particular social contexts and psychic stakes of working experience is required if one wants to take into account the various dynamics triggered by negative social experience at work. The psychic dynamics could lead an individual to take flight in overwork, perhaps ending in burnout or voluntary servitude. The social dynamics could undermine work collectives and the social conditions of the transformation of suffering into satisfaction as well as the social conditions of resistance against domination.

By *political* accuracy, we mean the capacity of a critical conception of work to have a grasp on the negative experiences and on the practical and cognitive dynamics that emerge from them. When the experience of work becomes problematic, there is a cognitive effort to make sense of the situation and to find solutions as well as practical efforts to adapt, to flee, or to transform the situation. If a social critique of work wants to reach its political objectives, namely contributing to social transformations that could make work experience more satisfying, it has to provide intellectual tools that could be helpful in the cognitive efforts emerging from negative working experiences and, hence, that could orient the practical efforts toward transformation rather than adaptation or flight.

There is, then, a threefold advantage in adopting the standpoint of working experience. But aren't they offset by greater disadvantages? If the method consists in spelling out normative expectations through the analysis of negative working experience, isn't there a risk of grounding the critical conception of work on expectations that would be either too particular or too vague? Could these expectations be universal enough to give rise to agreements about the legitimate transformations of the organization of work? Could these expectations be precise enough to define work situations that would imply more justice or autonomy? Such objections to the kind of particularist, pluralist, and pragmatic approach we are urging to the institution of more just, more autonomous forms of work organization have to be briefly addressed.[12]

We agree that it is unlikely that a consensus could be formed about what should be expected from work, particularly if work is conceived not only as employment but also as activity. Therefore, we also agree that it is probably impossible to find a set of universal expectations that could ground a consensus about what social justice at work could be. But we don't agree that discussions about social justice should only refer to universal expectations. Isn't it a political requirement to search for practical solutions when a significant group of persons suffer from the same social problem associated with similar negative social experiences? Isn't it legitimate, then, to take into account the normative expectations that remain unsatisfied in these social experiences, in order to understand what is at stake in these experiences and which types of social transformation would lead to more satisfactory experiences? The normative expectations upon which our critical conception of work is based may not be universal in the strict sense of the term, but if they are at stake in general worries about work, they are general enough to take up the political challenges raised by these worries.

Aren't expectations implicit in the experience of work we have been describing too vague to help deduce determinate solutions? Here again the objection misses the target. The objective of our critical conception of work is not to deduce what a just organization of work should look like, but to elaborate a model that could be useful to those who are interested in the transformation of the working situations they suffer from. Its aim is to help them to make sense of their negative experiences at work and to elaborate individual and collective reflection about the best solutions. In this respect, the critical conception of work has to be precise enough to capture the various types of normative stakes of the working experience (hence its particularism and pluralism), flexible enough to be applied in various working situations (hence its relative lack of determination), and general enough to promote a convergence of the various particular negative experiences into general claims about transformations of the organization of work.[13]

In our critical conception of work, two different norms, justice and autonomy, are taken in various senses and considered as providing complementary perspectives on negative working experiences. But the distinction between justice and autonomy could sound paradoxical since it is often taken for granted that autonomy is at issue in social justice. The general argument that supports this possible objection is grounded on the assumption that social justice means equal or fair satisfaction of universal expectations. And since there is a universal expectation of autonomy, everything that implies inequalities concerning autonomy would also translate into social injustice. We consider this definition as fully legitimate as an objectivist definition of justice. The reason we nevertheless distinguish the normative perspective of justice and that of autonomy results from the fact that we are not looking for an objectivist definition of justice but for a way of making sense of what is at stake in experiences of injustice and experiences of the restriction of autonomy at work. Now, these two experiences do not only have structural differences, they also relate to different social factors.

Experiences of injustice are characterized by their qualitative dimensions and by the fact that they occur when a social situation is no longer bearable.[14] These two specific dimensions are not captured by the objectivist definition of injustice as illegitimate social inequality. From the objectivist point of view, a wage inequality might be conceived of as more or less unjust, but from the standpoint of working experience it is unjust or not. From the objectivist point of view, the managerial evaluation of the performances of the employee could be more or less unjust, but for the employee it is either just or it isn't. Similarly, from the objectivist point of view, the distinction between just and unjust is primarily the matter of a discursively formulated critical reflection, whereas in the experience of injustice it is primarily the matter of a spontaneous feeling of injustice that may subsequently elicit reflection about the injustice of the situation. And when such a feeling occurs, something has become unbearable for those who feel it. "Unbearability" will typically not be a feature of the inequalities that become the subject matter of *impartial* reflection about justice and injustice.

These remarks supplement the point we made earlier about a methodological alternative we face between objectivist approaches to justice and approaches from the standpoint of experiences of injustices. There are specific features of the experience of injustice at work that deserve consideration and that remain out of the picture in objectivist approaches.

These remarks also show that the nature of the experiences of negation of justice and autonomy linked with work are significantly different. As we have noticed, except in extreme cases, experiences of negation of autonomy are usually experiences of *restrictions* of autonomy rather than *deprivation* of autonomy. There is a formal autonomy that is a structure of the working activity (due to the distinction between prescribed work and real work) as well as a structural restriction of autonomy that is a structural feature of it (due to structural domination in capitalistic employment). In the experience of working, a substantial form of autonomy is also at stake that concerns the appropriation of the content of my activity, and the correlated negation of autonomy is again a matter of degree. I could manage to distinguish in my own activity what is meaningful from what is not and try to center my activity on the former.[15] Of course, in the worst cases, my work can be meaningless in a higher degree, and this could lead to an experience of alienation: I could become a stranger to myself in my work. There are other forms of restriction of autonomy in precarious work and in unemployment, but they can also remain compatible with spaces of autonomy. The point in all this is that it is only when autonomy is conceived along the ideal of full autonomy that autonomy in work should be thought of in dichotomous terms. In the experience of working, however, it rather takes the form of a "more or less" rather than that of an "either/or."

Hence experiences of injustice and experiences of restriction of autonomy linked with work are clearly different in their form: one is qualitative whereas the other is quantitative, as it were. They are just as different in their content, namely in the type of problematic social situations they refer to. As we have noticed, experiences of injustice often relate to denials of recognition: a lack of recognition of my social status (in unemployment or in low professional statuses) or of the value of my contribution to society as a whole or to the firm (through insufficient wages or through inadequate managerial evaluations) or of my dignity. They shed light on work as a kind of experience and activity that is embedded in a network of social relations that are also relations of recognition. Things are different with autonomy.

It is true that the experience of a restriction of autonomy is sometimes connected to denials of recognition where autonomy outside of work is concerned. But at work, restrictions of autonomy are often not directly connected to recognition. They concern the material and technical organization of work, as when the practical question at issue is how this organization is compatible with a degree of individual autonomy. Or autonomy is impacted by the social relations constitutive of the work collective, as a condition of individual and collective autonomy. Or the relations of power are at stake in a dialectic between domination and resistance. These types of negative experience shed light on the technical dimensions of work, as well as on social relations of solidarity and power, rather than solely on recognition. In other words, experiences of injustice and of restriction of autonomy shed a different light on the social factors that contribute to negative working experiences.

All these distinctions, between the objectivist point of view and experience as a standpoint, between experience of injustice and experience of autonomy, are important if our critical conception of work wants to be phenomenologically, sociologically, and politically relevant. But here again, it could be considered that the advantages are less important than the disadvantages. Referring to a plurality of norms disconnected from each other may lead to a critical conception that is comprehensive and has a grasp on experience, but if there is no hierarchy between these norms, won't it become impossible to decide which claim is legitimate in a situation where various claims are in conflict? Once more, this objection misses the target. Our aim has been to elaborate a critical model that could contribute to promoting political discussions about work that would consider various dimensions of contemporary work-related issues. It has not been to provide rationally self-standing "criteria" for critique that would close the discussion once and for all. If a philosopher endorses a democratic conception of philosophy, then she should be wary of conceptual tools that would short-circuit the need for democratic deliberation. Struggling against the prejudices that obstruct the discussion of important social problems, struggling against critical models that imply one-sided accounts of these important social problems, elaborating tools that could help those who are interested in the transformation of these social problems to articulate their claims, *all this* and *only this* is fully consistent with a democratic conception of philosophy.

To sum up the argument of this chapter, we have been arguing that an experientialist model of critique provides a better framework for social criticism in relation to work than an objectivist model does. The experientialist model of critique—characterized as we have seen by its particularism, pluralism, and pragmatism[16]—has the crucial advantage of being able to capture what is at stake for those who actually experience the ills of the contemporary organization of work and can articulate these ills in such a way that could help them not only to make sense of what they experience at work but also to transform the social context of their negative experiences.

In putting forward this view, we are guided by a set of methodological orientations contained in the idea of a "critical theory of society," formulated with greatest clarity by the Frankfurt School (Horkheimer, Adorno, and Honneth in his early work). First, we take it that, in negative social experiences, some general implicit expectations could become explicit that are irreducible to institutionalized principles and that could offer new normative perspectives on the social world and contribute to the renewal of institutionalized principles. Second, we take it that a model of social critique should aim to become an instrument of social transformation, to be used by those who are practically interested in social transformation. Third, we take it that the social spheres and institutions are diverse enough to give rise to a diversity of negative social experiences that have to be considered in their specific social contexts. If a model of social critique is to help individuals make sense of the various normative stakes of their negative social experiences, and engage in practical efforts toward the transformation of the various social factors of these experiences, then a pluralist model of social critique is just what is required. Fourth, we take it that the normative principles of a model of social critique should not be defined by the test of public justification, but, on the one hand, by its cognitive capacity to articulate what matters in one's experience, what is the nature of the goods one wants to preserve or promote, and what ills one wants to diminish or eradicate, and, on the other hand, by its practical capacity to be useful in efforts oriented toward social transformation.

If we are to make headway with immanent critique oriented by these principles, there is no other way of proceeding than to use inductive and negativist methods: start with the plurality of social problems that a critical conception of work has to be able to address, then focus on the corresponding negative experiences to make explicit a set of normative expectations that could be articulated in normative standards of what work could and should be. Such is what we take the shape of a critical social theory of work to be, and it is in taking this shape that it earns its right to be called critical.

PART IV

Performance Evaluation

Chapter Seven

MANAGERIALISM VERSUS
COOPERATIVE MANAGEMENT

In the previous chapter, we delineated a conception of work that can frame a critical perspective on the various contemporary worries about work. In contrast to the standard model of critique within contemporary political philosophy and critical theory, this required us to develop a model of critique that is pluralist and particularist. That standard model, we argued, was responsible at least in part for the blindness generally shown by philosophers and critical theorists to the normative issues that specifically relate to work. But it is not just philosophers and theorists who overlook these issues: there is a general lack of *political* deliberation about them. One of our claims was that the critical conception of work we proposed could help to promote political discussions about work-related issues that matter for workers but that rarely feature in political discussions, be they in the public space outside work or the internal public spaces of work collectives. In the chapters that make up the fourth and final part of the book we shall try to make good this claim by considering how our critical conception of work can be applied to a major concern about contemporary work that rarely receives the political attention it deserves: the evaluation of performance.

There is widespread unease about the way contemporary work is assessed in terms of "individual performance," "standardized procedures" and the norms of so-called total quality management. These complaints concern not only the failure of these modes of assessment to reflect the reality of work but also the obstacles they present to productivity and good quality work. But while there is no doubt that these techniques of assessment are widely resented and criticized on an everyday basis among workers (often in the form of denunciation and ridicule), the reasons behind this resentment often remain implicit at this level of articulation. Furthermore, and partly because most criticism of assessment techniques remains at this level, practical alternatives to the current regime of performance evaluation are rarely proposed and discussed at the level of public political discourse. The whole issue thus fails to cross the political threshold. Our aim in this chapter and the following one is to show how, by means of our critical conception of work, this threshold might be crossed. We will try to demonstrate the way in which this conception of work might serve as a useful tool in efforts oriented toward an articulation of a *transformative* critique of the forms of individualized assessment that prevail in contemporary management. This will require us to speak not just in the register of theory but of criticism itself.

We can actually distinguish two aspects of the political deficit that afflicts work-related issues in general and performance evaluation in particular. One is semantic, the other properly normative.

The semantic aspect arises from the fact that, as we have already remarked, work is a type of action that is notoriously difficult to describe. It is therefore vulnerable to misdescription and linguistic distortion. Earlier we saw that the rich texture of actual work, in all its particularities, gets lost in the formalistic language used to describe prescribed work within the contemporary work organization. This language should not be thought of as a neutral, objective, or impartial one, but rather one that fits with and is shaped by the power structures of the contemporary workplace. If crafts workers were once able to use a rich and experience-based language to describe their productive activities, industrial work, and later on postindustrial work, has impoverished work culture insofar as it has replaced the languages of the crafts with a general, formalized prescription-based language. Now one of the reasons why it is so difficult to mount a compelling critique of contemporary managerial assessment methods is that it requires a counterdescription of the actual work. It is obviously easier to describe the quality of working activities in terms of performance measures or conformity with standardized procedures than to articulate a phenomenologically accurate description of the actual work activity. But without such a description how can it be shown that current managerial assessment is not really assessing the actual work responsible for levels of productivity or the quality of the goods and services?[1] The criticism of contemporary assessment techniques has to be grounded in a description of the particularities and peculiarities of actual work, a purpose we believe can be served by the account of working experience we outlined in chapters 3 and 4. As we explained there, actual work is structured by specific forms of recognition of the reality and value of the productive activities, including recognition by peers in the work collective and recognition by clients in service relations. But these forms of recognition are plainly at odds with the type of recognition that is involved in performance measurements and conformity to standardized procedures. In what follows, we will contend that the former types of recognition can provide the basis for an effective critique of contemporary methods of performance evaluation and point the way to alternative principles of assessment.

The second aspect of the political deficit characteristic of work-related issues, which the issue of performance evaluation also serves to illustrate, concerns the specificity of the norms to be invoked. Chapters 4 and 5 highlighted that the social critique of work is usually articulated in terms that are too general to capture what is distinctively at stake in normatively problematic working situations. The assessment issue confirms that what is required is a pluralist critical conception of work that refers to specific expectations of justice and autonomy at work. It is simply a fact that in contemporary workplaces assessment is experienced as a source of injustice. It is an experience of injustice to see one's own working activities assessed in such a way that the reality of one's work (the effort required to meet technical demands and temporal constraints, the personal investment necessary to prevent failures and solve problems effectively), as well as its value for the work collective, the firm, or the clients, is not recognized—or not accurately so.[2] Now the definition of justice that is at stake here cannot be captured except from the point of view of the recognitive expectations that are immanent in the working experience. A specific conception of justice is thus required if the criticism of contemporary performance evaluation is to reach its target.

But it would be a mistake to think that the norm of justice is sufficient to capture all the problematic dimensions of the experience of being subjected to contemporary performance evaluation. The malaise is also about the *domination* experienced through this form of assessment. It concerns assessment as a technique of power that increases the pressure on each worker and heightens competitiveness within the work collective. Individual performance measurements are not only a means of imposing on individuals a responsibility to increase the productivity of their own activity, in some kind of self-reification.[3] They are also a means of imposing on individuals a responsibility to become more productive than the colleagues with whom they nevertheless have to cooperate. Hence, assessment, as a form of power specifically targeting workers' subjectivity, is also a form of power that could be experienced as a drastic restriction of autonomy and as a negation of one's own will. This is what makes it a form of domination: it amounts to a restriction of my autonomy to the effort required to make myself more productive as measured by a given "indicator" and a negation of any intention on my part to actually care for the quality of the goods produced or service provided irrespective of the indicator or indeed the quality of the cooperative relations with my colleagues. Here again, in the criticism of performance evaluation as a form of domination, what is required is not a reference to autonomy in general but to the specific forms of individual and collective autonomy that are specific to work (the ones we analyzed in the previous two chapters).

Before considering the issue of performance evaluation as such, we have to recount briefly how this new form of power, the so-called *neoliberal* form, became embedded in the transformation of work undergone in the past few decades and to recall the ways in which they have affected working experience.[4] It is important to remind ourselves of the historically situated emergence of this kind of practice. This historical awareness is an important first step in our attempt to highlight the moral injuries and damage to subjective life they cause. While we share with others concerns over the accuracy and efficacy of current evaluation practices,[5] our emphasis is on the degradation of experience they are responsible for, that is to say, their negative impact on the quality of subjective life and the conditions that support it.

SUFFERING AT WORK AND NEW METHODS OF THE ORGANIZATION OF WORK

The introduction of individual performance assessments belongs to a series of developments that have negatively affected the subjective life of workers, and proved harmful for their mental health, which should be considered together. The others include the introduction of so-called *total quality management*, the *standardization of procedures*, and the *casualization of employment*. Let us briefly consider each in turn.

Beyond enjoining the members of a work organization to seek "continuous improvement," to "put the customer first," and so on, "total quality management"—an approach to management widely taken up by work organizations from the late 1970s—is, strictly speaking, in the service of an impossible goal. *Total quality* is a theoretical nonsense because, as we saw in chapter 3, in every labor process, whatever it is, there always occur anomalies, malfunctions, failures, bugs, unexpected occurrences that make up what we referred to as "the real of work." "Total quality" thus does not and cannot exist. It is an ideal. And when the ideal is taken as reality, as it is in this approach to management, and when this ideal is erected as the sine qua non of producing something worthwhile and putting it on the market, workers are forced to conceal the reality. Effectively, this means that a need to lie enters professional life, inevitably corrupting the rules and ethos of the trades and professions. This need to lie can give rise to much pain related to a sense of disloyalty, a betrayal of values, and loss of self-esteem. This "ethical suffering," that is to say a suffering experienced on account of participation in practices that offend one's sense of what is ethically acceptable, can be very difficult to live with and, as several studies have shown, can cause serious psychological damage.[6]

The *standardization* (or normalization) *of work procedures* in itself is not new—it goes back to F. W. Taylor's *Principles of Scientific Management* and the design of repetitive work under time constraints. However, it has been extended in recent times to service activities, though this is also a theoretical nonsense. For any service activity owes its quality and effectiveness to a cooperative relationship built between the provider and the beneficiary. For example, to treat a patient with insulin-dependent diabetes effectively, it is not enough merely to prescribe subcutaneous insulin injections, urine monitoring, control of glucose levels in the blood, a diet, a program of physical and sports activities, and so forth. This only constitutes the "prescribed work" for the patient. The quality of diabetes control depends rather on how the patient understands or interprets this "prescribed work." For the patient to understand the rationality of the treatment, she needs to get involved in a cooperative relationship with the doctor who should endeavour to teach her about diabetes, following her progress in this practice and in the technical mastery of skills that need to be integrated into her daily life. The doctor will then adapt her prescription to the patient's skills and material situation. For example, the doctor must do more than merely prescribe a diet rich in vegetables and low in carbohydrates, since some patients won't be able to afford such a diet. So the doctor has to adapt the initial prescription to fit the patient's economic status. Or if the patient's work requires her to travel a lot, the injection schedules will need to be revised. Effective treatment can thus only arise through cooperative interaction between the beneficiary and a care provider attuned to the specificities of her particular situation.

The standardization of care is in fact an aberration, the quality being dependent on the adaptation of the procedures to each individual patient. Formerly, the therapeutic choices made by a medical doctor were not controlled by someone else, or imposed on her externally. The practitioner based her options on her knowledge of medicine as a whole, from her experience with the population among whom she drew her clients and the rules and doctrines that constitute the medical art.[7] Today control through standardization has infiltrated and corrupted the service relationship between patient and doctor in the form of scripts that appear for each diagnosis on the computer screen. Under the threat of conflict with the insurance companies, social security, or professional bodies, the doctor is required to follow the script, even if she thinks it would be better to deviate from it for the benefit of a particular patient. The result for the doctor is a kind of deskilling or disqualification, which in turn gives rise to a lessening of interest in the medical profession and a diminished sense of its significance. Beyond this, looming again, is the specter of ethical suffering, due to the need to conform to these so-called protocols of "best practice," when she firmly believes that she would do things otherwise if it were just the interest of the patient that was at stake.

The precarization of employment is linked to these developments, since once the operational procedures, including those of service activities, become standardized, each operator is supposed to be able to execute them as well as any other, as if all operators were now identical. The interchangeability of workers in turn provides the employer with more power over the employees and is regarded as a complement to total quality management. But what this ignores is that, in many work situations, trust between members of a group (horizontal cooperation), between the teams and their leader (vertical cooperation), and among providers and beneficiaries (transverse cooperation) is a decisive factor in the quality and productivity of the work activity. And, of course, such relations of trust take time to establish: they require people who feel secure in their work and are unlikely to develop if the workers really believe the slogan that any time might be a "time to move on."

Individual performance evaluation asserts a claim to objectivity in the comparisons it makes between the performance of workers and the services they provide. It involves the use of putatively objective quantitative methods and measurement techniques. But here again we have a theoretical nonsense. In fact, the ability to address the discrepancy between prescribed work and real work, the invention of expertise, the unforeseeable ways of lending a hand, and the learning of tacit skills are all based on living labor. That is to say, actual work requires the engagement of subjectivity in the experience of the real, not only during the time of production itself but beyond, extending into time off work, the pressures and concerns that occupy us in our in private spaces, even in insomnia and professional dreams. In other words, the activities of living work, being individual and subjective, really are incommensurable with each other. We can only objectively measure through quantitative methods facts in the visible world. Since subjectivity does not belong to the visible world, it is not measurable. What is measured, even in the best cases of individual performance evaluation, is not the work but the result of work. But there is no proportionality between work and the results of the work.

For example, if I operate on older patients with significant medical or surgical history, the duration of stay and the number of postsurgical complications will obviously be higher than if I only operate on young athletes in sports clinics. And yet the actual work of the first is unquestionably more difficult and more dangerous than the second. But the results of the work, that is to say the measurable items of performance, say otherwise. This sort of quantitative and "objective" evaluation thus generates feelings of injustice and often functions as a denial of recognition of the efforts put into the work, as has already been analyzed in the previous chapters.

Total quality management, the standardization of procedures, and the precarization of employment, like individualized evaluation of performance, are all theoretically nonsensical, and have been shown to be so by the various ergonomic sciences of work. Why, then, have they not only been introduced but have tended to spread throughout the world of work?

There are two reasons.

The first is that the organization of work was until recently the preserve of engineers: organization engineers, methods engineers, design engineers, and so on. They were finally dethroned in the late 1990s by managers.[8] Previously the engineers did not confine themselves to conceiving and planning the organization of work. They also oversaw the implementation and execution of the organization of work they prescribed. So they were able to take part in a dialogue based on the employees' experience of the real of work. Such dialogue was certainly difficult, but it was possible, and it allowed the actual organization of work to evolve—not without hiccups, but to move forward nonetheless. The manager function, by contrast, inherently leads to a refusal to engage with the materiality of the work. Managers can claim to "drive" factories, administrations, institutions, universities, research centers from dashboards presenting in real-time the level of functioning and production of the organization in its entirety. They create centralized banks of quantitative data to track targets defined upstream in relation to performance recorded downstream, with checkpoints placed between the two stages, which are supposed to reflect the reality of the work process in its entirety. In fact, they have no knowledge of the actual work and do not want it.

The very idea that one can "manage" *any* working activity and *any* work organization by using basic, formal principles that are supposed to be universal in their reach and efficacy means that inherent in the very logic of such management is an opposition to feedback based on actual knowledge of the reality and material difficulties of actual work. Even if formal practices of feedback might sometimes be inscribed in particular management techniques, the deep logic of management in fact opposes real feedback coming from the actual field of work. For the same reasons, any deliberative space that may be put in place by managers will not serve the real needs of production and producers, will not be a real and efficient space of deliberation. Managers, who are not engineers or tradespeople but solely managers, oppose feedback and deliberative spaces that are necessary for the rational discussion and evolution of the organization of work. Indeed, in most of the dominant managing practices today, time devoted to discussion is hunted down as it is considered unproductive. And much of this comes from the fact that most managers simply do not have the technical skills that would enable them to participate in such discussions. Instead, many managing techniques today are based on the demand for ever more reporting, that is to say, for quantitative data on production time, production costs, and sales figures, on estimated budgets, which create a huge workload for those that do the actual work as they try to bring the figures in line with the "actual work." In the end, such figures give only a distorted and unfaithful picture of the actual work situation. But they require more and more frequent and finicky revisions that slow down and degrade productive activity itself. A key reason, therefore, for the extension of these new methods of management is that managers in fact do not have the skills to intervene rationally in the work organization that they are supposed to guide and organize. Any concrete difficulty in the work, whatever it is, is translated monolithically as a delay, which is inevitably treated in terms of workflow, resulting each time in the introduction of additional control mechanisms and sometimes an increase in administrative personnel responsible for putting these new mechanisms into effect.

The second reason is that the manager is now protected from disputes about the actual work of the subordinates and teams she leads. In compensation for the disadvantages and the dysfunction engendered by the all-powerful managerialism, the manager benefits from the weakening of the power of employees to negotiate compromises in the organization of work. This brings about much more room for domination.

Underneath the sustained assault on the legal framing of the working activity at the general legislative level in the last two to three decades,[9] the weakening of workers' bargaining power also resulted to a large extent from the pressure imposed on them to adopt the manager's language and de facto to abandon the language of work and activity. And methods of individual performance assessment had such an impact on working collectives that they also added significantly to this loss of power.

Indeed, individual performance assessments introduced generalized competition between workers. A performance below that of a colleague becomes an "objective" argument for sanction. Individual assessment works inevitably as a threat; one colleague's success is another's failure. All are led logically to relations of mutual suspicion. Competition among colleagues drifts from "healthy emulation" to reciprocal undermining and white-anting: retention of information, intentional transmission of distorted or falsified messages—no holds are barred in the struggle with the work colleague. This is true among workers at the various levels of the organization hierarchy. The higher up the hierarchy the more managers monitor each other, and they are right to do so, for there are no favors among leaders! Trust gives way to mistrust. Loyalty gives way to unfair competition. Mutual aid is done away with and, beyond that, mutual respect and civility in work disappear. There is no more talking to each other, no more greeting each other in the morning. It's every man for himself now.

For example, the engineers in an open-space office of the technical center at the company Renault, at Guyancourt, do not speak a word to each other. When one of them needs to respond to a reporting request from the hierarchy for information held by the engineer who works a meter away from him, he does not reply directly. He sends it by email. But he knows that the other will not rush to answer. So to show, in case of delay, that it is not his fault, he sends a copy of his message to his dozen managers whom he makes his witnesses: transparency demands it! The colleague is then obliged to answer forthwith. And likewise, to defend himself, he sends the copy of his response to all other recipients of the original message. Because the spoken, living word is no longer possible, these two engineers give extra work, twice, to a dozen people, as they too are expected to know of the exchange of messages. The end result is an avalanche of messages of all kinds for everyone that disrupts the work of each and causes an exhausting overload of work. It is in this technical center that four engineers took their own lives at their place of work in 2006. A few years later, the CEO of Renault-Nissan was found criminally culpable as the employer in these dramas, a verdict upheld in appeal and in the Supreme Court.[10]

The individual assessment of performance has always been the wish of the managerial organizers of work. Its formidable presence is due to a coming together of the victory of managers over the engineers, on the one hand, and to the miniaturization of computers and surveillance equipment (such as the "black boxes" that monitor the performance of aircraft pilots, which they call "the rat"), on the other.

Individual performance evaluation destroys relationships of trust and loyalty within work teams. Mutual respect, mutual support, thoughtfulness, and civility fade quickly, and, in the end, all solidarity and forms of togetherness disappear. Individual assessment installs solitude in the world of work, as well as fear and eventual hostility. Frequently now when an employee, worker, technician, engineer, or senior officer is the victim of unfair treatment or harassment, nobody moves. In the experience of harassment at work, the harassment itself is not always the hardest thing to bear. It is the silence of others, their treason, that is hardest to take. By not coming to the aid of a wronged colleague, each employee becomes an accomplice and will soon be a witness who will not testify. Beyond the passive consent to practices that offend their moral sense, each witness may experience a self-betrayal resulting in ethical suffering of the kind so often mentioned earlier. The latter has been identified as an intermediate link playing a major role in the occurrence of suicides in the workplace.[11]

The disadvantages of the individualized evaluation of performance through the degradation of the quality of the work, and its negative impact on the productivity and health of employees, have led some company managers to question this model of company governance. This is especially so of service companies, but not only them, where the work cycle is long and highly stable personnel is required (up to ten years, for example, for project managers responsible for town planning). For this kind of work, employees must remain in good health and must retain interest and enthusiasm for their work until their task is done. These areas of business have an interest in maintaining mental health and in ensuring employees are able to take some pleasure from their work.

We discussed the question of pleasure and health at work in chapter 3 and we will touch on it again in the next section. The enjoyment of work, and the mental health inseparable from it, rest on an organization of work that first loosens the embrace of, or indeed renounces, the evaluation of individual performance and strives instead to rebuild the foundations of working together—that is, cooperation. The prevention of mental ill-health at work cannot be delegated or outsourced to experts, doctors, psychologists, and psychiatrists. The function of the latter is limited to screening for psychiatric disorders and their treatment (the psychopathology of work). There did not use to be suicides in workplaces because mutual aid, kindness, solidarity, and togetherness between people at work implied individual and collective responsibility for the well-being of others. A colleague was not left to drift into isolation, sinking ever deeper into introversion and depression. Coworkers intervened, tried to make her express the reasons for her change in behavior, and collectively attempted to help her out. There is no substitute for this in preventing mental illness. But also, and beyond this, these relationships were the prerequisite of the psychodynamic recognition in work that we discussed earlier, consequently of pleasure at work and self-development and self-fulfilment through work.

THE TASKS OF THE MANAGER

Identifying the problems with contemporary methods of performance evaluation is one thing, coming up with a solution to these problems another. If we are to find one, we need to develop alternative forms of assessment. As mentioned at the beginning of this chapter, assessment is one way among others of recognizing the reality and the value of working activity. It is different from the types of recognitive relations between colleagues and clients for three reasons. First, it is a formal rather than informal type of recognition. Second, it is a hierarchical relation of recognition that can be supported by sanctions or rewards. Third, it is not directly involved in cooperation among colleagues and between colleagues and clients, but remains external and *post factum*, as a judgment about the type of working activity that has already been achieved. Hence two types of practical solution to the issue of performance evaluation could be considered: the first one would be to refuse all forms of managerial evaluation and to insist that the recognition of work has to be settled through the informal recognitive relations involved in cooperation among colleagues and between colleagues and clients. It would also mean that no management of work is required. But, even in the history of the many attempts made to promote worker control in the workplace, it has usually been acknowledged that some form of management has to be in place and that some formal and vertical recognition is required.[12] The second type of solution follows from this, and consists in reshaping the managerial formal and vertical type of recognition so that it could be grounded in the very principles that structure the relations of recognition embedded in cooperative working activity.

In what follows, we will elaborate a general model for such an alternative approach to managerial assessment. We will call it "cooperative management" to highlight, first, that it is grounded in the principles of recognition that are immanent to the cooperative working activity and, second, that it is put forward in the service of cooperation rather than simply to increase productivity at all costs. Given that contemporary managerial assessment, in a context of precarization and flexibilization of work, has deeply undermined work collectives, such a cooperative management can be characterized as a type of management that is primarily and for the most part concerned with the *reconstruction* and *maintenance of cooperation*.

In a first step, we will elaborate this conception of cooperative management from a normative point of view. We will describe what the manager should become if assessment were to be a tool at the service of cooperation.

Now to some readers it may appear politically too conservative, as a bowdlerising of the critical voice, to foreground the problem of management in the course of proposing a project of social transformation challenging the sources of the contemporary malaise around work. The management issue has always been taboo within the left.[13] But if one takes seriously the fact that work has to be managed, no program of social transformation, be it reformist or radical, could be consistent or plausible without tackling the management issue.

To other readers, on the other hand, our description of cooperative management may appear too utopian. This criticism, more likely to issue from the political right (though some antiutopian leftists might also raise it), rests on the assumption that without the kind of discipline imposed by managerial assessment, and the external incentives for productive work it provides, productivity will collapse and firms or other work organizations will go under. But in the next chapter we will look at evidence that contradicts this assumption, considering a case that illustrates how firms have fared that actually put cooperative management into practice. It is important to see that the conception of cooperative management we propose is not only a thought experiment, a hypothetical application of the theory of work experience that we outlined in chapters 3 and 4. It is also based on the results of interventions requested by management teams and companies to solve real, practical problems concerning the mental health of their employees (notably absenteeism and resignations of some of their most skilled employees) as well as dysfunctions of the organization of work.

In these cases, the workplace has become so "toxic" that, even from the perspective of the management, the need arose for experimentation in the organization of work aimed at *reconstructing the conditions of cooperation*, which had been badly degraded precisely by the current management methods. It is of great methodological significance for us that such experimentation has yielded undeniable practical results. For, as we have been insisting, it is a key desideratum of *critical* social theory not just to be able to present convincing social diagnoses but also to serve as a practical tool of progressive social transformation, that is, transformation that removes sources of domination and reduces social suffering. Experience shows that just this is what cooperative management can achieve. Rather than being a merely utopian ideal, our conception of cooperative management serves the interest in emancipation of workers suffering from the current management methods.[14]

But the model can also have a liberating effect on managers, insofar as they are themselves employees suffering under the pressure put on them by shareholders and the demands of high profitability. Whereas shareholders' interests only concern costs and productivity, and are disconnected from all experience of work, managers are confronted with the practical consequences of an approach to work focused exclusively on productivity and cost, and they could be led to the conclusion that their subordination to the shareholders' interests makes it impossible for them to work—that is, to manage cooperation—effectively. In the contemporary economy, the main social antagonism is arguably not between workers and management, but between shareholders and employees, even if employees are often shareholders themselves and even if the domination most employees are under is effected by power relations organized and maintained by management. For all these reasons, it is not unrealistic to conceive a broad and genuinely radical social transformation that would involve some kind of alliance between the managers and the managed and that would notably involve, or require, a transformation of management techniques.[15]

In our model of "cooperative management," the manager has several functions that we will now try to spell out.

Our assumption is that management should manage cooperation, and the various functions of the manager derive from this requirement. Cooperation, after all, does not arise by itself. It presupposes in particular that executives or managers who have the task of leading teams have a theory of cooperation available to them and that they implement it particularly in vertical cooperation between manager and subordinate or between leader and the work team.

Cooperation, when it works well, brings considerable productivity gains. But in order to be able to manage and promote cooperation, management methods need to be fundamentally changed in a way that brings the question of the actual work back to the center. This needs to occur at the level of the individual first: because despite his intelligence and zeal, it sometimes happens that a worker is not able to overcome the obstacles that the real of work presents to his technical capacities or that he hesitates on the approach to follow.

The *first* function of the manager, then, is to help her subordinates. It requires that she have knowledge of the concrete work to be done by her subordinates—inside knowledge, so to speak—and that she has the desire and the ability to transmit her experience and technical knowledge of the labor process, notably to the younger and less trained workers. A technically competent manager should ideally be able to replace each of her subordinates in the realization of a technical demand.

But work is not only an individual's relation to a task. As we saw, one works in general for others: for members of the team, for a manager, for subordinates, for clients.

Each worker uses his or her own tricks, depending on the particular shape of the worker's intelligence, age, gender, experience, tastes, talents, and so on. There is a risk of inconsistency, contradictions, or conflicts between workers of the same group or work collective. The zeal of one may affect the others' work. It is therefore necessary that the members of a team have guidelines to bring consistency to their particular intellects. Coordination essentially consists in distributing and harmonizing the tasks among workers of a team to set objectives for each, to rank priorities, to organize the course and sequence of tasks.

This is the *second* function of the manager: to coordinate intelligences to bring about their harmonization and even their synergy.

At the collective level, one finds again the gap previously identified at the individual level between *task* and *activity*. The prescription manifests itself at the level of *coordination*. But we know that workers never respect orders in their entirety. Even in the army, it is impossible to obey orders absolutely strictly. One needs to "interpret" them. But because the work involves others, the problem arises of a collective and shared interpretation of the practical meaning of the orders. When a collective reaches a common

understanding, *cooperation* takes place. Thus coordination and cooperation are two terms that reflect, at the collective level, the separation of task
and activity at the individual level.

The collective management of the gap between coordination and cooperation implies that everyone knows how the other deals with instructions
and the requirements of the leaders, how the orders are translated through
their particular skills and modus operandi. For this reason, at this level one
must move beyond the "tacit dimension" or the level of what up to now has
been able to remain implicit. Transparency is not enough: it is necessary to
establish *visibility*, that is, to seek to make visible and intelligible the modus
operandi of each member of the team.

But to make visible and to reveal one's tricks involves taking a risk: that
of being criticized or repudiated by one's colleagues. The effort of making
explicit and testifying to one's experience therefore presupposes *trust*
among workers. But this trust cannot merely be taken for granted: it must
be built and maintained. It is the result of a complex process that engages
not only horizontal cooperation but also cooperation along a vertical axis.

If one is to reveal one's modus operandi to others competently, one must
have the ability to defend its legitimacy and effectiveness. To testify to one's
good work presupposes an ability to justify it and thus *to articulate* and
defend one's point of view. This means that the argument that counts in favor
of a particular modus operandi will never be purely about its effectiveness. It
will involve other dimensions: respect for principles, loyalty, thoughtfulness
in regard to colleagues, and so forth. To present one's point of view competently, one must therefore be able to formulate and defend *opinions*.

Cooperation rests fundamentally on the confrontation of opinions
about modes of operation and interpretations of orders. This is possible
only if there is a functioning *deliberative space* where one says what one
thinks and where one listens to the perspectives of others.

The collective deliberation of procedures can lead to decisions about
what is acceptable and what is not, what is effective and what is less so, what
should be discarded or forbidden among the various deviations from the
prescriptions and tricks used by the workers. In the best case, deliberation
on the modus operandi leads to a *consensus*. In other cases, where a consensus cannot be found, arbitration becomes necessary.

The *third* function of the manager is to maintain the space of deliberation between team members. Such a space only really works if it takes on

two forms. First, there must be a formal space for discussion: for team meetings, staff meetings, briefings and debriefings, wrap-up meetings, and so forth. In this formal space, decisions on how to work together are duly registered and serve as references for the whole team. The second kind of space is informal and is localized in places workers spend time together: the cafeteria, the locker room, the kitchen, restrooms, festive spaces, and so on. In these spaces, decisions made in the formal space are commented on, criticized, made fun of, ridiculed. The informal space complements the formal space of collective deliberation and restarts the process of critique and questioning of coordination.

When an agreement is reached, by consensus or by arbitration, and is registered and stabilized, it constitutes a normative agreement. When several normative agreements are reached, they constitute a work rule. Where several work rules are formulated, they are rules of the trade.

A *"work collective," in the strict sense, comes about only on the basis of rules it has formulated for itself through a process of collective deliberation.* The activity of producing rules is therefore basically a bottom-up process. It can be designated by the name *deontic activity*. It is based on the possibility of challenging the prescribed organization of work. Such challenging does not interfere with coordination, but makes it evolve, making it both more realistic and more just with regard to each member of the collective. Any work rule refers simultaneously to the *efficiency* of cooperation in the objective world (productivity, quality, safety, security) and simultaneously to *living together* within the work collective. Such rules are always based on mixed arguments, dealing not only with efficiency but also with the psychological, social, ethical, and political preferences that each worker expresses. Living together and conviviality are not characteristics a company can import from elsewhere, like some sort of spiritual supplement to the internal labor process; they are not formed through top-down initiatives and exhortations external to the actual work; and they cannot be manufactured in specific locations separated from the places where work is actually completed. Rather, conviviality is a production of deontic activity. It shows that the conditions necessary for the exercise of singular intelligences are met despite the differences in each person's style. Moreover, conviviality based on collective deliberation and live speech is also the cement of living together, of respect for the other, thoughtfulness, mutual assistance, and solidarity. This is why cooperation based on *deontic activity* is *a fundamental element of mental health in the workplace.* To put it another way, deontic activity is what allows everyone not to feel alone either in face of the real of work or in face of one's superiors in the hierarchy.

A space of deliberation, testifying to one's work, speaking up to defend an opinion are possible only if trust exists. Trust rests mainly on a relation of equal value given to speaking and listening. The one who speaks takes a risk. There is fairness and equal value between partners involved in deliberation when those who listen take a risk equivalent to those who speak. The risk of listening is actually to hear and understand what is being said. For to hear and understand the arguments of the other, in fact, is to risk being destabilized in what was until then taken to be true and just; it is to risk having to change one's own position and beliefs.

The *fourth* function of manager is thus to maintain trust by exercising an ability to listen to subordinates, not only individually but also and especially in the presence of the team. To listen is a difficult skill that requires time, experience, and adroitness.

Arbitration, when there is no consensus, is rational only if it is based on the risky listening of the manager. But the arbitration decision is necessarily in favor of one opinion, and so at the expense of one or more held by others, who inevitably feel frustration or even resentment. The arbitration decision is therefore bound to face obstacles. These will be overcome only if a supplementary dimension exists that shores up the decision: namely, the authority of the leader, the discipline of the members of team, and finally loyalty toward the decisions she takes.

Authority is the main ingredient of vertical cooperation. It has two distinct origins. The first is the authority conferred upon the head from above, by the hierarchy and the management of the company. It is based not only on status and rank in the organization but also on the power to punish and reward subordinates. When authority is only sourced from above, it approximates to power based on fear and threat. Such a tendentious fear-based authority does damage to the space of deliberation, to trust, to questioning of the prescribed organization, to deontic activity, to conviviality and the health of workers. Reduced to its foundation from above, authority is just one form of domination. The second source of authority enables it to operate even in the absence of a power to punish. It is an authority founded from the bottom, meaning that it is conferred on the leader by the subordinates. This authority proceeds first from the technical competence of the manager, specifically her ability to provide advice and assistance to subordinates when they fail to tackle the obstacles presented by the real by themselves. This authority is thus based on technical competence, as considered previously in discussing the first function of the manager.

But the authority of the manager also depends on her ability to listen and make decisions, that is, to take responsibility for the consequences of her decisions. Responsibility for these consequences goes downstream and upstream. Downstream, it involves the ability, when a decision proves ineffective or wrong, to accept criticism by subordinates and to rectify the decision. Upstream, it involves the ability of the leader to go back to the company management with what she knows of the reality of work on the ground, gained from the experience of her subordinates, their efforts, and the collective interpretation of the directives that came from management. It involves not only bearing witness to her own experience of managing in the collective of managers, but defending the decisions taken by her teams based on collective deliberation until they are ratified by management. That means getting these decisions *institutionalized* and stabilized. The authority of a leader is based on the quality of such deontic activity directed upward. In doing this, the manager does a real service to her teams. She protects them by making visible and institutionalizing rules of work they helped to develop, and it shows that the word of her subordinates can have an effective impact on the evolution of the organization of work and the company or even on the expertise of the firm and its competitiveness with regard to other firms.

The *fifth* function of the manager requires the courage to take responsibility for decisions. It is therefore the opposite of a style of management reduced to the transmission of orders from above, by a boss who disclaims the responsibility that is owing to her from all the prescriptions she imposes on her subordinates. So the fifth function is deontic activity upward, which requires an ability to find expressive rationality, that is, the rhetoric whereby the team leader will make herself heard by the directors and get favorable compromises for the realization of the individual and collective intelligence of her subordinates. The manager, in the exercise of the authority conferred on her by her subordinates, is, in a sense, under the obligation of the latter. She is under the obligation of what she actually was able to understand by listening to them.

But she is also under the obligation of the company directors, to whom she owes loyalty, a loyalty that justifies the authority conferred by the top. It falls, therefore, on her to take back to her teams the guidelines coming from the company directorate. But she cannot merely pass down what comes from the top. It is up to her, as to any worker, to interpret orders based on the reality of living work as it unfolds in the teams she leads. She thus takes a risk in relation to her bosses, to whom she must be able to justify herself by testifying to her work as a manager.

This brings us to the *sixth* function of the manager: to relay downward the directives of the company, by assuming responsibility for the interpretation that she gives for the services she leads. This interpretation, and thus the deviation from the orders of the directors, she can only justify by reference to a supplementary fact: namely the company *ethos*.

The *ethos* provides a general framework for interpreting facts and for guiding and directing actions. One finds here an area badly abused by the new managerialism. The development of a genuine company "ethos" has been progressively abandoned. Profitability and margin targets now take precedence. A company, however, is not just a machine for producing profits to shareholders or the state. A company assumes a place in society and carries corresponding responsibilities: it either renews collective life or helps to destroy it; not only in its own domain but outside in the broader political community. The company must therefore deal with the relationship between its internal work organization and its own management, on the one hand, and their impact on the evolution of society, on the other. The development of an ethos serves this function, enabling the managers to interpret the directives they receive from the directors and adapting them to the specificities of each work situation. This is particularly the case within companies engaged in service activities and public services. But it can be shown that the same holds for industries engaged in various forms of production, such as the production of oil, petrochemicals, electricity, and agricultural and livestock products, that involve significant environmental challenges, raising issues of sustainable development and presenting risks to whole populations. The elaboration of an ethos is based, above all, on the participation of managers in discussions with the directors. And the contribution of the manager here is to seek continuity between the ordinary work undertaken within the company, on the one hand, and society, culture—or even beyond that, civilization—on the other.

Participation in discussion about the company ethos, that is, on the responsibility of managers in regard to the work and the broader community, is what constitutes the *seventh* function of the manager in a company.

Experiments that have been conducted in some companies, with the support of the directors, show that another style of management is possible: the style we designated under the title "cooperative management." This alternative orientation is not just superior from an ethical point of view. It is economically efficient and brings productivity gains, thanks to the renewal of cooperation in its three dimensions: *horizontal* cooperation within teams; *vertical* cooperation downward, between the manager and her team, and upward, between the manager and the general directors; and *transverse* cooperation with customers, patients, students, and citizens. Cooperative management is not just a utopian dream: it is ergonomically effective as well as a means of restoring trust and civility among employees, which in turn plays a fundamental role in maintaining mental health at work.

Chapter Eight

FROM THEORY TO PRACTICE

Intervention in an Enterprise

It is an important feature of the model of critique sketched in part 3 of the book that it can be used for practical, emancipatory purposes. If a critical theory lacks practical purport, if it simply lacks traction with the reality it aspires to transform for the better, then no matter what degree of conceptual sophistication it has reached, it remains seriously deficient as the kind of theory it is. We argued in chapter 6 that the model of critique that predominates in critical theory today—what we called the objectivist model—fares badly by this test, at least when it comes to tackling the injustices, deprivations of autonomy, and domination at stake in unemployment and the experience of work, experiences that are at the heart of the contemporary malaise around work. The alternative to this model of critique we sketched earlier—the experientialist model—in being guided by the content of these experiences, already has a better claim to be grounded in practice, or at least not to be so far removed from it. But the model of critical theory we are after needs to have a more intimate relation to practice than a foundation in actual experience. It needs to be more than a *diagnostic* tool. It must also show itself capable of *solving* practical problems, of helping us move from a situation that generates experiences of injustice, deprivations of autonomy, and domination to one that does not. In the last chapter, we saw that a type of managerial practice, wedded to notions of total quality, standardized procedures, casualization, and individual performance assessment, generates practical problems of this sort, and we hinted that an alternative form of practice, one oriented toward the reconstruction and maintenance of cooperation, might help solve them. But we have not yet shown what a solution to such problems would actually look like. To do so is the aim of this chapter.

In transitioning from theory to practice we need to change register and attend to the concrete details of a particular case. We are not concerned here with theory in isolation from a potential emancipatory impact, but with putting on display the actual emancipatory impact of a practical intervention consistent with the experientialist model of critique we have been defending. The discussion that follows thus departs from the more abstract philosophizing of previous chapters so as better to capture the specificity, complexity, and contingency of the practical problem at stake. While the details are, of course, specific to the case study, the problems that needed solving will be familiar to many, since they arose from the introduction of the managerialism, described in the last chapter, that has been adopted in work organizations across the globe. The case study will show, first of all, how destructive of workers' health, and, indeed, how economically counterproductive, current managerialism and its methods of performance evaluation can be. But it will also demonstrate how a different kind of management can rectify these ills. This alternative, cooperative mode of management is not only ergonomically, and therefore economically, beneficial. It also does justice to the subjective and normative demands of the beings involved in the work organization.

THE REQUEST

The request for an intervention came from the director of human resources of an urban planning and development company in September 2007.[1] After reading some of the previously published research in the psychodynamics of work on the relationship between work organization and mental health, he wanted to review a number of issues raised by the methods of evaluation used within his company. This research suggested that the introduction of methods of individualized performance assessment could give rise to serious psychological illness, even resulting in the emergence of suicides at work.[2] These methods of assessment had been introduced in his company ten years earlier. They had caused practical difficulties and were regarded as unsatisfactory. Although the company had not suffered events as extreme as suicides in the workplace, the HR director wished to prevent further deterioration of mental health among the staff. So the question was: how could an intervention based on the principles of the psychodynamics of work be made that could remedy the pernicious effects of the individual evaluation of performance?

As mentioned, the company making the request was an urban planning and development business, responsible for designing and implementing rehabilitation projects and projects for developing new towns. The company is also the owner of land either acquired by it or entrusted to it by the state, which it sells to new towns or developers. Finally, it provides financial management services in relation to land entrusted to it by the state. It is a public company, but its salaried staff are employed under private law. It is led by a CEO appointed by the board of directors. The CEO is assisted by an executive director who is also chief financial officer. The executive committee is composed of eight members: three operational managing officers who divide the control of urban work projects according to their geographic location; the leader of the real estate department, which deals with sales and acquisitions of land and manages the real estate portfolio; the leaders of the accounting and the human resources departments; as well as the CEO and executive director.

The economic context of the company is characterized by a reduction of income from the management of the real estate portfolio. Much of the land had been sold in previous years and upcoming profits were forecast to be much more limited. Competition had increased significantly in recent years in part because of the recent creation of agencies for public works and private development companies and the creation by new towns of mixed-economy companies linked to local communities.

Concerns regarding the recruitment of skilled staff had emerged. Competing companies sometimes offered higher salaries than those paid to the staff of the company we are talking about. As a result, recruitment now focuses on young project leaders. They acquire vocational training and experience in the company and are then "head-hunted" by competing firms. There is therefore a problem of turnover, which can seriously hamper work on urban projects that can last for periods of around a decade. In order to be undertaken successfully, such projects require stability in their project leaders and team members.

At the request of the company, a team of three researchers was established, consisting of a specialist in the psychodynamics of work, an economist of work, and an ergonomist.

PRINCIPLES OF THE INTERVENTION

The intervention was based on the following two principles. First, the effort put in by each worker to giving an account of his experience of the actual work and formulating his opinions, sharing them with the other members of the peer group, was to be recognized as having a genuine revelatory power. To speak to a group that listens is the most powerful means of thinking through one's own experience. This is how the individuals can work through their *subjective experience of the real*. Second, when the individuals involved in a collective agree to engage in this effort to talk and listen, new ideas for the organization of work always emerge. This process is what in the previous chapter we called deontic activity or the collective elaboration of *the rules of work* or *trade rules*. The team of intervening researchers make no recommendations of their own. The intervention puts its trust in the genius of the individual intelligences and collective intelligence of the participating workers and is strictly limited to catalysing the functioning of the *space of collective deliberation*. The solutions are not the doing of consultants or experts; they are developed, each time, by the workers themselves.

Hence the center of gravity of the action of the three researchers departs from the practice of external expertise that characterizes the usual way of dealing with "health risks" and "psychosociological risks" within an enterprise. The intervention is certainly not intended to help workers improve their ability to deal with stress by transforming their "bad stress" into "good stress," as is usually the case with clinical interventions in companies nowadays. The intervention is limited to catalyzing collective deliberation by helping participants to transform their working experience into a subject matter of collective deliberation, an experience structured by know-how and knowledges that usually remain tacit.

What is at stake is fundamentally a struggle against the various obstacles that make it difficult to cross the threshold of explication. On the one hand, actual work is subjected to a semantic deficit, as noted in the previous chapter. On the other hand, in working situations where suffering is experienced, and where it is no longer possible to work without invoking individual and collective psychic defenses against the work, some kind of denial of the actual situation, and a resistance to thinking it through, can occur. Hence it may not be easy to help those involved in the deliberation to exercise their ability to analyze and think through their own experience of the real (of work). It is at this very ordinary level that the critical conception of work we advanced in chapters 5 and 6 can make its contribution. Lack of success in thinking through the obstacles to technical mastery of the process of work condemns one to repetition of the same or even to worsening the problematic situations. Conversely, collective deliberative thinking allows one, as a rule, to find new solutions to overcome the obstacles that the resistance of the real opposes to the mastery of the work process.

The fundamental principle of the intervention is thus that rational solutions to the resistance that the world poses to human efforts to control it are those working individuals discover by themselves and that they adopt together. There is no inherent antagonistic opposition between work (*poiesis*) and action (*praxis*).[3] Working together, or the collective bridging of the gap between coordination and cooperation, is, on the contrary, a major pathway open to rational action. Action, as an emergent property of working together, is based on the confrontation of the opinions of each member of a work collective and, as such, is the kind of activity that characterizes participation in a democratic public sphere. We will return to this key idea at the end of the chapter.

FINDINGS AND ANALYSIS

Guided by these principles, the pilot study for the requested intervention exposed the following. First, there were difficulties in cooperation among five of the seven departments, with a scarcity or complete disappearance of team meetings and spaces of collective deliberation. Second, major difficulties had arisen from the introduction of new accountancy software with cascading effects at all levels of the organizational hierarchy, with increases in workload, many dysfunctions, multiple delays in disbursements, receipts, billing, and so on. Third, the occurrence of a number of administrative and procedural "incidents" in the accounting department (AD), in the operational branches, and in the legal unit had come to light.

Fourth, tensions had arisen within the board, which resulted in it no longer functioning as a space of deliberation but merely as a "reporting and registration chamber." Fifth, there were significant problems of work overload, with a number of workers reporting health problems. Nevertheless, employees' attachment to the company was maintained.

At the end of a seminar organized by the researchers for the executive committee, the director of the AD made her department the object of another pilot study. There had recently been two "incidents," considered serious, that she thought the investigation might help to explain. The investigation of the AD began in September 2008 and ended in March 2009. It consisted of individual interviews with the majority of the members of the AD; repeated collective interviews (four in all), bringing together the director and her management team; single collective interviews with some of the support teams; and some investigation of all the other teams.

In regard to the management team, the investigation sought to elucidate the conditions under which the incidents occurred, in particular one concerning an accounting hole involving a large amount of unrecovered debt and unpaid claims. To account for this hole, it was necessary to carry out a detailed analysis of each accounting line and to identify each time the reasons why receipts either had not been recorded (due to the difficulties caused by the new software) or could not be recovered. This was particularly so for unpaid rental payments whose precise origin could vary considerably because of the complexity of the collection process, some coming directly from tenants, others from organizations granting accommodation assistance allowance, which for different reasons could refuse to provide the assistance.

The elucidation and analysis of the accounting hole therefore involved a considerable workload that presented itself as an unforeseeable disruption of the work allocated to the AD. This was thus a paradigmatic case of what has been referred to as the real of work. To avoid this overload of work, the analysis of the accounting hole was evaded and the claim was treated as an *exceptional expenditure*. Now its amount was, in fact, higher than the maximum level tolerated in public finance law. The director of the AD was directly responsible to the executive committee and board of directors.

The second incident related to the settlement of a contract. The accounting rules had not been followed; in particular there had been no prior confirmation of the absence of a potentially opposing third party, as required by law. As a result of this, the invoice was settled with a company that ought not to have been credited (as it was in a state of bankruptcy). The amount was high. The responsibility fell on the accounting director, with a possibility that she would have to cover the loss from her own funds in case the matter had been formally pursued. The failure to comply with accounting rules was *concealed* from the director by her team *for a period of one year.*

The incident initially seemed to be the responsibility of one of the director's assistants, or both, to the extent that the second assistant had not sought to deter the first from passing the accounting hole as an "exceptional expenditure" and did not oppose this wrongdoing despite it being a higher amount than the maximum tolerated in the code of public finance.

In seeking to understand the origins of the incident, the comprehensive approach afforded by the psychodynamics of work referred the investigators back to the *meaning* of the situation as much as to the observable facts of the matter. For it was on the basis of the meaning the assistant assigned to the situation at the time that he probably made the decision to conceal the hole from the director, as explicable as an exceptional expense. It is likely that he knew full well that he was committing an offense. If he did, what were his reasons? How is it that nobody on the team intervened? How is that no one went up to the director of the AD to warn her?

These questions suggest that cooperation within the AD was not functioning properly and that, as such, the offense is not the sole responsibility of the assistant but signals the passive complicity of the other members of the AD or an important communication failure between the members of this department. If this cheating that bordered on fraud did not draw the attention of anyone, it may be because the trivialization of cheating had already become so deeply entrenched. If several employees spotted it but decided not to intervene, that would suggest a climate of "every man for himself" had enveloped the team; there was no longer mutual support, solidarity, or even mutual trust.

To determine what was going on here, we returned to the work itself and especially the difficulties in the work activity that might explain why employees adopted behaviors that interfered so much with the smooth running of the department. Collective analysis of the work in the presence of the researchers brought up several types of difficulties.

First, there were difficulties related to the information tools. Constant difficulties arose in the work of all members of the AD, in particular at the level of the director's assistant, since the introduction two years earlier of new accounting software. This information tool was very difficult to use and continually got "bugs," despite considerable efforts by an ad hoc unit to improve the functioning of this software with the help of a consultancy firm. Difficulties in the transfer of data stored in the previous software system and many incompatibilities required makeshift fixing and left many holes. In addition, there were difficulties collecting relevant data, which were compounded by the extraordinary complexity of the management system for the social housing stock, with many unpaid bills, clashes between the various institutions involved in the family rental assistance procedures, and so on.

Second, there were difficulties associated with the sheer accumulation of tasks. We just mentioned an ad hoc unit deployed to improve the functioning of the computing software. This unit involved the two assistants of the director of the AD. But they were both also charged with having to provide support to all the employees of the company when they encountered difficulties with the operation of the accounting software. They somehow became "resource persons" for the software. And beyond one-off "troubleshooting," which accounted for a significant portion of their working time, it would come back to them to take responsibility for the training of the company personnel, one by one, for handling the said software.

It was assumed that the introduction of the new software would facilitate the work of all the employees. Everyone in each department needed to be able to process accounting operations, especially project managers who manage the budgets of the operations for which they have responsibility. Before the introduction of the software, there was a financial and accounting unit within each business unit. One of the expected advantages of the new software was the simplification of procedures it would bring, enabling each project manager to take responsibility for all the financial and accounting tasks. As a result, the financial and accounting units that had existed in each business unit were disbanded. Project leaders and members of their teams now constantly encountered difficulties with the software, which took up much of their time and disrupted their work. They had to rely on the accounting director's assistants for troubleshooting, which might have allowed the assistants to provide the necessary training to the project managers and their teams. But, in reality, the troubleshooting took so long that the assistants ended up doing all the work themselves, without providing any training. In other words, they now had to do most of the work formerly done by all the finance and accounting units. From this state of affairs, a *considerable overload of work* arose for the two assistants of the accounting director.

A third set of difficulties arose in the area of cooperation. The two assistants of the accounting director were constantly at the service of the members of the other departments of the company. Everyone recognized their availability and their helpfulness, to the point that they took advantage of them, never hesitating to interrupt them in a task they were performing. Even at lower levels in the hierarchy, no one hesitated to enlist the help of the assistants. Therefore the accounting service, which should first be in the service of external clients, ended up giving priority to internal clients and requests.

As a result, significant delays in relation to deadlines with external companies were often recorded, giving rise to criticism of the AD by the other departments. Thus, conflicts arose between the assistants and the director around the determination of priorities. In order to meet their own priorities rather than the director's, the assistants sought to protect themselves from her requests or orders, and to that end would retain information from her. So there arose a major problem of *vertical cooperation,* with a deficit in the authority of the director manifested by a weakening of loyalty from her subordinates, disobedience, and ultimately violations of professional accounting rules.

The support teams also stopped functioning properly.[4] There was little to no *horizontal cooperation,* with priority now given to upward cooperation with the managers at the expense of horizontal cooperation within each team. There was little flexibility, no possibility of swapping each other's work, and so on, resulting in lengthening delays in the processing of receipts and billing. Everyone got caught up in the retention of information. A *defensive individualism* had set in to counter the suffering caused by the deterioration of relations among colleagues and between staff at the different levels of the company hierarchy.

SUFFERING AND DEFENSE MECHANISMS

Let us look a bit more closely at the forms of suffering and defenses against suffering in the AD. Suffering was evident among several employees. Some were consuming psychotropic drugs, including antianxiety drugs that were constantly visible on their desks. The workdays grew longer. Among executives working at home, weekends were spoiled by the obligation to work on cases, generally on Sundays. Time with family and children had been reduced; domestic tensions had arisen.

The suffering related to work overload had several sources. These included malfunctions and inefficiency of the accounting software and the obligation to be at the service of many people within the company, which in turn disrupted their ongoing work. For the assistants of the director, there were two de facto superiors above them: their department director first, but also the chief financial officer, who had a hierarchical superiority over the director of the AD. The latter ended up checking all the files that she entrusted to her assistants and so asked for additional documents and many additional reports (adding to a loss of trust in the director and her assistants).

Another source was the rise in the number of reproaches and criticisms coming from different departments of the company against the AD, either because the processing period was too long or because the AD was considered excessively scrupulous, even fussy, or because the staff in the AD, although they were available, were constantly overloaded and not always friendly. As is easily understandable, the reproaches made the employees within the AD feel as if they never did well enough despite their undeniable efforts to work quickly and efficiently. This suffering thus arose from nonrecognition of the work they did, which also triggered feelings of injustice.

A climate of mistrust was another source of suffering, particularly between the director and the assistants. Each side was on the defensive, creating divisions and conflicts in the team. Overall, the assistants were wary of the director and tended to stand against her. Support staff were also wary of the director, but, as there was a general climate of suspicion about the skill level and quality of the work done, the tendency was not to communicate with colleagues and to direct all ordinary questions to the director to make sure they were "covered." Horizontal cooperation was ineffective, which increased the workload. But vertical cooperation didn't work either. The director no longer had authority over her own department. The assistants considered her incompetent and disorganized because she intervened in every transaction regardless of clearly identified priorities.

Conversely, the director was actually not available to help, support, and guide the work of her staff because she was so occupied in control and monitoring tasks. Chronically overloaded by the situation, she was led to cut down all time for discussion. There was no more space for collective deliberation, no more team meetings, at any level of the AD. And in fact the loyalty of assistants to the director also eroded, even if they remained generally loyal to the company. Loss of authority and the loss of trust did not result in malicious conduct or a desire to hurt the director (at least it hadn't yet). Rather, everyone simply felt alone with their responsibilities. Loneliness is certainly one of the major causes of vulnerability in regard to suffering at work.

What about the defense strategies used against this suffering? They reflected the different sources of the suffering itself. On the side of the director, errors, breaches, delays, the reluctance of assistants to escalate the difficulties and report anomalies—that is, a lack of vertical cooperation— only made the failures of the assistants more apparent. As is usual in these cases, the director developed a defensive strategy that has been identified in other professional environments exposed to similar malfunctions as the "spontaneous pejorative psychology of the executives."[5] What doesn't work well in the work is "psychologized." Increasingly ignoring the real of work that the assistants attempted to face, the director considered them more and more incompetent, disloyal, and unaware of the responsibilities entrusted to them. In short, they came to be seen as hopeless, possibly recalcitrant, and ill-willed, refusing to obey orders and requests.

On the side of the assistants, a siege mentality against a common enemy formed, which translated into the absence of team spirit, withholding information, withdrawing from everything except routine tasks, the over-load of work being the excuse for absences of communication and mutual assistance with the director. Furthermore, the assistants, to counter the claims or the requests of the director, exploited their position in the hier-archy by privileging requests or orders from other branches of the com-pany, which they prioritized at the expense of their director.

Because these two strategies of defense oppose each other as mirror images, communication between levels in the hierarchy became increas-ingly tenuous. This is the reason why, unable now to discuss the issues linked to the reality of the actual work, each individual was made to interpret the actions of the others all by himself. In other words, there were no longer *problems of work* in a strict sense; there were only "people problems"— problems of personalities. Aggression emerged sporadically, exacerbating the tendency to interpret everything in terms of the faults in the other's character as their being obtuse or unintelligent or malicious.

And, indeed, the less one can communicate about the problems of work through speech, the more one yields to the temptation of deprecatory "interpretation." When the accounting hole occurred, of course, the assistants became aware of it and were very upset. But in this situation, encumbered as it was by a "pathology of communication,"[6] it was impossible to open up to the director. The problem, whose origin was complex, as we have seen, did not admit of a simple or quick solution. The "makeshift" approach of passing this hole for an "exceptional expenditure," if it had remained unnoticed, would have allowed them to avoid significant work of retroactive investigation, on the one hand, and conflict with the director on the other. The assistants undoubtedly took a serious risk: namely to see their makeshift approach fail, which would have put them in serious personal trouble. But on the side of the director, the concealment of the accounting hole had a completely different significance: namely that this irregularity, serious in regard to public accountability, made her personally financially liable.

In the shadow of this "conflict between leaders," support services staff were essentially deprived of any reliable recourse to a recognized authority. As a result, each was afraid of not being up to her task, of making mistakes, and of not being able to count on anyone given the atmosphere of generalized suspicion. Each therefore adopted an individual defense strategy to withdraw to the performance of the more routine, well-controlled tasks, where there is no risk to take. Given the chronic overload of work, there was still a sufficient quantity of these routine tasks to occupy all of one's working time. Everyone turned away from any difficult or unusual matter that required deliberation, while still being able to claim that the prescribed tasks of the job took up all of their time. This defensive individualism increases loneliness and gradually destroys all traces of conviviality between colleagues. Several employees among the support staff fell ill (depression, hypertension requiring a stoppage of work, and so on).

IMPACT OF THE INVESTIGATION

The main problem for the investigation came from the defense strategies already described. How were we to set up a group involving the director and the assistants when each one is wary of the others and each has a strongly pejorative view? There was no longer any communication between the various parties, and nobody wanted any. Yet the methodological principle of the investigation was based on the voluntary activity of the participants. The director was there voluntarily, as she made clear before the executive committee. But the assistants were not.

Collective discussion would only be possible if all partners agreed beforehand that failures do not only result from the incompetence or ill will of the participants but also, perhaps, from genuine difficulties in the work—the real of the work—that no one currently knew how to fix in the AD. And they had to agree that in order to identify these difficulties—the real of the work—it would require everyone to speak effectively of their personal experience regarding the difficulties faced in carrying out their work. And it would only be at the conclusion of the investigation that what was at stake in the serious incident of the accounting hole would become clear. To reveal a hidden accounting hole was one thing; to elucidate the process that led to this "dubious manipulation" on the part of competent and honest people would be another.

After several individual interviews with each of the employees concerned, an agreement was obtained for a working session between the director and her assistants, in the presence of the researchers, to analyze the real of the work in the AD. For such a setup to work, "conditions of mutual understanding" must be established between the participants, that is to say, conditions where each shows an authentic curiosity for what others may say of their subjective experience of the actual work. These conditions are those of communication in the higher sense of the term, that is, of a communication oriented toward the search for a shared understanding of the pathogenic situation. It was pathogenic in the double sense of the word: first, in that it generated a *pathology of communication,* which here took the form of a disappearance of conviviality and communication stalled by defense strategies (pejorative psychology of executives, on the one hand, siege mentality against the common enemy, on the other); second, in that this organization of work actually put everyone in a situation of *psychological suffering.*

Conditions of mutual understanding, ideally, are formed before beginning the working sessions, when the people involved participate on a voluntary basis. This often happens, but, as we have seen, not in this case. It was in fact as the discussion progressed in the working sessions that the conditions of mutual understanding took shape. Everyone was asked by the researchers to give an account of what posed the biggest specific problem in the cases and tasks they had to treat. Failing to speak to colleagues, the participants mainly addressed the researchers; although everyone knew that they also talked to colleagues on the side. During the course of the discussion it became clear that the difficulties associated with the work constraints had become overwhelming for all participants, but in a manner specific to each, which everyone was in fact unaware of until then.

In addition to the specific questions raised by the materiality of each person's tasks, it turned out that no one in the work collective knew how to solve some of them. One of the key elements came from the excessive number of requests arriving at the AD, both from outside companies and from other departments within the company. How to deal with this excess? None of the solutions adopted by any one person was acceptable to all the others. It was recognized that since it was to be expected that these requests would continue to come, it would be useful to establish a hierarchy of urgent demands and priorities. However, none of the participants had a formula that would work on its own.

If each person is left to deal with things in his own way, inconsistency and conflict is inevitable. Therefore, prioritization had to become a regular object of debate or collective deliberation, where everyone could actually give their opinion on the basis of their place in the work process. In the end, if there was no consensus on priorities, then arbitration by the director would be needed, but in the presence of her assistants, by giving arguments and justifications for her decision. If some requests remained unfulfilled and there were complaints as a result, it would then fall on the team as a whole to respond. "Faults" and criticisms could be collectively endorsed precisely because the decision about the work process had been reached collectively. The cohesion of the work organization would then be based on a collective deliberation of the management team; nobody would have reason to feel personally responsible. Several working sessions were necessary for these conclusions to become apparent. As a result of these working sessions, the director, with the agreement of her assistants, established a weekly management meeting. The meeting was basically devoted to the analysis of the real of the work as it presented itself to each of the participants. In doing this, the team gradually acquired new skills in the analysis of the individual and collective work.

These meetings were kept up. The second fundamental lesson of these spaces of deliberation was that direct communication, using live speech, in the effective presence of the participants, could not be replaced by the use of information and communication technologies. What was discussed and decided in these spaces of deliberation was neither information nor reporting, neither email messages nor balance sheets. To speak of the real of one's own work is always a matter of screening one's experience for what is central and what is tangential, what is urgent and what can wait, what is most worrying (or most painful) and what is insignificant. As such, in a few minutes or a few hours, a huge saving of time was made compared to the time taken by each individual on the mass of information, emails, documents, and requests that pile up on each other, causing reciprocal disruption without ever announcing themselves as a cause of additional workloads. Prioritization is no longer a matter of the information available; it is the result of deliberation about *experiences* of the real of the work of each person under the constraints of the real. Each person knows what priorities and objectives are to be achieved by the next session and is focused on these tasks, so that everyone can be aware of the progress of the collective work at each step. The cooperation thus reconstituted is the best guarantor against individual errors because the exchange of experiences and subjective difficulties generally permits areas of darkness to be revealed that may go unnoticed for an isolated individual.

Trust being restored, the director could let go of the need to check and control everything. A considerable reduction in workload resulted from this. This is one of the main reasons why in the end collective deliberation and live speech saves time—by saving all the time lost in the dispersion caused by the continuous avalanche of the flow of information.

Time released by the newfound trust now allowed the director to focus on the specific tasks that concern her as director, namely the work process involved in public accounting. A part of her time will now be devoted to team meetings, another part to technical assistance she can give punctually to one or other of her colleagues when she is faced with a problem on which she hesitates or that she is unable to resolve by herself. This also rebuilds the authority of the leader based on technical competence and the ability to provide assistance to subordinates. Time is also allocated to the preparation of reports for the executive committee on the operation of her department, on the work actually done by her team, and on the support she needs to improve its functioning.

One year after the intervention, the director of the AD was able to take responsibility for the accounting department of another company, similar in nature but of a smaller scale, for a scheduled time corresponding to one-third of her total working time. Furthermore, in the company where she was previously in a situation of serious work overload, she now heads its department with only one assistant instead of two. The productivity gain obtained by the restructuring of cooperation was therefore even more significant than the most optimistic forecasts. The work climate in the department changed radically: it became much more relaxed. The improvement in terms of both the mental health of the workers and the productivity of the work were confirmed by the director five years later.

TRANSFORMING THE WORK ORGANIZATION

This experiment is not a unique case. Since then another urban planning company in great difficulty requested intervention of the same type and benefited from the same effects in the quality of cooperation and productivity. Other businesses, including a commercial enterprise distributing musical instruments, have adopted the same principles of cooperative management with benefits in terms of pleasure at work and enduring financial recovery. Despite two brilliant results, these experiments remain limited and occasional for reasons that we will clarify. In order to do so, we should first say something about the specificity of the company involved in this experiment.

The activity of this company is a service activity. Its quality and relevance for its beneficiaries depends on the capacity of the company employees to adapt to the demands of its clients. The nature of these demands is not always transparent. Clients may formulate them without knowledge of the land involved or the full environmental, social, and human implications of the operations they intend to perform. It thus falls to the employees of the company to clarify them and to inform the client about the indirect consequences of the operations or land development work required. The responsibility of the members of the project team does not solely concern the implementation of a given plan. The employees of the company are also expected to work with the clients on the initial request and often also to advise on operations to be undertaken. One finds here the issue of transversal cooperation, that is, cooperation between the provider (the planning company) and the beneficiary (the population and its elected representatives, local authorities, and so on). This cooperation consists in the project manager getting the beneficiary to agree to work with her on the development project, its design, budget, organization, the choice of companies to be involved, and so forth. That is, they must agree to learn the language of land use and planning and to acquire knowledge in a number of areas concerning urban planning, soil and water treatment, the environment, and related matters. Only then can the negotiation of trade-offs between provider and client start on the basis of a rational deliberation.

But for such cooperation to take place, the project manager must establish relations of trust with the customer and prove herself worthy of trust. And account must be taken of the fact that competition exists with other private development companies, competition that stiffens as new companies aiming to establish a market enter the scene, more concerned perhaps with lowering their prices than ensuring the quality of work, the sustainability of the development, and the long-term interest of the population. It is therefore necessary for the project manager to be able to justify the higher prices that she asks for the projected operations, by explaining to the clients the differences between the quality of the service she offers and what the competitor offers. In other words, she must find the right rhetoric for winning the argument in this context. What the project manager needs to acquire, then, is a good knowledge of the population, the land, the local associations, the elected representatives, the local traditions, the history of the place, and so forth. And in so doing she must learn to adjust the service to be offered. It is in proportion to the quality of the work performed by the project manager and her team that relationships of trust are built between them and the clients, which will serve as the basis for operations that will last several years.

It is then up to the land development business and its leaders to listen to the experience of the project managers, because it is basically through them that they can get knowledge and experience of the field. The quality of vertical cooperation, in particular in the bottom-up direction, but also cooperation with other departments of the company, is crucial for this. We can easily see that this whole process rests first and foremost on a subjective commitment from the head of the project and the members of her team to undertake the work. *The quality of the cooperation, as well as the health of the workers, therefore appears as one of the strategic resources* on which the creation of value in dealing with the clients rests. As managers become aware that cooperation and health are economic issues, it makes sense for them to experiment in ways that can lead to transformations of the organization of work.

But this also points to one of three main limits to the kind of intervention we have been considering. For of course it is not true of all firms in the contemporary neoliberal world that they seek to increase their competitiveness by improving the quality of the services they offer.[7] On the contrary, most try to become more competitive by reducing costs. The contemporary economic trend is clearly toward increasing competitiveness by cost reduction, irrespective of the impact this may have on the quality of cooperation within the company or between the company and the client. It may well be the case that such a way of making profit is not sustainable in the long run. But another distinctive feature of the contemporary neoliberal economy is the seeking out of opportunities for short-term profit, whatever the consequences for the business itself, let alone the broader society. It is clearly not in all firms that the *quality of the cooperation* and the *health of the workers* can be conceived of as strategic resources or as predominantly economic issues.

The second limit is that, in our opinion, the transformation of the organization of work required today is not just a matter of changes *internal* to an enterprise that serve to make that firm more *competitive*. After all, to become more competitive necessarily means becoming more competitive than others, at the expense of the workers working in those other, less competitive firms. The practical impact of our critical conception of work is not intended to be higher profits, but a transformation of the factors that make working an experience of injustice and domination, which could also affect health. In the contemporary neoliberal firm, injustice and domination at work are linked with operations of power that favor individual performance assessment and competition between workers. Conversely, evaluation in the service of the work collective paves the way to more justice, and cooperative management paves the way to a subversion of the relations of domination within the workplace. Indeed, this subversion requires that the transformation of power relations within the workplace is not only motivated by managers' attempts to make cooperation more efficient. If the transformation of power relations is to be an experience of emancipation from domination, it has to be connected with, or initiated by, mobilizations of the workers themselves in their struggle against injustice and domination. The dominated cannot be emancipated by anyone but themselves. Let us recall one of the main implications of the critical model of work sketched in part 3. To be relevant as critique, the criticism of work has to take the standpoint of the normative insights and practical dynamics that emerge from experiences of injustice and domination at work. Of course, it should not be forgotten that managers are workers, too, and that they could suffer from their working conditions. But since they are key instruments in the current domination of work and at work, they cannot be the main protagonists of the struggles against domination and injustice. The dominated cannot be emancipated by those in power.

In other words, work organization and the health of the workers should not be thought of only as economic issues but also as political issues—as political issues within firms as well as outside of firms. Within firms, even those in which the organization of work and the health of the workers are not conceived by managers as solely economic issues, the workers should be able to claim that another organization of work is possible, and our critical conception of work, as well as the experimentation described previously, could help them do this. But the goal to be achieved is broader and more demanding: it is a transformation of the work organization toward more justice and less domination not only in one or several firms but in all of them. This is a political issue that must be tackled through deliberation and debate in the political public sphere, not only in the public space internal to work collectives.

A third limit of the experiment concerns the process of transformation of the work organization. In all the dimensions of cooperation we have discussed—that is, vertical cooperation within the accounting department, transverse cooperation with local authorities, and horizontal cooperation within management teams (as well as within a project team)—each decision involves not only the involvement of a leader but also the involvement of the other workers. The various levels of the cooperative community are also concerned. All the dimensions of cooperation can only be capitalized

upon by the company under the condition of the development and institutionalization, step by step, of new work and trade rules based on the
evolution of the field. The transformation of the work organization undergone is then a step-by-step and complex process depending on the participation of various actors in a more and more cooperative community, as
well as consent over the new rules, and a process of institutionalization of
new norms and power relations. The third limit does not only concern the
fact that such a process requires a radical transformation of the managerial
culture that is characteristic of the neoliberal firm. Managers will have to
deeply transform the habits of working, learned at university or management
school, that manifest and reproduce the power relations of the neoliberal
firm. They will also have to change the managerial norms they have internal-
ized and have been told to make their subordinates internalize. It is indeed
not easy to change one's habits, one's practices, and one's relation to norms.

Being a progressive transformation, the transformation of cooperation
can be described as being of a reformist kind in terms of its political implications. But given that it calls for deep transformations in the work culture
and the power relations characteristic of the neoliberal firm, it also amounts
to a radical kind of political transformation.

As soon as radical politics is at stake, strong obstacles are to be expected.
The problem is not only that of the intrinsic difficulty of the transformation of institutionalized power relations and the corresponding work
culture; it is also one of social forces that serve to perpetuate the status
quo. We have analyzed a situation where a consensus has been reached
between managers and other workers to reshape the firm in order to make
it a more cooperative community. Such consensus is surely difficult to
reach, but nevertheless possible, as we have seen. But, in a capitalist economy, those who have economic power in the last resort are not managers
but capital owners, that is, in the neoliberal contemporary world, shareholders interested above all in high rates of short-term profit. There is a
structural tension, if not a contradiction, between the social interests of
those who, in the last resort, rule the firm and those who are interested in
making cooperation better in the workplace.

As a general political orientation, the project of transforming firms into
cooperative communities and to make society as a whole more cooperative

could be labeled socialism.[8] At its origins, socialism was not only a struggle for more social justice but also for a transformation of an economic system based on market competition as well as for another form of work organization. It is simply a fact that the socialist movement, and more generally the left, has over time renounced the issue of how to tackle the transformation of the organization of work.[9] In this respect, what is at stake in the transformation of work we are advocating is a return to some of the primary motivations and aims of the socialist project. Since this social transformation requires deep changes in the working culture, the power relations and the managerial norms that define neoliberalism as the dominant contemporary form of economic and work organization, what is at stake here is a struggle against neoliberalism.

Critics of neoliberalism have tended to focus, not unreasonably, on macro-economic inequalities,[10] and on forms of subjectivation through norms of "self-entrepreneurship" or other forms of marketized subjectivity.[11] But actualizing the socialist project in the context of neoliberalism means transforming the economy not only at the macro-level, and at the level of general "subjectivation processes" across all institutions, but also at the level of the specific forms of power (such as individual performance evaluation, standardization of procedures, normalisation, and precarization) that structure the work organization, and to work toward alternative forms of work organization. Actualizing the socialist project requires that the organization of work becomes again a subject matter of political deliberation and social experimentation. The intervention that this chapter has just described does not claim to offer a general solution to these problems, but rather serves to illustrate how the critical conception of work sketched in this book could be used practically to foreground the political stakes of the organization of work and to experiment in ways of transforming the neoliberal firm.

_____

In the last two parts of the book, we have put much emphasis on the fact that there are issues concerning justice and autonomy that are specific to the working experience. This is why we have advocated a "bottom-up" approach, starting from experience rather than from general definitions of justice and autonomy, if a critical conception of work is to adequately capture the many problematic dimensions of contemporary working experiences and is to provide a useful contribution to practical solutions. This emphasis on the specificity of work as a form of experience was also motivated by the fact that in contemporary political discussions it is usually taken for granted that the norms of justice and autonomy are not really relevant as soon as a critique of work is concerned or, indeed, that there is nothing specific in the experience of injustice and domination at work that would call for specific conceptions of justice or autonomy. By contrast, we have tried to show that some experiences of injustice and domination are specific to the working experience and, as a consequence, that they call for a specific critical conception of work.

In the last chapter, we presented a concrete case study that demonstrates that the critical conception of work we have delineated provides cogent analytical tools to articulate some of the more concrete and pervasive worries about contemporary working situations. This particular case also showed that these analytical tools can help agents and institutions transform the work organization in a way that leads to less unjust and less dominated conditions. In contemporary political discussions, there is a striking silence about the content and possibility of a work organization that would be more adjusted to expectations of justice and autonomy. The silence is even more resounding in relation to the ways in which real social experimentation oriented toward such a goal might be conducted. Indeed, while there is a general consensus concerning the fact that the very idea of democracy implies that experimentation should be undertaken in order to make the social world better, and that these social experiments should be guided by public deliberations and the participation of those concerned,[1] this very consensus splits—or, indeed, interest in these matters disappears—as soon as work is concerned. Not only is there a striking lack of political interest in discussing work from a critical point of view, there is also a surprising lack of political imagination concerning social experimentation at work and democratic ways to conduct such social experimentation. This double lack makes problematic not only the ways in which the issue of workplace democracy is usually articulated but also, as we will now briefly intimate, the whole debate about the democratization of actually existing democracies.

Readers might find it surprising or maybe disappointing that we turn so late to the issue of politics, to what shape a more democratic work organization might take. But, before these political questions can be debated, a full picture has to be drawn of the complex and ambiguous features of the working experience, or so our conviction has been. This is especially the case given all the misconceptions about work experience that circulate in contemporary academic discourse as well as in many institutional forums of public debate. The return of work we advocate is notably a return of work to the forefront of scholarly interest and a return of work to public and policy debates that do full justice to the impact work has on modern individuals and communities.

In relation to political issues, therefore, the purpose of our book has deliberately been a preparatory one. We could have entitled our book "Critical Prolegomena to a Contemporary Politics of Work." For our primary goal has been to show *why*, and the *different ways in which*, work deserves to be taken into account in democratic deliberations. We have sought to propose specific analytical tools to help take work into consideration in such deliberations in a way that would do justice to its complexity and its ambiguity. Our purpose was not to describe *how* work should be taken into consideration and what kind of democratization of actually existing democracy this consideration of work would imply. By way of a conclusion to our book, however, we can provide some general, schematic, and provisional insights about the ways in which our approach would help address political issues from the perspective of what we have termed the centrality of work.

FROM INJUSTICE AND DOMINATION TO WORKPLACE DEMOCRACY

In contemporary political discussions, the issue of democracy is at the center of attention, either because one wants to defend democracy against its enemies or because one wants to democratize actually existing democracy and make it more democratic. Most of the time, however, the possibility, let alone the specific form, of democracy in the workplace is not really taken into consideration. The situation is similar to that of the discussions concerning justice and autonomy. Either it is considered that democracy is not a relevant concern in workplaces or, when it is thought to be relevant, that democracy should be institutionalized in firms in just the same ways it is institutionalized in representative democracies, namely with some kind of parliament representing the interest of the workers and controlling the use of power. In this latter case, when workplace democracy is thought through a "Firm-State Analogy,"[2] the issue in question is how to generalize existing forms of political democracy to a specific institution that remains largely undemocratic. Such a generalization of democratic practices into workplaces would no doubt represent an increased democratization of contemporary societies, and for that reason we should support this kind of democratization, like any other kind of democratization. But in our opinion, this model of democratization suffers from a twofold shortcoming: first, it assumes that there is nothing specific in the challenges that the democratization of work faces; second, it assumes that the challenge of "democratizing democracy" concerns the extension of existing forms of democracy rather than a radicalization of democracy.

In many ways, however, the working experience raises specific democratic challenges. The preceding chapters have shown that the experience of domination at work relates to forms of structural domination since workers are basically forced to earn a living and therefore enter in a contract that establishes their subordination. A long tradition of workplace republicanism that is being revitalized today has sought to emphasize this form of domination at work as one of the main challenges for a broader project of a democratization of democracy.[3] But domination at work also relates to other power apparatuses that are embedded in the very materiality of the working activity itself: in the rhythm of the machines, the control of individual productivity via computers, the procedures of assessment, and so on. Therefore, even in this specific workplace republican tradition, all the dimensions of domination at work have not been taken into account. This inability to tackle the variety of challenges corresponding to the various dimensions of the experience of domination at work is even more true of conceptions of "representative" or "deliberative" democracy.

Conversely, the work experience brings into play highly specific democratic resources. We have pointed out that cooperation should be contrasted with mere coordination of the working activity by the management insofar as work usually requires an internal public sphere where deliberations about the best ways of translating tasks (or prescribed work) into activity (or real work) can take place. We have also shown that the working experience produces a specific knowledge about cooperation and that particular justice expectations on the part of the workers concern the possibility of having their say about cooperation. It follows from these various points that what is at stake in expectations for more democracy in workplaces is not only some control of the use of power by management, and not only to have one's right respected and one's interests represented, but also to be recognized as a contributor to cooperation, as someone who has a specific knowledge, a knowledge that authorizes one to participate in deliberations concerning the very organization of cooperation. Hence what is at stake in such democratic expectations represents not just an extension to work of the forms of democracy that exist outside of the workplace but, in fact, also a deep transformation of these democratic forms, an extension that constitutes a radicalization as well, since it concerns the very relationship between the governing and the governed. As shown in the last two chapters, the power of the manager is something very specific: it is required not only from the point of view of prescribed tasks and the prescribed division of labor within the workplace but also in order to make sure that the transformations of prescribed coordination into cooperation does not become dysfunctional. Given that this type of power is used in situations that regard particular processes of problem solving, and particular ways of preventing mistakes, democratic control of managerial power cannot simply mean control by some kind of parliament internal to the firm via regulations voted by such a miniparliament. It needs to include participation of the workers in the processes through which cooperation is organized. In other words, it means not only regulation of the relations between those who govern and those who are governed in the firm but also a subversion of this very division between the governing and the governed, the managing and the managed. This is why it represents not only an extension of democracy to firms but also a radicalization of democracy.

This conception of workplace democracy is consistent with the main claims of chapter 5. To recall, justice at work doesn't concern only individuals as citizens having political rights (justice as respect of universal rights) and consumers expecting a fair distribution of wealth (justice as distributive justice) but also individuals as producers or contributors to the cooperation within workplaces (contributive justice). Equally, autonomy at work doesn't mean simply having an opportunity of choice and the possibility of self-realization but also the possibility to participate in the individual and collective process of transformation of prescribed work into real work. Our particularist, pluralist, and pragmatist critical conception of work aims not just to capture the various stakes of injustice and domination at work and thereby to be useful in social experimentation oriented toward more justice and autonomy at work. This critical conception of work also sheds a new light on the issue of workplace democracy, that is, on the ways in which these social democratic experiments might be conducted. It leads to a conception of workplace democracy as a means of satisfying norms of contributive justice and as a way of developing the democratic dynamics of deliberation rooted in the work collectives.

But the issue of democracy intersects with work-related issues in many other ways than simply with regard to workplace democracy. The functioning of political democracy, understood as a way of organizing the state and its relation to society, is also affected by what happens at work. The moral and political dimensions of work, through its formative effects on subjects, imply that workplace democracy should not just be considered from the point of view of the possible extension, or indeed radicalization, of political democracy into workplaces. The relationship between work experience and democracy also goes in the other direction, or so we think our critical conception of work can show. Workplace democracy can contribute to democratizing political democracy itself and also, even more generally, lead to more democratic ways of life.

FORMATIVE EFFECTS OF WORK AND THEIR MORAL AND POLITICAL IMPLICATIONS

Earlier in the book we highlighted the formative effects of work mainly from a psychological and sociological point of view. We have shown how unemployment and working conditions going wrong can deeply affect health and psychic life. We have also pointed out that unemployment tends to deprive subjects of fundamental dimensions of the social experience. At, and through, work, one not only learns technical skills but also develops affective, moral, and intellectual capacities that condition the type of life one will live after hours. In other words, work triggers learning processes that have not only psychological and sociological implications but also moral and political ones. These implications can be aptly articulated using the language of virtue ethics.

Virtues, as Aristotle contended, consist in habits that enable a subject to behave in the right way in particular circumstances. The analyses we have offered throughout our book help to establish the important claim that the formative effects of work notably concern the decisive role that work plays in the process of incorporating virtues defined in this Aristotelian way. These formative effects relate to the fact that, as an experience of genuine cooperation, work can be a learning process for what philosophers have characterized as some of the main virtues, namely tolerance, solidarity, courage, and justice. However, as we have amply documented, genuine cooperation meets many obstacles in contemporary work organizations. And so, just as work can be a decisive vector for creating habits of tolerance, solidarity, courage, and justice in subjects, it can conversely create quite contrary habits and lead to the development of the opposite qualities of being intolerant and hostile, egoist and servile, even weakening the sense of justice.

In order to engage in genuine cooperation with one's colleagues, one has to accept discussion with them about the best means to achieve a common goal. One has to be open about one's own ways of transforming prescribed work into real work and thereby subject one's own activity to their criticism.

One has to be willing to embrace differences within cooperation and to receive critical judgment on the part of colleagues. These colleagues, in turn, might be too different from us to possibly become friends. Workers expect to work with "good colleagues," but everyone knows that some of our "good colleagues" could never become "good friends," and nobody expects this to be otherwise. This shows precisely why and how the work experience can be a place in which a learning process can occur leading to the cultivation of tolerance. Conversely, when the work conditions and the structuration of the work collective make genuine cooperation impossible, suspicion and mutual hostility grow between colleagues. As suggested in chapters 1 and 2, it is likely that the worries related to bullying and disrespect result, at least partly, from a contemporary organization of work that tends to make genuine cooperation impossible and that gives rise to suspicion and hostility among coworkers. However, when a habit becomes entrenched in an individual through his life and activity in a particular institution, this habit will also be carried by the individual through the rest of his life. When the main part of one's daily life consists in a process whereby one learns suspicion and mutual hostility, how could the rest of one's life remain unaffected?

Genuine cooperation also presupposes solidarity. What holds the work collective together is not just a shared technical knowledge, the sense of working toward a common goal, and the possibility of discussing problems faced together. The work collective owes its unity as well to the fact that one can count on one's colleagues to help solve problems and prevent errors and mistakes. Practical trust in the other as a possibility of help and support is a crucial aspect of life in a work collective. But, as noted in the last part of the book, in the contemporary neoliberal situation the work experience tends to offer less and less a learning process of solidarity and more and more a process of mutual competition. Work then becomes a learning process of egoism and instrumentalizing the other rather than a learning process of solidarity. This also has an impact on the habit of behaving courageously and justly. If working always entails refusing to simply follow prescriptions, a form of disobedience is a structural feature of the experience of work. Since domination is equally a structural feature of many places of work in the capitalistic context, this core of disobedience can also make the work experience a place in which to learn to resist domination. In order to refuse simply to obey orders, and to resist threats related to pecuniary sanctions or even the possibility of being fired, one has to behave courageously. But, in the long run, such courageous behavior is possible within a workplace only if there is support from the work collective, that is to say, solidarity. When the work collective is undermined, the work experience can no longer be a learning process of courage, and it is likely that it becomes in fact a learning process of voluntary servitude, a voluntary servitude at work that, once again, will have direct and powerful side effects on life outside work.

The same argument applies to justice and habituation to injustice. When cooperation is backed by a network of solidarity, it could become a habit to give due recognition to the efforts spent by the colleagues and to the solutions they have been able to discover in order to make cooperation more efficient or more satisfying. And when courage to resist is made possible in the long run, it can also become a habit to publicly criticize the injustices suffered by oneself or by colleagues. But, conversely, when solidarity reverses and transforms into distrust and competition, when courage reverses and transforms into voluntary servitude, the capacity to give just recognition to colleagues and the ability to resist injustice will most likely not remain unaffected. Moreover, the habituation to unjust relations between colleagues and with the management could affect the very sense of justice. The working experience can become a process of learning the banality of injustice. Such a process cannot but impact on the whole of social life on the level of ordinary interaction as well as on the level of political deliberations.[4]

It is precisely because work is a learning process that deeply impacts subjective life in its social, moral, and political dimensions that we have contended in chapter 3 that the self is also a working self or, to put it in other words, that there is a kind of centrality of work. Taking this centrality seriously doesn't have only psychological, sociological, and moral implications. It also has deep political implications, and this not only because it provides a strong argument to take the problems encountered by men and women at work seriously. In fact, taking this centrality seriously also implies a different definition of what a democratic society is than those usually acknowledged.

In our opinion, a democratic society is not just a society in which citizens benefit from political rights (freedom of expression, freedom to vote, freedom of association, and so on) but also a society in which citizens could be engaged in learning processes that yield courage to resist domination, behavior that conforms to standards of tolerance, solidarity, and justice, openness to other people's opinions and readiness to discuss them, and readiness to criticize authority. To be able to accept others' views, to have an effective sense of justice and solidarity, to have one's conduct guided by habits of discussing and criticizing amounts to a set of conditions without which the political institutions of society lose much of their value. But these political institutions do not by themselves produce such habits, or at least not in a sufficiently profound way. True, there is no reason to believe that the learning processes that underpin such habits take place only within the workplace. Indeed, there is much historical evidence that revolutionary episodes, and more generally political mobilization, also engage such processes. The institutions of political democracy can also have deep formative effects, for example when general elections are highly disputed and confront projects that seem radically opposed to each other. But these are all exceptional episodes. In the long run, in the day-to-day life of everyday subjects, the learning processes at work have deeper effects on these conditions of a democratic society than other socialization processes.

Hence there is a circle between political democracy, workplace democracy, and democracy as a form of life. As John Dewey, one who most consistently established this circle, put it: "the identification of democracy with political democracy is responsible for most of its failures."[5] By this he meant precisely what we have just been advocating, namely the very aims of political democracy presuppose a set of democratic habits that political institutions cannot produce by themselves. As a result, Dewey argued, democracy should in fact be considered as a "way of life" rather than simply as a way of organizing state power and its relations with society.[6] The consequence of the view of democracy as a way of life is that every institution of society as well as ordinary practices should be organized in conformity with the democratic virtues of tolerance, solidarity, justice, and collective deliberation in order that democratic habits could be widespread enough to give democratic ideals their flesh and blood. But as we have seen, all institutions are not comparable in terms of the depth and lastingness of their learning processes. Work seems to have deeper formative effects on democratic habits than most other forms of social experience; workplaces, we want to argue, are a central learning place of democracy. And this is true not only in the positive, to the extent that work can make democratic habits possible, but also in the negative, insofar as deleterious work can corrode democratic habits and strengthen their corresponding vices: intolerance, voluntary servitude, the acceptance of injustice, and even evil being done to others. Therefore, in this respect also, critical theory should probably follow Dewey when he argued that democracy cannot become in reality what it is in name until it becomes workplace democracy.[7]

NOTES

INTRODUCTION

1. See, among the many examples of this kind of inquiry, Clive Jenkins and Barrie Sherman, *The Collapse of Work* (London: Eyre Methuen, 1979); Stanley Aronowitz and William DiFazio, *The Jobless Future* (Minneapolis: University of Minnesota Press, 1994); Michael Dunkerley, *The Jobless Economy?* (Cambridge: Polity, 1996); Jeremy Rifkin, *The End of Work* (London: Penguin, 2000); Ulrich Beck, *The Brave New World of Work* (Cambridge: Polity, 2000); Kathi Weeks, *The Problem with Work: Feminism, Marxism, Antiwork Politics, and Postwork Imaginaries* (Durham: Duke University Press, 2011); Erik Brynjolfsson and Andrew McAfee, *The Second Machine Age* (New York: Norton, 2014); Martin Ford, *The Robots Are Coming: Technology and the Threat of a Jobless Future* (New York: Basic, 2015); Jerry Kaplan, *Humans Need Not Apply* (New Haven: Yale University Press, 2015); Nick Srnicek and Alex Williams, *Inventing the Future: Postcapitalism and a World Without Work* (New York: Verso, 2015). For healthy skepticism about the end of work hypothesis, see Shaun Wilson, *The Struggle Over Work* (London: Routledge, 2004).
2. See for example Beck, *The Brave New World of Work*, pp. 42–43, Rifkin, *The End of Work*, pp. 11–13.
3. ILO Global Employment Trends 2014, Annex 3, p. 111.
4. Alfred Marshall, *Principles of Economics*, 8th ed. (London: MacMillan, 1961), p. 54.
5. A fiction Marx famously sought to correct Adam Smith on. See Karl Marx, *Grundrisse* (London: Penguin, 1993), p. 611.
6. An interpretation in the sense of an application that is responsive to the particular demands of a situation, not in the sense of an intellectual entertaining of something. On the role of interpretation in rule-following and the idea of self-applying rules, see the classic discussion in Ludwig Wittgenstein, *Philosophical Investigations* (Oxford: Basil Blackwell, 1953).

7. Those inspired by John Rawls, *A Theory of Justice* (Cambridge: Harvard University Press, 1971), though the extent to which Rawls himself embraced procedural liberalism is debatable.

8. See Charles Taylor, *Sources of the Self* (Cambridge: Cambridge University Press, 1989).

9. See Michael Walzer, *Spheres of Justice* (New York: Basic Books, 1983).

10. See Alasdair MacIntyre, *After Virtue*, 2d ed. (London: Duckworth, 1984).

11. Though it is Kymlicka's textbook interpretation of Taylor that is largely responsible for the wide take-up of this idea. See Will Kymlicka, *Contemporary Political Philosophy* (Oxford: Oxford University Press, 1990).

12. See Charles Taylor, "Cross-Purposes: The Liberal Communitarian Debate," in his *Philosophical Arguments* (Cambridge: Harvard University Press, 1995).

13. See Walzer, *Spheres of Justice*.

14. Richard Rorty and Robert Brandom, though more Hegelian liberals than communitarians (Brandom calls himself a "progressive rationalist"), are two of Dewey's more celebrated champions who have neglected this aspect of Dewey's legacy. See Richard Rorty, *Consequences of Pragmatism* (Minneapolis: University of Minnesota Press, 1982); and Robert Brandom, *Reason in Philosophy—Animating Ideas* (Cambridge: Belknap, 2009).

15. See Jürgen Habermas, *The Philosophical Discourse of Modernity* (Cambridge: MIT Press, 1987).

16. See Jürgen Habermas, *The Theory of Communicative Action*, vol. 2 (Boston: Beacon, 1985); and Hannah Arendt, *The Human Condition* (Chicago: University of Chicago Press, 1958).

17. See, above all, Andre Gorz, *Farewell to the Working Class* (London: Pluto, 1982).

18. Indeed we would argue that a focus on work, done in the right way, is not only consistent with feminist, environmental, and anticolonial critical impulses but also a means of sharpening and amplifying them.

19. See Max Horkheimer, *Critical Theory: Selected Essays* (New York: Continuum, 1999).

1. UNEMPLOYMENT AND PRECARIOUS WORK

1. See ILO, *Global Employment Trends 2014* and *World of Work Report 2014*.

2. See ILO, *Global Employment Trends for Youth 2013*.

3. The exact figure was 20.9 per cent of those aged fifteen to sixty-four. See "Australian Aboriginal and Torres Strait Islander Health Survey: Updated Results, 2012–13," Australian Bureau of Statistics, cat. no. 4727.0.55.006

4. See David Dooley and Joann Prause, *The Social Costs of Underemployment: Inadequate Employment as Disguised Unemployment* (Cambridge: Cambridge University Press, 2004).

5. See ILO, *Global Employment Trends 2014*, p. 42. For example in the EU, "the proportion of involuntarily accepted temporary employment increased by 1.1 percentage points between 2008 and 2012 and the share of involuntary part-time employment grew by 2.4 points in the same period." The US shows a similar trend. A survey conducted by the Australian Bureau of Statistics in September 2013 also found

that the phenomenon of insufficient work (as indicated by the length of its duration and the number of people in it) was on the rise ("Underemployed Workers,
Australia," ABS cat. no. 6265.0).

6. See Philip Eisenberg and Paul Lazarsfeld, "The Psychological Effects of Unemployment," *Psychological Bulletin* 35 (1938): 358–90.

7. See Connie R. Wanberg, "The Individual Experience of Unemployment," *Annual
Review of Psychology* 63 (2012): 369–96.

8. K. I. Paul and K. Moser, "Unemployment Impairs Mental Health," *Journal of
Vocational Behavior* 74 (2009): 264–82, 280.

9. See, for example, David Fryer, "Psychological or Material Deprivation: Why Does
Unemployment Have Mental Health Consequences?," in E. McLaughlin ed.,
Understanding Unemployment (London: Routledge, 1992), pp. 103–25.

10. See, for example, Marie Jahoda, *Employment and Unemployment: A Social-
Psychological Analysis* (Cambridge: Cambridge University Press, 1982).

11. See, for example, Marie Jahoda, "Economic Recession and Mental Health: Some
Conceptual Issues," *Journal of Social Issues* 44, no. 4 (Winter 1988): 13–23, 17.

12. See Marie Jahoda, Paul F. Lazarsfeld, and Hans Ziesel, *Marienthal: The Sociogra-
phy of an Unemployed Community* (Chicago: Aldine Atherton, 1971).

13. See, for example, K. I. Paul, E. Geithner, and K. Moser, "Latent Deprivation
Among People Who Are Employed, Unemployed, or Out of the Labor Force,"
Journal of Psychology 143, no. 5 (2009): 477–491; K. I. Paul and B. Batinic, "The
Need for Work: Jahoda's Latent Functions of Employment in a Representative
Sample of the German Population," *Journal of Organizational Behavior* 31 (2010):
45–64.

14. See Cristobal Young, "Losing a Job: The Nonpecuniary Cost of Unemployment in
the United States," *Social Forces* 91, no. 2 (December 2012): 609–34. The drop in
subjective well-being consequent on unemployment is "on an order of magnitude
greater than the effect of changes in the family structure, home ownership, or
parental status."

15. Ibid., p. 615.

16. See Jahoda, *Employment and Unemployment*, pp. 8–9.

17. "We all need some tie to reality so as not to be overwhelmed by fantasy and emotion. Under current conditions, the vast majority derive five ties from employment
as latent by-products: time-structure, social contacts, the experience of social purposes, status and identity, and regular activity." Jahoda, "Work, Employment,
Unemployment: Values, Theories and Approaches in Social Research," *American
Psychologist* 36, no. 2 (February 1981): 189.

18. See, for example, the discussions in Arne L. Kallerberg, "Precarious Work, Insecure
Workers: Employment Relations in Transition," *American Sociological Review* 74
(February 2009): 1–22; and Guy Standing, *The Precariat* (London: Bloomsbury,
2011).

19. We leave to one side the conundrum of whether zero hour contracts, which are
increasingly used, have this character.

20. See, for example, Kallerberg, "Precarious Work, Insecure Workers"; S. Paugam,
Le Salarié de la précarité (Paris: PUF, 2000); Klaus Dörre, Karin Scherschel, Melanie
Booth, Tine Haubner, Kai Marquardsen, and Karen Schierhorn, eds., *Bewährungspro-
ben für die Unterschicht?* (Frankfurt: Campus, 2013).

21. See, for example, K. Doogan, "Long-Term Employment and the Restructuring of the Labour Market in Europe," *Time and Society* 14, no. 1 (65–87): 2005; Ralph Fevre, "Employment Insecurity and Social Theory: The Power of Nightmares," *Work, Employment, and Society* 21, no. 3 (2007): 517–35; Francis Green, "Subjective Employment Insecurity Around the World," *Cambridge Journal of Regions, Economy, and Society* 2, no. 3 (2009): 343–63.

22. See K. Doogan, *New Capitalism?* (Cambridge: Polity, 2009); and Green, "Subjective Employment Insecurity Around the World."

23. As presented on the OECD website, September 2014, http://stats.oecd.org.

24. See Standing, *The Precariat*, p. 11, though, as we go on to explain presently, using a different terminology. Serge Paugam, another leading theorist of precariousness, also draws a distinction between precariousness in relation to job ("précarité de l'emploie") and precariousness in relation to work ("précarité du travail") (Paugam, *Le Salarié de la précarité*, p. 356). The need to distinguish security in relation to work from security in relation to employment has also been made effectively by Dale Tweedie in Tweedie, "Making Sense of Insecurity: A Defence of Richard Sennett's Sociology of Work," *Work, Employment, and Society* 27, no. 1 (2013): 94–104.

25. See, for example, Richard Sennett and Jonathan Cobb, *The Hidden Injuries of Class* (New York: Knopf, 1972), p. 201; and Richard Sennett, *The Culture of the New Capitalism* (New York: Yale University Press, 2006), p. 175.

26. See, for example, Standing, *The Precariat*; K. Dorre, K. Kraemer, and F. Speidel, "The Increasing Precariousness of the Employment Society—Driving Force for a New Right-Wing Populism?," *International Journal of Action Research* 2, no. 1 (2006): 98–128.

2. WORK-LIFE IMBALANCE, DISRESPECT AT WORK, AND MEANINGLESS WORK

1. What we mean by this will become clearer in the context of our discussion of "A Critical Conception of Work," part 3 of this book.

2. See Eurofound, *Fifth European Working Conditions Survey* (Luxembourg: Publications Office of the European Union, 2012). The survey is based on interviews with forty-four thousand employees across thirty-two European countries.

3. See Eurofound, *Second European Quality of Life Survey: Family Life and Work* (Luxembourg: Publications Office of the European Union, 2010).

4. See *OECD Factbook 2014*, p. 142.

5. In noting this, we do not mean to say that what counts as "long" or "short" by way of working hours should be measured according to some putatively natural, universally applicable standard, say a thirty-five- or forty-hour week. We are not assuming that we *ought* to think of a thirty-five- or forty-hour week as "normal," a fifty-hour week as long, and so on. We are simply drawing attention to some population level facts, insofar as we know them, about how many hours people actually do spend in employment.

6. The source for all these figures is the OECD Better Life Index, http://www .oecdbetterlifeindex.org/topics/work-life-balance/ (accessed October 2014).

7. We should emphasize that the phenomenon in need of explanation here is not the difficulty people have maintaining a work/life balance while working what are generally considered "normal" working hours. For many people the "norm" of the thirty-five- or forty-hour week is far from striking the right balance for them. The issue we are concerned with here, the thing that needs some explaining, is the counterintuitive correlation between reduction in working hours and increasing discontent about work-life balance.

8. For example, the increasing amount of time spent traveling to work, as rising property and rental prices in urban centers forces people who work there to live further away; and employment in multiple jobs, which can be more deleterious to work-life balance than the equivalent time spent in employment in a single job.

9. See Francis Green, *Demanding Work* (Princeton: Princeton University Press, 2005).

10. As observed by Francis Green, "Work Effort and Well-Being in an Age of Affluence," in R. J. Burke and C. L. Cooper, eds., *The Long Work Hours Culture* (London: Emerald, 2008), pp. 115–36. The figures cover fifteen member countries of the European Union prior to enlargement in 2004.

11. Eurofound, *Fifth European Working Conditions Survey*, p. 53.

12. Green, "Work Effort and Worker Well-Being." See also Eurofound, *Fifth European Working Conditions Survey*, pp. 124–26.

13. Cited in Tarani Chandola, *Stress at Work: A Report Prepared for the British Academy* (London: British Academy, 2010), p. 56.

14. See P. Bongers, A. M. Kremer, and J. ter Laak, "Are Psychosocial Factors, Risk Factors for Symptoms and Signs of the Shoulder, Elbow or Hand/Wrist? A Review of the Epidemiological Literature," *American Journal of Industrial Medicine* 41 (2002): 315–42; and A. Hauke, J. Flintrop, E. Brun, and R. Rugulies, "The Impact of Work-Related Psychosocial Stressors on the Onset of Musculoskeletal Disorders: A Review and Meta-analysis of Fifty-four Longitudinal Studies," *Work and Stress* 25, no. 3 (2011): 243–56.

15. See Hauke et al., "The Impact of Work-Related Psychosocial Stressors."

16. "The State of US Health, 1990–2010: Burden of Diseases, Injuries, and Risk Factors," *Journal of the American Medical Association* 310, no. 6 (August 2013): 596.

17. S. Stansfeld and B. Candy, "Psychosocial work Environment and Mental Health—A Meta-analytic Review," *Scandinavian Journal of Work, Environment, and Health* 32, no. 6 (2006): 443–62.

18. J. P. E. Bonde, "Psychosocial Factors at Work and Risk of Depression: A Systematic Review of the Epidemiological Evidence," *Occupational and Environmental Medicine* 65, no. 7 (July 2008): 438–45.

19. For an overview of some of the conceptual issues arising from the definition of burnout and its relation to depression, see Marc Loriol, "La construction sociale de la fatigue au travail: L'exemple du burn out des infirmières," *Travail et Emploi* 94 (2003): 65–74; and Arnold B. Bakker, Evangelia Demerouti, and Ana Isabel Sanz-Vergel, "Burnout and Work Engagement: The JD-R Approach," *Annual Review of Organizational Psychology and Organizational Behavior* 1 (2014): 389–411.

20. In some cases, to the extent of destroying it entirely. In Japan, the phenomenon of *karoshi*, or "death from overwork," is a serious social issue in its own right.

21. See K. M. Lindblom, S. J. Linton, F. Fedeli, and Bryngelsson, "Burnout in the Working Population: Relations to Psychosocial Factors," *International Journal of Behavioral Medicine*, 13: 1, 2006, 51–59.
22. See T. D. Shanafelt, S. Boone, L. Tan, L. N. Dyrbe, W. Sotile, D. Satele, C. P. West, J. Sloan, and M. R. Oreskovich, "Burnout and Satisfaction with Work-Life Balance Among US Physicians Relative to the General Population," *JAMA Internal Medicine* 172, no. 18 (October 8, 2012):1377–85.
23. The terms *emotional labor* and *affective labor* are also used to designate this type of work. See Arlie Russell Hochschild, *The Managed Heart* (Berkeley: University of California Press, 2012).
24. The prevalence of this phenomenon is indicated by data in the *Fifth European Working Conditions Survey*, which show that 41 percent of male and 37 percent of female health workers across the twenty-seven countries of the EU reported positively to having to hide their feelings always or most of the time. This is a higher proportion than any other sector. Education is the second highest.
25. Dieter Zapf and his colleagues have provided strong evidence for thinking that the specific demands of emotional work lie behind the high incidence of emotional exhaustion and "depersonalization" that characterizes burnout in the caring and service professions. See Dieter Zapf, Claudia Seifert, Barbara Schmutte, Heidrun Mertini, and Melanie Holz, "Emotion Work and Job Stressors and Their Effects on Burnout," *Psychology and Health* 16 (2001): 527–45.
26. See Pascale Molinier and Anne Flottes, "Travail et santé mentale: Approches cliniques," in *Travail et Emploi* 129 (2012): 51–66.
27. For some details on the extent of media coverage and the plethora of academic research, see Ståle Einersen, Helge Hoel, Dieter Zapf, and Cary L. Cooper, eds., *Bullying and Harassment in the Workplace*, 2d ed. (Boca Raton: CRS, 2011); and Ralph Fevre, Duncan Lewis, Amanda Robinson, and Trevor Jones, *Trouble at Work* (London: Bloomsbury Academic, 2012).
28. P. Lutgen-Sandvik, S. J. Tracy, and J. K. Alberts, "Burned by Bullying in the American Workplace: Prevalence, Perception, Degree, and Impact," *Journal of Management Studies* 44, no. 6 (2007): 837–62, p. 854.
29. See R. Hodson, V. J. Roscigno, and S. H. Lopez, "Chaos and the Abuse of Power: Workplace Bullying in Organizational and Interactional Context," *Work and Occupations* 33, no. 4 (2006): 382–416; and Einarsen et al., *Bullying and Harassment in the Workplace*. The 10–20 percent estimate hides a high-degree variation in the prevalence of bullying found in these studies both within and between countries, as is evident from the review of a sample of them in M. B. Nielsen, A. Skogstad, S. Matthiesen et al., "Prevalence of Workplace Bullying in Norway: Comparisons Across Time and Estimation Methods," *European Journal of Work and Organizational Psychology* 18, no. 1 (2009): 81–101.
30. Eurofound, *Fifth European Working Conditions Survey* (Luxembourg: Publications Office of the European Union, 2012), p. 57; Eurofound, *Fourth European Working Conditions Survey* (Luxembourg: Publications Office of the European Union, 2007), p. 35.
31. See M. Milczarek and European Agency for Safety and Health at Work, *Workplace Violence and Harassment: A European Picture* (Luxembourg: Publications Office of the European Union, 2010).

32. Though whether work-related suicide generally results from bullying or from other "moral" sources, which may vary between cultures, is another matter. For example, bullying would certainly seem to be only part of the story for the *karojisatsu*, or work-related suicides, in Japan, and probably not the most important part. The adequacy of the concept of bullying for grasping the social and psychic structures at stake in moral suffering in the workplace will be discussed in the remainder of this section.

33. Though if the relationship is violent, it is almost certain to be a "him."

34. See Philippe Davezies, "Les impasses du harcèlement moral," *Travailler* 11 (2004): 83–90.

35. Fevre et al. observe that while there is evidence to suggest that Norway has had some success in reducing bullying levels through antibullying legislation, antibullying policies have been less effective in the UK and in other Scandinavian countries. See Fevre et al., *Trouble at Work*, p. 13.

36. Among these, disabled people and people with long-term serious illnesses were shown to be particularly at risk. Gender and ethnicity were shown to be less significant factors in determining vulnerability to work-related ill-treatment.

37. See for example Eurofund, *Trends in Job Quality in Europe* (Luxembourg: Publications Office of the European Union, 2012).

38. Adam Smith, *The Wealth of Nations* (New York: Modern Library, 1937), p. 735.

39. See Frederick Winslow Taylor, *The Principles of Scientific Management* (New York: Harper, 1911).

40. See Harry Braverman, *Labor and Monopoly Capitalism: The Degradation of Work in the Twentieth Century* (New York: Monthly Review Press, 1974).

41. See Ralph Fevre, "Employment Insecurity and Social Theory: The Power of Nightmares," *Work, Employment, and Society* 21, no. 3 (2007): 517–35.

42. See for example Marie Jahoda, *Employment and Unemployment* (New York: Columbia University Press, 1982); Robert E. Lane, *The Market Experience* (Cambridge: Cambridge University Press, 1991); and Francis Green, *Skills and Skilled Work* (Oxford: Oxford University Press, 2013).

43. See, for example, Martin Baethge, "Arbeit, Vergesellschaftung, Identität: Zur zunehmenden normativen Subjectivierung der Arbeit," *Soziale Welt* 42, no. 1 (1991): 6–19; Hans J. Pongratz and Günther Voß, "From Employee to 'Entreployee,'" *Concepts and Transformations* 8, no. 3 (2003): 239–54; and Stephan Voswinkel, "Admiration Without Appreciation: The Paradoxes of Recognition of Doubly Subjectivised Work," in Nicholas H. Smith and Jean-Philippe Deranty, eds., *New Philosophies of Labour* (Leiden: Brill, 2012).

3. THE TECHNICAL DIMENSION

1. F. W. Taylor, *Principles of Scientific Management* (New York: Norton, 1967).

2. Most notably Adam Smith, *The Wealth of Nations* (London: Penguin), 1:109–26. See the impact this image made on the young Hegel, "Philosophy of Spirit 1803–04," in *Hegel's System of Ethical Life and First Philosophy of Spirit*, ed. and trans. Henry Silton Harris and Thomas Malcolm Knox (Albany: State University of New York Press, 1979), p. 248; and "Philosophy of Spirit (1805–6)," in *Hegel and*

the Human Spirit, trans. Leo Rauch (Detroit: Wayne State University Press, 1983), p. 121.

3. See the two classical accounts of factory work by philosophers in the 1930s and 1960s: Simone Weil, "Factory Journal," in *Formative Writings: 1929–1941* (London: Routledge, 2009), 149–226; and Roger Linhart, *The Assembly Line* (Amherst: University of Massachussets Press, 1981).

4. See Mike Rose, *The Mind at Work* (London: Penguin, 2005).

5. Any worker, even a worker engaged in the most routine clerical or sevice provision tasks, has some activity to perform, activity that is responsive to the demands of a situation, some of which have a technical character. If by "skill" is meant responsiveness to technical demands, it does indeed follow that there is no such thing as completely unskilled work. But we must be careful not to draw the wrong conclusions from this. First, it does not follow, of course, that all work is equally skilled. Clearly, the technical demands thrown up in work situations vary enormously in their complexity, in the amount of training that is requried to respond effectively to them, and so on. Some techniques are harder to master than others, and some may require hardly any training at all. Second, following from this, the understanding of skill as responsiveness to technical demands is not incompatible with the "de-skilling" hypothesis and the transformation of high-skill craft work to low-skill industrial and postindustrial work. It is useful for certain purposes to distinguish between skilled and unskilled work, and that is fine so long as we do not make the mistake of taking unskilled work to involve no technical aspect at all, and no subjective relation to the technical dimension. Third, it certainly doesn't follow from the inescapability of the technical dimension that all work is equally *meaningful*, or that there is no real problem about the prevalence and distribution of meaningful work because all work requires some subjective engagment with technical demands, as if such engagement dissolves the worries about meaningless work discussed at the end of the previous chapter. Two thoughts need to be held onto in order to avoid succumbing to such a fantasy. First, as just noted, the complexity of technical demands varies enormously, and the "meaning" work has for a subject will depend in part (and only in part) on the challenge those demands make. Second, a subject's investment in work activity is by no means always beneficial for the subject; the subject may flourish or wither in responding to the demands of the job. We look into this in more detail in the next chapter.

6. A good review in English can be found in V. de Keyser, "Work Analysis in French Language Ergonomics: Origins and Current Research Trends," *Ergonomics* 34 (1991): 653–69. See also Kim Vicente, *Cognitive Work Analysis* (New York: CRC, 1999), pp. 87–108.

7. This conflict between external prescription and the reality of the task as lived from the inside is vividly illustrated in the introduction to Kim Vicente's widely used handbook on the ergonomics of work cited in the previous note. Even in such highly controlled work environments as a nuclear plant, there might in fact not be just "one best way" to do things. Even there, contingencies can demand interventions by workers that no amount of prescriptive work can predict. See Vincente, *Cognitive Work Analysis*, p. xiii.

8. This ideal type of worker is particularly prevalent in detective stories in American cinema, with many famous characters developed on those lines. Dirty Harry is the archetype here: he plays "dirty" (violates all the normal procedures, even flaunts the law), but in the end it is he and his "dirty" methods that bring about justice. He is simultaneously the worst and the best cop.

9. This is a feature of human experience particularly highlighted by the phenomenological tradition. See, for example, Jean-Paul Sartre, *Being and Nothingness* (New York: Washington Square Press, 1984), pp. 9–16; Maurice Merleau-Ponty, *The Phenomenology of Perception* (New York: Routledge, 2012), pp. 310–11; and Michel Henry, *The Essence of Manifestation*, trans. G. Etzkorn (The Hague: Martinus Nijhoff, 1973).

10. See Paul Ricoeur, *Time and Narrative*, 3 vols (Chicago: University of Chicago Press, 1988).

11. See Martin Heidegger, *Being and Time* (Oxford: Blackwell, 1962).

12. See Charles Taylor, *Sources of the Self* (Cambridge: Cambridge University Press, 1989), chapter 3.

13. Georges Canguilhem, *The Normal and the Pathological* (New York: Zone, 1991), pp. 196–200.

14. It is probably for this reason that Dewey defined work as "the key to happiness." See John Dewey, "Democracy and Education," in *The Middle Works of John Dewey, 1899-1924* (Southern Illinois University Press, 2008), 9:318.

15. Christophe Dejours, *Le Corps d'abord* (Paris: Payot, 2003).

16. See, for example, the classical text by Marcel Mauss, "Techniques of the Body," in M. Locke and J. Farquhar, eds., *Beyond the Body Proper. Reading the Anthropology of Material Life* (Durham: Duke University Press, 2007), pp. 50–68.

17. See, for instance, Pierre Bourdieu, *Pascalian Meditations* (Stanford: Stanford University Press, 2000).

18. What Freudian psychoanalysis refers to as primary narcissism; see, for instance, Freud, "On Narcissism: An Introduction," in *The Standard Edition of the Complete Psychological Works of Sigmund Freud*, ed. James Strachey, 24 vols. (London: Hogarth, 1957), vol. 14 (1914–1916): *On the History of the Psycho-Analytic Movement, Papers on Metapsychology and Other Works*, pp. 67–102.

19. If these examples lead to the accusation that our model is masculinist because the examples are those of masculine professions, we can only retort that the masculinist assumption is in fact in the very idea that only men can perform these jobs or indeed enjoy them as we describe here.

20. See Sigmund Freud, "Instincts and Their Vicissitudes," in *Standard Edition*, 14:117–40. To see how Freud's conception of psychic work can be related to productive work, see Christophe Dejours, *Travail Vivant*, vol. 1: *Sexualité et travail*, 2 vols. (Paris: Payot, 2009), 1:45–62.

21. Clearly, care work, of all the kinds of work, most eminently includes an encounter between bodies and thus libidinal dimensions. For an analysis of these dynamics, see Pascale Molinier, "Care as Work: Mutual Vulnerabilities and Discreet Knowledge," in Nicholas H. Smith and Jean-Philippe Deranty, eds., *New Philosophies of Labour* (Leiden: Brill, 2012), pp. 251–70.

22. Dejours, *Travail Vivant*, 1:159–83.

23. See Benedictus Spinoza, *The Ethics*, book 3, prop. IX in *The Collected Writings of Spinoza*, trans. Edwin Curley, 2 vols. (Princeton: Princeton University Press, 1985), 1:498.

24. See Thorstein Veblen, *The Instinct of Workmanship and the State of the Industrial Arts* (New York: Cosimo, 2006).

25. Veblen elaborated his theory of the instinct of workmanship precisely by way of counterposition to the classic and neoclassic economic theory of work. See also Dale Tweedie and Sasha Holley, "The Subversive Craft Worker: Challenging 'Disutility' Theories of Management Control," *Human Relations* 69, no. 9 (2016): 1877–900; and Dale Tweedie, "Is Call Centre Surveillance Self-Developing? Capacities and Recognition at Work," *Travailler* 30 (2013): 87–104.

26. See Philippe Zarifian, *Le Travail et la compétence: Entre puissance et contrôle* (Paris: PUF, 2009), pp. 7–29.

27. See the diary of the nineteenth-century carpenter Louis-Gabriel Gauny, as analyzed by Jacques Rancière, in *Proletarian Nights: The Workers' Dream in Nineteenth-Century France* (London: Verso, 2014), pp. 49–67.

28. See, for example, Christophe Dejours and Isabelle Gernet, *Psychopathologie du Travail* (Paris: Masson, 2015).

4. DYNAMICS OF RECOGNITION

1. See, for example, the depictions of *homo faber* and the *animal laborans* in Hannah Arendt, *The Human Condition* (Chicago: Chicago University Press, 1958).

2. Christophe Dejours, *Le Choix* (Paris: Bayard, 2015), pp. 113–66.

3. See Axel Honneth, *Struggle for Recognition*, trans. Joel Anderson (Cambridge: Polity, 1995).

4. See G. W. F. Hegel, *Elements of the Philosophy of Right*, ed. Allen Wood, trans. H. B. Nisbet (Cambridge: Cambridge University Press, 1991).

5. See Pierre Bourdieu's "Preface" to Paul Lazarsfeld, Marie Jahoda, and Hans Ziesel, *Les Chômeurs de Marienthal* (Paris: Minuit, 1981).

6. See E. C. Hughes, "The Social Drama of Work," *Mid-American Review of Sociology* 1, no. 1 (Spring 1976): 1–7.

7. See Kendra Briken, "Suffering in Public? Doing Security in Times of Crisis," *Social Justice* 38, nos. 1/2 (2011): 128–45.

8. See Karl Marx, *Capital: A Critique of Political Economy*, vol 1 (London: Penguin, 2004).

9. *Reconnaissance* in French contains that sense more explicitly.

10. "I do not rely on the generosity of the baker to provide me with bread: the exchange that takes place between us is mutually advantageous but each of us engages in it only for our own self-interest." Adam Smith, *The Wealth of Nations* (New York: Modern Library, 1937), p. 119.

11. The norm of "public service" is an ideal that can have real purchase for workers in the public sector of modern economies, see Philippe Zarifian, *Le Travail et la compétence: Entre puissance et contrôle* (Paris: PUF, 2009).

12. See the famous example of the "Friday cars" in the European car industry that was rife with conflict.

13. Axel Honneth, "Work and Recognition: A Redefinition," in *The I in We* (Cambridge: Polity, 2012), pp. 56–75.

5. JUSTICE AND AUTONOMY AS NORMS OF WORK

1. Among critical theorists, Jürgen Habermas and Axel Honneth seem to share this view. See for instance Jürgen Habermas, "What Does Socialism Mean Today? The Rectifying Revolution and the Need for New Thinking on the Left," *New Left Review* 183 (1990): 3–21; and Axel Honneth "Labour and Recognition. A Redefinition," in *The I in the We* (Cambridge: Polity, 2012), pp. 56–74. On Habermas, see John Sitton, "Disembodied Capitalism: Habermas's Conception of the Economy," *Sociological Forum* 13, no. 1 (1998): 61–83.

2. Significant exceptions to this characterization include Russell Muirhead, *Just Work* (Cambridge: Harvard University Press, 2004); Paul Gomberg, *How to Make Opportunity Equal: Race and Contributive Justice* (Malden, MA: Blackwell, 2007); Beate Roessler, "Meaningful Work: Arguments from Autonomy," *Journal of Political Philosophy*, 20, no. 1 (2012): 71–93; Ruth Yeoman, *Meaningful Work and Workplace Democracy* (London: Palgrave Macmillan, 2014); and especially Andrea Veltman, *Meaningful Work* (Oxford: Oxford University Press, 2016). There is much in these discussions that we find congenial. But the philosophical accounts, such as they are, tend to focus exclusively on problems of *normative analysis*, that is, analysis of the norms of justice and meaningfulness as they apply to the sphere of work. The tendency is first to identify the core meaning of a norm in the abstract (justice as fairness, for example, or meaningfulness as a property of a certain kind of life) and then to see how that norm might be applied to the case of work. Normative analysis of this sort can certainly yield insightful results. But, in our view, in order for such normative analysis to serve the purpose of *critique*, it must 1. be closely tied to a *social diagnosis* (analysis of what, actually, is going wrong with work) and 2. have *practical intent* (plausibly help us to do something about what is going wrong). Critique of work, in this sense of empirically informed, practically oriented normative analysis, remains a rarity.

3. A highly influential formulation of the former view is to be found in Hannah Arendt, *The Human Condition* (Chicago: University of Chicago Press, 1958), while the latter view is presupposed by many liberal theorists of justice, thus screening out the organization of work from the scope of their theories.

4. And for this reason, the problem with liberalism in regard to the social organization of work is not just its quietism. It is not just the unduly restricted scope of liberal theories we are pointing to here, as if things would be fine if the scope were widened, as if the norms apt for the organization work were just a neglected topic, a neglect born of social and anthropological prejudice. More fundamentally, it is the adequacy of the conceptual framework that is at stake. Liberalism (or at least the proceduralist model of liberalism that has become the orthodoxy) is famously agnostic about questions of "the good life," and this agnosticism justifies a doctrine of the neutrality of the state. But we have seen that the relation between work and the good or, as we have just put it here, between working and the self, is not well conceptualized as a matter of *choice*, and to interpret it that way is to miss

much of its social and political significance. Since agnosticism about the good and a commitment to the neutrality of the state are such basic features of procedural liberalism, it is not just accidentally but intrinsically ill-equipped to grasp the social and political significance of the normative conflicts that underlie the contemporary malaises around work. We shall discuss this at greater length in chapter 6.

5. This is not to say that all the normative expectations involved in the negativity of the experience of work can necessarily be *reduced* to demands for justice and autonomy. It is not clear that expectations of individual fulfillment through meaningful work, or for authentic self-realization through work, for instance, are ultimately *nothing but* demands for justice or autonomy. But expectations of justice and autonomy do nevertheless permeate the spectrum of negative experience we characterized earlier as the malaises of work, and it is this permeation that concerns us here.

6. Many sociological studies have dealt with the ways in which workers criticize the work organization and working conditions. In addition to the sources mentioned in chapter 2, see, for instance, François Dubet, Valérie Caillet, Régis Cortéséro, David Mélo, and Françoise Rault, *Injustices: L'expérience des inégalités au travail* (Paris: Seuil, 2006).

7. Such feelings need not be inconsistent with positive answers to survey questions such as "do your present skills correspond well with your duties?," which, as we saw in chapter 2, might be taken as indicators of high levels of work satisfaction. For one might not believe that one's qualifications and background even count as skills in a sense relevant to the question. One can have disappointed expectations rooted in a discrepancy between one's actual work and one's particular professional or educational background without believing that one is "too good" for one's actual work.

8. On this particular type of underemployment, see Douglas C. Maygnard and Daniel C. Feldman, eds., *Underemployment: Psychological, Economic and Social Challenges* (New York: Springer, 2011).

9. Thomas Piketty, *Capital in the Twenty-First Century* (Cambridge: Harvard University Press, 2014).

10. This is why complaints about inequality, as opposed to people not "having enough," should not be brushed off as the result of muddled egalitarian moral thinking; see Harry Frankfurt, *On Inequality* (Princeton: Princeton University Press, 2015). What (rightly) triggers the moral indignation of many people about the extreme inequalities of wealth we witness today is that such inequality cannot possibly reflect the worth of the activities of those who earn the wealth. This is why socioeconomic inequality, and not just people "having enough," matters from a moral point of view.

11. R. Castel, *From Manual Workers to Wage Laborers: Transformation of the Social Question* (New Brunswick, NJ: Transaction, 2003).

12. See especially Nancy Fraser's contributions to Nancy Fraser and Axel Honneth, *Redistribution or Recognition? A Political-Philosophical Exchange*, trans. J. Golb, J. Ingram and C. Wilke (London: Verso, 2003).

13. The relation between being poor and misrecognized has been highlighted by Georg Simmel, "The Poor," *Social Problems* 13, no. 2 (Autumn 1965): 118–40. The same relation is at play in contemporary social welfare; see S. Paugam, *La disqualification sociale* (Paris: PUF, 1991).

14. A classical analysis of the hierarchy of professions in hospitals and of the ways nurses experience the low level of recognition of their work is provided in E. C. Hughes, H. McGill Hughes, and I. Deutscher, *Twenty Thousand Nurses Tell Their Story* (Philadelphia: Lippincott, 1958).

15. The term *profession* is used here in its broadest sense. In a narrower sense, it should have been said that occupational groups expect to be recognized as a profession, that is, as an organized and socially useful vocational group. On this relationship between professionalization and struggle for recognition, see E. C. Hughes, *On Work, Race, and the Sociological Imagination* (Chicago: Chicago University Press, 1994), chapters 1 and 2.

16. See, for instance, R. Kosugi, "Youth Employment in Japan's Economic Recovery: 'Freeters' and 'NEETs,'" *Asia-Pacific Journal*, Japan Focus, May 11, 2006.

17. For an analysis of experiences of alienation in this particular sense, see Rahel Jaeggi, *Alienation* (New York: Columbia University Press, 2014).

18. See for instance R. Hodson, *Dignity at Work*; and I. Ferreras, *Critique politique du travail. Travailler à l'heure de la société des services* (Paris: FNSP, 2007).

19. And on the decline of the "industrial citizenship" normative model of work in the twenty-first century more broadly, see Guy Standing, *Work After Globalization* (Cheltenham: Edward Elgar, 2009).

20. The idea that the norm of justice implies the satisfaction of a series of basic needs is quite intuitive, and it has been one of the main justifications of welfare policies; see for instance F. Rosen, "Basic Needs and Justice," *Mind*, new series, 86, no. 341 (January 1977): 88–94. For the purpose of the present argument, there is no need to discuss in more detail what these needs are and how a reference to individual needs could be introduced into a definition of justice. It suffices to show that this connection makes sense and to add that situations in which these needs are not met define some specific experiences of injustice.

21. See Paul Gomberg, *How to Make Opportunity Equal: Race and Contributive Justice* (Oxford: Blackwell, 2007); and Andrew Sayer, "Contributive Justice and Meaningful Work," *Res Publica* 15, no. 1 (2009): 1–16.

22. See, for instance, Ashley Braganza and Andrew Myers, Jaideep Motwani, Dinesh Mirchandani, Manu Madan, and Angappa Gunasekaran, eds., *Business Process Redesign, a View from the Inside* (London: ITBP, 1997); J. Motwani, D. Mirchandani, M. Madan, and A. Gunasekaran, "Successful Implementation of ERP Projects: Evidence from Two Case Studies," *International Journal of Production Economics* 75, nos. 1–2 (2002): 83–96. On "appropriation" as being a constitutive dimension of working activities, see P. Bernoux, *Mieux-être au travail: Appropriation et reconnaissance* (Toulouse: Octarès, 2015).

23. See, notably, M. Burawoy, *Manufacturing Consent: Changes in the Labor Process Under Monopoly Capitalism* (Chicago: University of Chicago Press, 1979).

6. TWO MODELS OF CRITIQUE

1. See John Rawls, *A Theory of Justice* (Cambridge: Harvard University Press, 1971).
2. See Jürgen Habermas, *The Inclusion of the Other* (Cambridge: Polity, 1998).

3. See Axel Honneth, "Democracy as Reflexive Cooperation: John Dewey and the Theory of Democracy Today," *Political Theory* 26, no. 6 (1998): 763–783.

4. See G. W. F. Hegel, *Elements of the Philosophy of Right*.

5. See Philippe van Parijs, *Real Freedom for All* (Oxford: Clarendon, 1998).

6. John Rawls, *A Theory of Justice* (Cambridge: Harvard University Press, 1971), p. 529.

7. Adina Schwartz, "Meaningful Work," *Ethics* 92, no. 4 (July 1982): 634–46.

8. Schwartz, "Meaningful Work," p. 638.

9. See also Beate Roessler, "Meaningful Work: Arguments from Autonomy," *Journal of Political Philosophy* 20, no. 1 (2012): 71–93.

10. See, for instance, David Courpasson, *L'action contrainte: Organisations libérales et domination* (Paris: PUF, 2000).

11. For such a critique, see Axel Honneth, "Recognition as Ideology," in B. van den Brink and D. Owen, *Recognition and Power. Axel Honneth and the Tradition of Critical Social Theory* (Cambridge: Cambridge University Press, 2007), pp. 323–47.

12. Honneth raises such objections in "Labour and Recognition: A Redefinition," where he seems to be taking them as fatal for the experientialist model of critique we are proposing, despite acknowledging the many advantages of that model. Honneth is ultimately persuaded by Habermas's scepticism toward the kind of critical conception of work we are after, and which Honneth himself once had in his sights, as formulated, for example, in Jürgen Habermas, "Reply to My Critics," in J. B. Thompson and D. Held, eds., *Habermas: Critical Debates* (Cambridge: Polity, 1982). For Honneth's fledgling critical conception of work, see Axel Honneth, "Work and Instrumental Action: On the Normative Basis of Critical Theory," in Honneth, *The Fragmented World of the Social* (Albany: SUNY Press, 1995).

13. Having generality in this sense, that is, in being able to show how general claims about the need for the transformation of the organization or work can arise, does not make the model "generalist" in the sense we have ascribed to the objectivist model. The "generality" of the latter refers to something else: the criteria of objective social criticism.

14. See E. Renault, *L'Expérience de l'injustice* (Paris: La Découverte, 2004).

15. For a sociological study regarding such efforts, see A. Bidet, *L'engagement dans le travail: Qu'est-ce que le vrai boulot?* (Paris: PUF, 2011).

16. By "pragmatism" we mean here a basic methodological orientation to practice, such that the worth of a social theory is bound up with practical consequences of having it. It is thus an important desideratum of the model of social critique we are proposing that it really be useful in the right way, that is, suited for the practical purpose of transforming the organization of work for the better.

7. MANAGERIALISM VERSUS COOPERATIVE MANAGEMENT

1. On this question, see Christophe Dejours, *L'évaluation du travail à l'épreuve du réel* (Paris: Inra, 2003).

2. See, from the point of view of mainstream management literature, Caroline Ann Rowland and Roger David Hall, "Organizational Justice and Performance: Is Appraisal Fair?," *EuroMed Journal of Business* 7, no. 3 (2012): 280–93.

3. See Axel Honneth, *Reification: A New Look at an Old Idea* (Oxford: Oxford University Press, 2012).

4. See Richard Sennett, *The Corrosion of Character* (New York: Norton, 1998).

5. See, for instance, Samuel Cuthbert, *Get Rid of the Performance Review: How Companies Can Stop Intimidating, Start Managing, and Focus on What Really Matters* (New York: Business Plus, 2010); Tom Coens and Mary Jenkins, *Abolishing Performance Appraisals: Why They Backfire and What to Do Instead* (San Francisco: Berrett-Koehler, 2002); T. Baker, *The End of the Performance Review: A New Approach to Appraising Employee Performance* (London: Palgrave Macmillan, 2013).

6. See, for example, the account of technicians in charge of the quality control of materials used in the construction of nuclear plants in Dejours, *L'évaluation du travail à l'épreuve du réel*. See, in relation to nursing, K. Hoe,Y. Kang, and Y.-R. Park, "Moral Distress in Critical Care Nurses: A Phenomenological Study," *Journal of Advanced Nursing* 71, no. 7 (2015): 1684–93.

7. See J. Dumesnil, *Art médical et normalisation du soin* (Paris: PUF, 2013). See also S. Carmel, "The Craft of Intensive Care Medicine," *Sociology of Health and Illness* 35 (2013): 731–45.

8. See also Thomas Klikauer, *Managerialism: A Critique of an Ideology* (London: Palgrave Macmillan, 2013).

9. See Michel Husson, ed., *Travail Flexible, Salariés Jetables* (Paris: La Decouverte, 2008).

10. Trial of Touzet-de Barros against Renault SA, Tribunal des affaires de sécurité sociale des Hauts de Seine, jugement du 17 décembre 2009.

11. D. Rolo, *Mentir au travail* (Paris: PUF, 2015); Christophe Dejours, ed., *Psychopathology of Work: Clinical Observations* (London: Karnac, 2015), chapter 6.

12. Already in *Capital*, vol. 1, in the chapter on cooperation, Marx wrote: "all directly social or communal labour on a large scale requires, to a greater or less degree, a directing authority, in order to secure the harmonious cooperation of the activities of individuals, and to perform the general functions that have their origin in the motion of the total productive organism, as distinguished from the motion of its separate organs. A single violin player is his own conductor: an orchestra requires a separate one." Karl Marx, *Capital: A Critique of Political Economy*, vol. 1 (London: Penguin, 2004), pp. 448–49.

13. J. Lojkine, *Le tabou de la gestion: La culture syndicale entre contestation et proposition* (Paris: Atelier, 1996).

14. On the interest in emancipation, see Jürgen Habermas, *Knowledge and Human Interests* (Boston: Beacon, 1971).

15. Indeed, this idea of an alliance between the working class and the managerial class is at the heart of the proposal put forward by G. Duménil and D. Lévy in *The Crisis of Neoliberalism* (Cambridge: Harvard University Press, 2013). See also Jacques Bidet and Gérard Duménil, *Altermarxisme: Un autre marxisme pour un autre monde* (Paris: PUF, 2007).

8. FROM THEORY TO PRACTICE

1. The intervention, conducted over several years, was led by Christophe Dejours and Christian du Tertre. A more comprehensive account of the intervention can be found in Christophe Dejours, *Le Choix. Souffrir au travail n'est pas une fatalité* (Paris: Bayard, 2015).
2. See Christophe Dejours and Florence Bègue, *Suicide et travail: Que faire?* (Paris: PUF, 2009).
3. On the complex relations between *poiesis* and *praxis* in Aristotle, more complex than is usually acknowledged, see James Murphy, *The Moral Economy of Labor: Aristotelian Themes in Economic Theory* (New Haven: Yale University Press, 1993).
4. The support teams are composed of secretaries, bookkeepers specialized in various areas of public procurement, private markets, billing, collection, etc.
5. See Christophe Dejours, "Contributions of the Psychodynamic Analysis of Work Situations to the Study of Organizational Crises," *Industrial and Environmental Crisis Quarterly* 7, no. 2 (1993): 77–89.
6. See Jürgen Habermas, "Reflections on Communicative Pathology," in *On the Pragmatics of Social Interaction: Preliminary Studies in the Theory of Communicative Action*, (Cambridge: MIT Press, 2001).
7. By the terms *neoliberal* and *neoliberalism* we mean not just the dominant form of governance within contemporary work organizations, but the whole new configuration of capitalism that has risen to global prominence since the 1970s, replacing the social compromise reached between the different classes following the Second World War. Neoliberalism therefore designates a specific set of economic conditions revolving around the regained power of the owners of capital over other classes in the structuring of economic activity. Neoliberalism also designates a broader reorganization of modern societies revolving around the dismantling of the principles and institutions of the welfare state, which made available a number of social securities for the majority through the collective management of individual life issues and material and symbolic resources. See David Harvey, *A Brief History of Neoliberalism* (Oxford: Oxford University Press, 2005).
8. See Axel Honneth, *The Idea of Socialism* (Cambridge: Polity, 2017). See also F. Fischbach, *Le sens du social, les puissances de la coopération* (Montréal: Lux, 2015).
9. See B. Trentin, *La Cité du travail: La gauche et la crise du fordisme* (Paris: Fayard, 2012).
10. See Thomas Piketty, *Capital in the Twenty-first Century* (Cambridge: Belknap, 2014).
11. See, for example, Wendy Brown, *Undoing the Demos: Neoliberalism's Stealth Revolution* (New York: Zone, 2015); and Pierre Dardot and Christian Laval, *La Nouvelle Raison du Monde* (Paris: Découverte, 2010).

CONCLUSION

1. It should be noted however that the idea of democratic experimentalism inspired by Dewey can be meant in very different senses; see the opposite views on this propounded by C. Sabel, "Dewey, Democracy and Democratic Experimentalism,"

Contemporary Pragmatism 9, no. 2 (2012): 35–55; and G. F. Pappas, "What Would John Dewey Say About Deliberative Democracy and Democratic Experimentalism?," *Contemporary Pragmatism* 9, no. 2 (2012): 57–74.

2. For such a conception of work place democracy, see H. Landemore and I. Ferreras, "In Defense of Workplace Democracy: Towards a Justification of the Firm-State Analogy," *Political Theory* 44, no. 1 (2016): 53–81.

3. See, in particular, A. Gourevitch, "Labor Republicanism and the Transformation of Work," *Political Theory* 41, no. 4 (2013): 591–617; and *From Slavery to the Cooperative Commonwealth. Labor and Republican Liberty in the Nineteenth Century* (Cambridge: Cambridge University Press, 2014).

4. See Christophe Dejours, *Souffrance en France: La banalisation de l'injustice sociale* (Paris: Seuil, 1998).

5. John Dewey, "Reconstruction in Philosophy," in *The Middle Works of John Dewey, 1899–1924* (Southern Illinois University Press, 2008), 12:200.

6. John Dewey, "Creative Democracy," in *The Later Works of John Dewey, 1925–1953* (Southern Illinois University Press, 2008), 14:224–30.

7. "There is no need to beat about the bush in saying that democracy is not in reality what it is in name until it is industrial, as well as civil and political." John Dewey, "The Ethics of Democracy," in *The Early Works of John Dewey, 1882–1888* (Southern Illinois University Press, 2008), 1:246.

INDEX